# The Structure *of* Literature

# The Structure *of* Literature

*By* PAUL GOODMAN

THE UNIVERSITY OF CHICAGO PRESS

The University of Chicago Press, Chicago 37
Cambridge University Press, London, N.W. 1, England
The University of Toronto Press, Toronto 5, Canada

 *Published 1954. Composed and printed by* The University of Chicago Press, *Chicago, Illinois, U.S.A.*

I DEDICATE THIS BOOK

TO FOUR TEACHERS

RICHARD McKEON

*who taught me to notice the actual experience, when he showed that by the object of sight Aristotle means the oval of vision*

RUDOLF CARNAP

*who taught me to make structural definitions*

MORRIS COHEN

*who taught me that if you want to make sense you had better take all the important factors into account*

DR. J. KLEIN

*who taught me what criticism is, when he asked our high-school class on "Macbeth," "Who is the 'he' in 'He has no children'?"*

# Table of Contents

[ CHAPTER I ]

# Methods of Formal Criticism

## [ *Formal, Genetic, and Final Modes of Analysis* ]

IN THIS BOOK I INTEND TO DISCUSS A NUMBER OF PARTICULAR poems chosen to illustrate the range of fictional literature and to show how each poem hangs together as a combination of parts. Without being pedantic about it, I shall stick rigorously to this one line of explanation of literary works, "formal analysis." Yet I want to treat the things that make literature important, moving and concernful, to us. In the analyses will occur such terms as "good," "base," "serious," "laughable," "joyful," "pitiful," "fearful," "sin," "miracle," "passion," "sentiment," "educational," "feelingful," "philosophical"; in all these cases, however, the reader will find, perhaps to his surprise, that I mean nothing but certain combinations of literary parts, ways of modifying the rhythms, different repetitions and returns, kinds of sequence in the plot, and exhaustion or expansion of the possibilities of combination. A serious reader will have to ask, "If he means only this, why bother?" Right off, then, let me try to show that it is plausible to make literary explanations of this kind. My point is not that formal analysis is the best mode or the only mode of criticism, for I am persuaded that several other ways of criticizing literature are valuable, but simply that it is reasonable, and relevant, to write a long book of formal analyses.

Consider first some other modes. When a man puts together parts to make an object, we usually know important information about the parts independently of their combination into this particular object; and we sometimes know something about the process of combining the parts. This chair is made of wooden sticks glued together according to a plan taken (as the photographic negative) from the human posture of sitting generalized. Or Boas importantly explains a certain design on pottery by showing that it is the pattern of a previous basketry; or Choisy casts light on the magical planes of the Egyptian colossi by showing that they used to cut the blocks with wire or string. To give a literary example, Dr. Tillyard shows how the imagery and the thought of *Richard III* are a system borrowed from Elizabethan cosmological politics. In these cases we learn about the object before us by answering the questions: "What parts were put together?" "Where did they come from?" "By what process were they put together?"

On the other hand, we can always profitably ask about something made, "What did they make it for?" "To achieve what end?" "To solve what problems?"—and these questions will importantly probe the parts and their combination. When we know that this hammer is to drive a nail, we understand why the head is heavy, why the handle is long to give leverage, why the head must be wedged on, why there is a claw. New York skyscrapers are designed to solve the problem of small space, high land value, and getting some light into the streets (to be sure they do not solve the problem). Or, to give a literary example, Dryden explains the fate of Dido as a means of recalling the triumph over Carthage in Virgil's general aim to flatter the Romans and give them an image of themselves as they bowed under the Augustan servitude. Or, again, in the context of Greek civic therapy, Aristotle explains tragedies as a means of abreacting pity and fear and such emotions.

Such genetic and final explanations are prima facie reasonable in discussing artifacts, and they cast light. If now, in discussing literary artifacts, we pass them by and stick to the formal question, "How do the parts imply one another to make this whole?" we must feel that thus we can account for a good deal, very many of the details and the unity of the whole. And indeed we can. An immense volume of criticism, ancient, medieval, modern, and contemporary, has devoted itself to formal and technical discussions. There has always been a disposition to treat art works as "whole animals" and "ends-in-themselves." With whole animals we are interested more in the organic physiology than in the dismembered parts or the utility of the beasts; with ends-in-themselves we do not much ask, "What for?" To return to our question, "How is this plausible with these artifacts?"

I mean to be asking a naïve question; naturally the answer will involve broad and matter-of-course considerations. Let us briefly consider three things: the experiencing of literature (or any fine art); the meaning of "imitation" and the sense in which literature is and is not an "imitation of life"; and the use of the art for the artist and the audience.

## [ *The Plausibility of Formal Criticism* ]

### FROM THE NATURE OF THE EXPERIENCE

The experience of a work of literature or other fine art is immediate, fairly isolated, and a kind of awares identification.

We take in a work immediately as we sense something immediately; we do not think away from an art work or a sensation to get further clues or information, but the experience grows just by attending to what is presented. It is in this meaning that poems make "sensuous" (as Milton said) a wide range of nonsensory experience.

Unlike most sensations, however, the art work is perceived

in isolation. It is not at once taken as a quality of some substance in a situation. We give it our attention, and it fills our attention, more and more excluding, as the experience grows, any awareness of our surroundings in the theater or that we are reading a book. This isolation is, I think, the simple truth in the advice to "maintain the illusion"; it is not that the art experience is illusory but that this part of our reality is heightened and the rest temporarily excluded.

We identify with the world of the work as our space and time and sensory existence. (I do not mean "identify with the hero," which is largely an unconscious process to which some people are subject.) Our experience is the immediate presentation, the aesthetic surface. And this experience is, in a peculiar way, neither active nor passive or not merely active or passive: we are passively "presented with" the work but in such a way that we are at once actively recognizing and understanding and cannot draw back; we actively pay attention but are at once forestalled by an immediate presented surface that wins our attention, that falls into place, that answers our questions at the very instant they are asked, so that we cannot make the work an object. In the height of aesthetic absorption we are simply aware—not aware of what is "out there" or of what is "in us."

Then we can see the plausibility of looking for the importance of the experience in the internal structure of the presented work. When we are absorbed, the motions, proportions, and conflicts presented are the motions, proportions, and conflicts of our experiencing bodies (at rest, in isolation). And these motions, conflicts, and resolutions of experiencing *are* the various feelings, attitudes, and concerns that are important for us. Thus it is plausible to say, as we shall, "Fear *is* such-and-such a sequence in the complex plot," or "The characteristic attitude of Catullus *is* the Phalaecean rhythm."

Are the emotions felt by identifying with the motions and rests of the aesthetic surface the same in kind as the gross emotions felt in the environment with muscular response uninhibited? I think so, for the most part. (I should perhaps, in the end, distinguish emotions where the motoric part is very strong, like hot anger or lust.) But certainly the art emotions are much more subtile and differentiated than most environment emotions; this is, I think, mostly because there is less anxiety and withdrawal, and the meaning of the emotion can flower. "The dictionary words for the emotions are crude and few; to express the emotions that are felt in sensitive experience requires nuance and reticence, and much objective reference. Works of plastic and musical art are pure language of the emotions, elaborated to statements of conviction."[1]

Let me distinguish my view here from two contemporary views that are close to it. I do not mean that the events in the work are causes of which the feelings of the audience are effects. (I take it that this is the position of I. A. Richards.) I think such a formulation is a mere prejudice of "modern physical science" and clutters up criticism with an apparatus of local motions of waves and particles and of electrical and hormonal discharges most of which have yet to be discovered. The reality is simpler: what is in the art medium is presentable; we properly attend to it, and it is our present; our present is concernful. I do not mean, again, that the plot, characters, or images of the work are "objective correlatives" of our concerns. (So T. S. Eliot and others.) This view is as if to say, "There is seeing, and there is its objective correlative, color." But, in the actuality of seeing, the color is a part of the seeing, not the object of it, as anyone can verify by being aware of his oval of vision and of a color in it. So the image

1. Perls, Hefferline, and Goodman, *Gestalt Therapy,* II, chap. xii, 6.

and its plot are part of our experience, and in the conditions of experiencing art they make up the greater part of it; and this is concernful. The effect of speaking of objective correlatives is to withdraw from the dust and heat of art life and to speak of the image as if it were remote and ideal rather than a special and risky condition of the ordinary.

Now, arguing in this way for the plausibility of the formal internal analysis of works, as touching the experience itself, I seem to be proving that *other* modes of analysis are irrelevant and implausible. This is not my intention. The genetic and final modes of analysis also treat importantly the actual aesthetic experience. They deal, for instance, with the unaware habits and dispositions in the experience. We speak of "paying attention," but in fact we can become absorbed in only what meets our underlying needs. We speak of "excluding our surroundings," but this is possible only within the limits of not arousing anxiety. An artist makes what solves his inner conflict; he cannot integrate what fails to solve it. There is a convention of what people expect, will comprehend (or even notice), will pay money to support. Thus, not merely to tell the history or sociology of the theater, but to explain what in fact goes on in a theater, it is vital to consider the theatrical tradition, the status of the players, the architecture of the theater, the composition of the audience, the morals and politics of society. These are not among the topics of this book; nevertheless, they will often come into the discussion indirectly, for every important factor in the actual experience appears (positively or negatively) in the plot and other combinations.

### THE CONCEPT OF IMITATION

We call an artifact an imitation when the plan according to which it is put together is abstracted from something known independently, the model. The copy is "like" the model. Thus, a chair could be called a kind of contrary imitation of the human body sitting; or, more usually, a portrait is an imitation of its subject.

Now throughout the ages, until the recent development of a theory of absolute music and nonrepresentational plastic art, most art works in all media have been prima facie considered as imitations: "imitations of life," "imitations of nature," "imitations of the passions," "imitations of men in action," "imitations of the ideal." The artifacts are recognizably like some model or at least hint at a model. It would seem, then, that an intrinsic study of them as formal combinations would be implausible, for in discussing imitations the chief questions concern the relations of the copy to the model: "Is it an accurate copy? "Does the copying heighten our understanding of the original?" "Is it a worthy model?" Such questions have, of course, been asked; and I am persuaded that, subtilely employed, this line of inquiry casts light on even works of music and plastic art that seem quite absolute.[2]

Yet, surprisingly, in the history of criticism many of the critics who take it for granted that art is imitation nevertheless devote little attention to the extrinsic relation of model and copy. Pretty soon they make it clear that there is a "truth of poetry" independent of the model, and they go on to various kinds of literary analysis. Consider roughly the method in Aristotle's *Poetics:* Poems, he says, are imitations. He is going to talk about plays, and he classifies them from the kinds of men, the models. He draws the parts of tragedy (and comedy) from the prima facie analysis of imitating: Action, Character, Thought, are the "object" imitated; Dic-

2. For instance, when an abstract painting is regarded psychologically as a projection, the less representational it is, the more clearly it is likely to reveal personality.

tion and Melody and Acting are the means and manner, the medium of the copying. Nevertheless, having begun in this way, he devotes almost no attention to the question of an accurate or heightened likeness. His analysis is mostly structural: What are the combinations possible and why? What is the unity of the plot? The chief use of the doomed historical families is that they provide good meat for working the complex plot. At certain climactic points he appeals to final causes, the tragic effect on the audience or the proper pleasure of each kind. What has happened to the original framework of Object and Means of imitation?

But it is just *because* important parts of the combination have been taken from life and concernful parts of life, famous dooms, the foibles of society, strong feelings on common and extraordinary occasions, it is just because the works *are* imitations that the poet can prima facie neglect the extrinsic reference of accuracy and concentrate on making a self-contained whole; and so, after him, the critic. In its conditions of sensuousness, isolation, and identification the poem carries on a free experiment. The humane relevance of the experiment is guaranteed by the origin of the parts, but the success and importance of the experiment reside in the new qualities of the actual experiencing, its clarity, grace, neatness, magnitude, surprise, inevitability, insight; and these qualities, I have tried to suggest, may be adequately analyzed in the structure of the work itself. The story of Macbeth is borrowed from Holinshed because obviously a murderous usurper is interesting. But Macbeth in *Macbeth* is not a copy of that king but a real part of a real world. This world is only an aesthetic surface; one is not supposed to leap onto the stage and join Malcolm's army; but then our experience is so managed that we do not want to. Certainly Macbeth is more literally real than my neighbor in the next seat.

Let me put this another way. The objects of imitation are only too well known in history and from day to day; but what happens (for us) if we give them another turn in the conditions of artistic combination and awareness? It is said that, to be weighty and relevant, the imitation must remain believable; and many play-reviewers, in the manner of Horace, check on credibility by referring back to the models in human nature and society. I would suggest, rather, that credibility can be regarded as an intrinsic unity in the ongoing experience. The problem is not what demands on credibility the poet makes by going beyond habitual experience (verisimilitude) but *how,* making the demands, he supports the ongoing theater experience with his language and construction. A strain on credibility is the same as a lack of invention in the combination. This is obvious, for the most banal three-acter or magazine story is incredible, but *Pelléas* or *The Trial* remain perfectly credible, weighty, and relevant.

Paradoxically, it is just in the cases of not obviously imitative art, absolute music, or nonrepresentational painting and sculpture, that purely formal criticism seems dissatisfying. People want not only an explanation of their experience but a proof of its human importance. So concert programs and gallery brochures are chock-full of biographical anecdotes and abstruse metaphysics. A psychologist must conclude that people are made anxious by being simply moved, and they cling to the concept of truth-to-life as a way of minimizing guilt; toward the artist they feel resentment.

The logical extreme of taking the model for granted and *therefore* finding all the novelty and excitement in the combination is to say that Nature imitates Art, rather than the other way. (So Whistler and Wilde.) Or to speak of Art for Art's Sake, like the Parnassians. Yet the more conservative doctrine of Matthew Arnold comes to the same thing—that literature is a criticism of life. He means to say that we learn humane conduct and feeling by the comparison of daily behavior with our literary touchstones; we do not judge literature by comparison with daily behavior.

Many of the so-called New Critics of recent decades, on the other hand, seem to take the following tack. Starting from the world presented in the work of art, they show that this world is, or is not, up to the "values" of the critic (which are moral, gentlemanly, and often ante bellum). Correspondingly, the medium itself is treated as an example of the tradition of literature by a close "textural" analysis of the vocabulary, syntax, imagery. The work is taken as a sign of the times and is called on to prove its pedigree. The ordinary world is astray and is not, as such, worth imitating; books, art-working, and the experience of art are not taken for granted but must prove themselves as belonging to a better world; the hope is that they will spearhead a counterattack. In Arnold and Wilde the books are taken, with a certain defiance, for granted; the world must prove itself. In Aristotle, Dryden, or such older worthies it is taken for granted that there are books and that they play, well or badly, a customary role in society.

### ARTIST, AUDIENCE, AND COMMUNICATION

In this book I embrace the old-fashioned view: that books are of course drawn from aspects of life, that art has a valuable use, and that we may enhance this use by examining the works as objects interesting in themselves. But what a strange thing to have to make such an assertion! (It is the obverse face of our preoccupation with method and rigor of method.)

For the artist the work "solves an inner conflict," "rids him of the neurotic symptom by turning it outward"; the audience shares his deep experience with him, and so indirectly, as

Freud beautifully promises, he wins fame, fortune, and the love of women. This doctrine of Freud has been taken to mean that the chief relevant analysis of the work is psychoanalytic, to explore not the surface of the work but its latent wish—a mode of genetic and final interpretation. But this has not been the practice of the good psychoanalysts; they have explored the latent meanings to explain not the work but the failure in the work. To the extent that art-working *solves* the "inner" conflict, it does so, like any other activity, by changing the environment to express the repressed need; this the artist does by spontaneous action in his public medium. Thus, if we want psychologically to explain the artist's success rather than his failure, we analyze the art-working itself and its completion in the work itself, for this is how the old unfinished business is finished at last in the open. Such analysis is, precisely, formal analysis of the work, considering always that a literary gesture is a motion of the soul in the world. And we may have confidence that, precisely with the great artists, we know the essential man, the soul in power and act, by knowing their immortal works.

For the audience the experience of art has always been taken to be "recreation," in isolation, as we have said, from ordinary affairs and responding with simple awareness and identification. As such, intrinsic analysis of the experience is prima facie plausible, just as to explain a recreative game we give the rules of the game. But of course the theater is not a game, nor is the game "merely" a game. Plays and games are social rituals, drawing on deep sources of refreshment, repeating crises without anxiety, reaffirming the social solidarity; *therefore,* they are recreative. Even so, the intrinsic analysis of the play itself is a good entry into explaining what goes on; for the fact is, and has always been, not that the ritual plays and games mirror society, but that society learns and relearns its convention from the rites. This is as true of a Hollywood movie as of a primitive dance.

Finally, what is communicated between the artist and the audience? Certainly the artist does not know what he means to say; he does not know how to solve his "inner" conflict, for then it would not be an inner conflict, raging unawares to him. He solves it by making the work; but even then, unless he has a rare faculty of criticism, he does not know what he has done, certainly not to talk about it and answer questions. Simply he feels that something is finished, and he is justified. The audience is equally in the dark; its explanations of a powerful aesthetic experience are either halting and taciturn or have the charming babble of a free association, mixed in with snobbery or self-condemnation for "having been taken in"—everything but a description of what was felt. Nevertheless, something definite was shared, the work itself, for that is all there was.

I have thus tried to show the plausibility of attending to the intrinsic structure of poems, as well as examining their sources, their purposes, their relevance to life, and their meaning to artist and audience. Indeed, I would venture to state that it is only when the formal structure has been thoroughly explored that the other questions can be sharply formulated and answered with point and depth. (Some of the ensuing analyses ought to make this clear.)

## [ *Some Terms of Formal Analysis* ]

Let us go on to a rough statement of some terms of formal analysis and then take up the various moments of applying them *(ante rem, post rem,* and *in re)*. The over-all question is a simple one: "How do the parts interrelate to constitute one whole object, so that, as Aristotle says, 'the transposal or removal of any one of them will disjoin and dislocate the object'?"

Where the parts are in a temporal flow, as in poetry, we look for the beginning, the middle, and the ending, where "the beginning is not necessarily after anything else and has something else after it; an ending is what is after something else as its necessary or usual consequent, and with nothing else after it; and a middle is what is after one thing and leads to another" (Aristotle).

But if the parts, as we have said, organically imply one another and the whole, how are the beginning and ending possible? (Similarly in a painting, how can there be a boundary?) This paradox is reflected in the difficulty of the playwright in making the opening scene interesting and in the disposition of the audience to carry the feelings and situations out into the street, which proves that the situation is unfinished. The solution for the beginning is, first of all, conventional and not artistic: when the curtain rises, it is the beginning; the first page is the beginning. Then the spectacle and costumes, which are nontemporal yet have formal implications, allow the spectators to gather meanings for a time. Meantime the poet either proceeds, like Racine, with an exposition that is half in the play and half a kind of prior program note or, like Shakespeare, creates some formal combination out of just a few data, as a striking sentiment or a surprising exclamation—the beginnings of *Hamlet* and *Macbeth* are famous examples—and this, combined with the spectacle, has us into the play. (In music, where the elementary combinations are simple, it is extremely easy to launch into the world of the work.) Still another possibility is to formalize the difficulty itself and have a prologue.

Ideally, the ending of a poem is necessary, for it follows on the exhaustion of the possibilities of combination that the artist has allowed to claim attention; the ending is the last possibility. Once the atmosphere of necessity dominates the scene, and there is no more suspense or choice, we have passed into the ending. On the other hand, if another combination were importantly possible, we would not be satisfied that *this* is the ending. (The case is again clear in music, where a strong re-establishment of the tonic allows for nothing but recapitulation and coda.)

The relationship of being after parts already presented and leading to other parts we call "probability," as there is a probability that Macbeth will seek out the Witches again after the incidents, character, speeches, and atmosphere presented in Acts I–III. The formal analysis of a poem is largely the demonstration of a probability through all the parts. Or better, in the light of the previous paragraphs, in the beginning anything is possible; in the middle things become probable; in the ending everything is necessary. (But we shall find, of course, that "probability" means one thing in tragedy, another in comedy, etc.)

However, although the principal structure in most poems is the temporal sequence, there are always important nontemporal formal relations. Consider the proportion, of either contrast or likeness, established between foil characters in a play, as the family of Laertes-Polonius-Ophelia is a foil to the family of Hamlet-Claudius-Gertrude and makes us see that "family problems" are important, just as the foil of Hamlet and Horatio implies "temperament." Or contrast two of the important formal properties of characters, their consistency and their appropriateness. A character is consistent when his later decisions, speeches, and actions follow from what we have been led to expect of him—or, if they are inconsistent, this implies that something had made him change: this is probability. But a character is appropriate when the traits assigned to him are compatible, as in the convention of Roman comedy it is appropriate for an old man, but not a youth, to be also a miser. Here there seems to me to be no temporal probability generated in the poem, yet there is a unifying relation. Therefore, as a more general term than "makes probable," let us use the term "implies" to indicate that a part combines with another; thus, young man and spendthrift imply each other; or confronting Horatio's stoical serenity and Hamlet's melancholy implies temperament, and this is crucial in a tragedy retarded by sentiment.

The returns and repetitions of verses have important non-temporal implications, for instance, attitude or character. (Feeling, which is a temporal motion, is expressed rather in the modifications of the verses, as we shall see.) For the most part, character is just such repetitions and returns, of rhythm, diction, thought, etc. Passion is the breakdown of character in the complex sequence of the plot.

(I mention probability and implication as important unifying relations, but I do not intend to define them further or to seek out other kinds abstractly. The bias of this essay is inductive; I shall analyze unique poems, and I prefer to discuss the unities important only in the case before me. Further, the obvious question, "What *is* a unifying relation and what kind of unity does a work of art have?"—this question belongs to metaphysics and epistemology and will get no answer here.)

What are the parts of a poem? We saw how, starting from the concept of imitation, Aristotle found the parts in the object and means of imitating: Action-Character-Thought, Speech-Music-Spectacle. But why are not these "means" parts of the object imitated, for example, "the kind of vocabulary Lincoln might have used" or "the way New Orleans looked at that time"? And certainly much of the presented action and thought exists in the poem to advance the plot. Therefore let us start from the art work as we experience it and find the working parts in what actually claims our attention. For instance, sometimes in written poems the visual appearance of the words is not a part; most often (when there are verses) it mildly implies a tone or attitude, recalling the attention again and again in an almost insensible way; in calligraphic poems the visual appearance powerfully implies both image and thought. By "powerfully implies" I mean that the critic would not be able to say very much of the formal structure of his experience if he omitted this part. Let us call such parts as imply something "parts of the poem," to distinguish them from merely conventional or physical parts (if such exist). The parts of the poem are the aesthetic surface.

We must remember that every part that catches the reader's attention and enters into the reality of his experience will be expressive in some way, either controlled or uncontrolled. Therefore, if the poet does not need this particular implication for his whole, he must try to neutralize or even delete the part. One can neutralize by making the other parts stronger; or one can often neutralize simply by disarmingly not caring about it and inviting the audience not to care, as with the Chinese property man. In this respect, the remark of Aristotle that Herodotus versified would be no less history and no more poetry is not accurate; the verse would certainly imply the character and attitude of its rhythm. Suppose, for instance, it were a comic doggerel—would not many episodes become satirical?

Any system of parts that carries over, continuous and changing, from the beginning to the end let us call the "plot." In a short poem every part, including the rhythm, the diction, the imagery, carries over through the whole, continuously modified, and the whole structure is plot; this is the formal meaning of Poe's statement that only a short poem is a poem—he meant that it has one growing feeling, and feeling is just this modification of all the parts. Often, again, in Shakespeare the profusion of images is so handled through a long play that it forms a systematic structure and is part of the plot; we shall analyze the case in *Richard II.*[3] Usually, however, the case in a long poem is as follows: The rhythm and diction establish the character, but it is the character that persists and grows from act to act, making probable new speeches with changed rhythm. In most plays diction and spectacle (acting) give the character and advance the action, but it is the relations of character and action, and the change from characteristic thought to philosophic thought, that are the plot. I do not mean that the plotted part is more essential or anything like that, for it is the ever new speeches that unify the plot and advance it, and the climactic moments may well be single speeches of recklessness or despair or joy uttered in conditions prepared by the plot. But simply it is the plot that adds up, is carried in the memory, and keeps providing conditions. In principle, since every part has many implications, it would be possible for an agile critic to start anywhere and demonstrate the entire formal structure; nevertheless, it would be a tour de force to prove the necessity of the rapid patter of a comic finale in terms of the interplay of all the previous rhythms rather than in terms of the comic action of the middle.

There is also what Aristotle calls the "proper magnitude." The proper magnitude is nothing but the expansion of all the formal possibilities of the parts, so that there is a necessary ending. The work should be long enough to solve the formal problem that it poses. Where the poet presents us many parts widely differing in their formal implications—as the

3. See below, chap. ii, p. 64.

several kinds of serious and comic in *I Henry IV*—the combination has more magnitude than where there are fewer and more similar parts, as *Richard II*. It is not that there are more words and scenes but more improbabilities becoming probabilities, so that the experience is more probing and grand.

## [ *Generic Criticism* ]

I have begun to sketch out a formal approach. Now, given such an approach, how to come to grips with the actual works? We can bring our forms to the work, or we can invent them afterward, or we can find the formal structure in our actual experience of the work. Let us call these "genre criticism," "practical criticism," and "inductive formal analysis." Each of these is extremely useful for some purposes.

The history of formal criticism, especially since the Renaissance, has been a study of genres: What is it to be a tragedy? A comedy? A pastoral? What is the appropriate diction for each kind? What are the appropriate characters? What is the correct style of acting?

Expressed systematically, this generic mode of formal analysis seems to mean the following: The critic learns an elaborate organon or instrument of criticism, a battery of questions and topic with which he tests any work and makes it say what kind of thing it is and whether it is a correct example of the genre, giving the proper pleasure. How is such an organon arrived at? We start with the kinds of parts that are put together in poems—the different actions of life, the different characters of men, the vocabularies and styles of speech and gesture, etc.—and we explore into the general potentialities of each kind of part to combine into new artificial wholes. For instance, if we combine a serious action with noble characters and lofty language, we get a line of tragic and epic genres. But suppose we keep the lofty language and substitute a base action; these are mock-epics, Varronian satires. And, if we add serious thought to Varronian satires, we get a kind of philosophical satire. In Shavian comedy the action is comic, the characters ordinary, and the thought serious. In the "realistic" plays of Ibsen the action is serious, the characters and language ordinary, the thought serious.

A moment's reflection will show that such an organon can easily proliferate into hundreds or even thousands of genres; and a master can apply it with considerable nuance and without forcing the poem into a strait jacket. This is especially so in an Augustan age, where the aim of the artists is the refinement of the basic types. And such an organon is useful in daily reviews of average current work, where there is a conventional norm and where the different works are marked by new twists.

But the most profitable use of such a theory of pure literature is in teaching writing (not reading). The teacher of creative writing is always faced with the problem of what to teach and whether the art can be taught at all. At this level the technique of literature can be taught, just as one teaches techniques of painting or musical composition; and it is just at this level that most contemporary writers seem to me to be extremely ignorant in comparison with other artists today and other writers of other times. They do not know, they have not tried out, the possibilities of literary expression. What I have in mind is controlled experimentation, according to the theory of literature, rather than the free experimentation on a set topic that is the usual exercise. For instance, students ought to experiment with the simple elements: Write the paragraph in the past and historical present tenses and notice the difference in feeling; make changes that will emphasize the differences; try to make a transition in the paragraph from the past through the present to the future tense. Or describe the scene in pentameters and then in trochaic dimeters and make the other changes required.

## [ *Practical Criticism* ]

But it is the inventive artist, and not the theorist or his students, who finds new ways of putting things together, just as it is the artist who brings new subject matter altogether into the province of literature that was never thought of as literary or was even excluded as impossible. A student learns the possibilities of technique, but an artist works just beyond his technique and creates what he did not know. In a new work that is powerfully fused in the imagination, all the parts are altered to a new whole, and we say that "every masterpiece is a new genre."

For criticism of such works the critic does wisely if he does not stray from his actual art experience, the poem itself, and does not blind himself with a theory of literary possibilities. He comes to the work, of course, with his previous experience and knowledge; and, the more imaginatively and speculatively he has studied what has been done, the more likely he is to take in what is now done for the first time. But his use of this generic knowledge is habitual and heuristic; it tells him where to look, not what to find.

We can understand the nature of practical criticism if we consider in what conditions a practical critic operates. In principle there are four possible relations of the experience and the analysis of it. We may have a theory of a work but no such work before us; this is the hypothetical use of the abstract theory of genres by a teacher, an "experimental" artist, or, again, a collector who wants to fill out his menagerie. Contrariwise, we may have a unified art experience but no understanding of it; this is the condition of every perceptive reader, for we read to enjoy and not to explain what we enjoy, until we are asked a question. It is also the condition of the critic surprised by a new powerful expression and faced with the problem of explaining it. Third, we may both have a unified experience and recognize in it its formal structure; this is what I call "inductive formal analysis." Lastly, we may have confusion before us and no confidence that any structure we may entertain will clarify what we cannot make out; this is the case of a bad work, something this is called an object of art for physical or conventional reasons but that has no form. (Of course, the chaos of one generation of critics is the creation of the next. The condition that seems essential to judge a work as "bad" is, therefore, not incomprehension but comprehending only too well, seeing *through* it; we perceive enough formal combination to account for the parts that the poet has assembled and failed to integrate, and we understand the extrinsic social and psychological pressures that have made him attempt much and achieve little.)

The practical critic operates in the passage between the second and the third cases; he is surprised by something new, and he copes with it as best he can. This is the task of the good book-reviewer. The important thing is for him to do justice to his actual experience and convey it to his readers, pointing out especially what is strange that they are likely to miss and what has been therefore made different that they are likely to misunderstand. He must shun like the pest the kind of generic criticism that comes to the experience with a theoretical possible art work that, to be sure, he would write if he could write but that has no relation to what he knows he is feeling, so he becomes a liar and takes it out resentfully against the daring author. On the other hand, there is no call for the reviewer to make a full-blown formal analysis, a literary essay on a work that is still unknown and untypical; his purpose is to introduce the work, to get it abroad. Such a role is vital in a society (at present a rapidly dwindling subsociety) where new books are important and taken for granted as necessary sustenance. And the reviewer operates in conditions of practical urgency, performing a service to the artist and audience that is most useful when the iron is hot.

The practical urgent responsibility has its fruits for the critic. To my mind—and judging my own work as a critic, such as it is—the very best criticism, the most acute, the most loving, the most moved and most moving criticism, that is written in America is in the good book reviews, not in the literary studies and not in treatises like the present one. One of the reasons that readers turn first to the back of the magazine is that, over certain names, there is more thought and spirit there.

### [ *Inductive Formal Analysis* ]

The recognition of the formal structure in the present work is the task of inductive formal analysis. This differs from generic criticism in starting from and staying with the actual whole-and-parts as combined rather than starting from the various possibilities of combination. It has, roughly, an habitual approach rather than an organon. It differs from the practical criticism we have been describing by persisting in the analysis, for its own sake, until a kind of definition is reached, and returning on the experience with the understanding arrived at, so the experience becomes richer, and comprehending and enjoying are the same. So Goethe used to ask, "How the devil does he do that?" and then he could really enjoy the play.

The definitions reached in inductive formal analysis are

of the kind "Works like *this* one," for example, "tragedies like *Oedipus Rex.*" Any definition is of a class, and we must hold that the genre of "works like *Oedipus*" can have many examples; but, in fact, there may be only one example, perhaps *can* be only one example. Or, to put it the other way, we seem to have here an individual substance that is known, not like other substances through a most differentiated species in a system of more general ones (as Socrates is known as a "man," an "animal," etc.), but the features of the art work are so uniquely determined and known through and through that we call it by a particular name, "like *Oedipus,*" and indeed we mean *Oedipus.* It is the individual itself that we know.[4]

The established classics are the best works for this mode of analysis. Through long use of them, years of interpretation and imitation, we may have confidence that we can get to know them through and through. Also many habits of form and style that are unnoticed and indeed unnoticeable in contemporary poems can be isolated after the lapse of time and

4. The logical status of the formal structure of a work of art is a peculiar one in that through it an individual actual experience seems to be knowable and namable. Consider the opposite extremes. On the one hand, we recognize a friend or study an historical event, but we do not pretend for a moment to define them. On the other hand, there is the system of definitions of a science, but the terms defined are infimae species, not individuals. Thus again we see the peculiar genius of art, for the artist makes a particular work, and this particular work is at the same time a communicable *term* for the intellect. By analogy we could say that we know our friend in a psychoanalytical case history of him; but the analogy collapses into an identity, for a case history becomes persuasive by becoming a novel. Kant grasped the problem firmly when he asked how we get to have individuals for judgment at all; and he answered it with the *Critique of Judgment,* the theory of aesthetic experience and whole animals: we get knowable individuals in art (constitutively) and in organisms (regulatively). Finally, the works of genius, fine art, are *exemplary:* they are models, as we have been saying, "like *Oedipus*" (*Critique of Judgment,* I, Sec. 46).

shown to be working in the classics. But it is also the case that we do not read the classics with close attention to themselves in their own terms but rather with the preconceptions of our own genres and literary expectations; with such reading they do not really hang together, and we are prone to make allowances for them and admire dismembered passages that ring familiar. With a close reading, however, aimed at finding the formal structure of that old experience, we are surprised at what *strange* pieces they are, and also how well made, and also, in the end, how human and modern.

This book is a collection of inductive formal analyses of classical poems. They are arranged according to an abstract theory of genres borrowed from Aristotle (serious actions, comic actions, sentimental actions, considerations of diction, special problems); and frequently, especially at the beginning of each analysis, there is generic discussion about the kinds of parts in possible combinations. But mostly I go on to determine the parts uniquely in each poem: "serious" means one thing in *Oedipus,* another thing in *Philoctetes,* another thing in the *Aeneid,* and still another thing in *Richard II;* and so with the other terms.

The chief use of this mode of analysis is teaching reading or, what comes to the same thing, the history of literature as a living tradition. Inductive formal analysis is a discipline in taking great men (and audiences) in their own terms. The customary history of literature traces the changes in the parts and in the conventions—changes in subject matter, in genre, in technique—and all this is very valuable, especially if it is integrated with the story of the changing political and moral institutions. But what it omits is the fact that, after all, the history was done and suffered by men like ourselves; that is why we study it. It has been argued that we cannot possibly understand the past, because those men had their own "pattern of culture"; so they did. But through their art, if we stubbornly insist that their experience had some formal structure or other, we do understand the pattern.

From this, too, we can see why the formal analysis of works is prerequisite for the nonformal analyses, whether genetic or final, historical, social, or psychological. In the nature of things we are constrained to notice and overlook, emphasize and devalue, according to our own personal, social, and scientific interests. For instance, the now famous thought of Iokaste on dreaming (*Oedipus Tyrannus* ll. 980 ff.) is not even noticed in the commentary of Sheppard or Jebb; yet to Freud it was almost the climax of the plot. If, now, we assume that the artist and the audience shared a whole experience, we are obliged to demonstrate in detail the formal relations that made up that experience, however absurd or repugnant to ourselves. This may alter our bias, and then we can go on to explain what it was that happened.

[CHAPTER II]

# Serious Plots

IN THIS CHAPTER WE DISCUSS FOUR SERIOUS PLOTS. "SERIOUSNESS" is taken as a relation between agents and actions, the relation of "being essentially involved." Yet in each case the seriousness is a different structure of plot, the involvement of the characters is different, and they are different as characters. We must keep in mind what is actually happening in each work. In *Oedipus Rex* the characters are moving the plot; in *Philoctetes* the characters cannot move the plot; in *Richard II* something besides the characters is also moving the plot. And in the *Aeneid* and other epic poems we shall see how the heroes have a different kind of structure and move a different kind of plot.

I have chosen *Oedipus* because it is a good example of the "complex plot" that is the specific subject of Aristotle's *Poetics;* so, in analyzing this play, I can borrow from, comment on, and add to the doctrine of the *Poetics.* Contrariwise, I have chosen *Philoctetes* to show how, even with a play from the same culture, by the same poet, the analysis of the *Poetics* is inept, and we must start inductively afresh, using Aristotle's methods rather than his doctrine. For the same reason I have included some generic observations on epic poetry to show that to explain epic poems we must look elsewhere than the *Poetics.* I chose *Richard II* first because it is Shakespeare's; and then this play in particular as a useful introduction to *Henry IV* in the next chapter.

These are analyses of plots, the substructures that "carry

through the poem," as explained above.[1] I here make only topical remarks on the verses, style, imagery, scene, etc., not because they are less important, but that I prefer to discuss them where they can be seen in completed motion in chapter v. The imagery of *Richard II* is treated a little more formally just because it is part of the plot.

## [*"Oepidus Rex": Complex Tragic Plot*]

### "OEDIPUS" IN THE "POETICS"

The definition of tragedy given in *Poetics* vi, "A tragedy is the imitation of an action that is serious and complete, etc.," is drawn partly from generic considerations, partly from the history of Greek plays, and partly from a conception of the purpose of theater. But the more specific Complex Tragedy, that with reversal or discovery or both, seems to be an explanation of *Oedipus Rex;* it is almost an induction from it. This play, says Aristotle, has the best kind of discovery, that attended by reversals (xi. 1452ᵃ32). Such a combination will indeed rouse pity and fear and is the tragic kind of action (xi. 1452ᵃ38). In *Oedipus* it is the arrangement of the incidents, not the extraneous appeal to spectacle, that gives the tragic pleasure (xiv. 1453ᵇ5). Further, the best kind of discovery is that arising from the incidents themselves in a probable way, as in *Oedipus* (xvi. 1455ᵃ18). And, again, the protagonist must be a man not pre-eminently virtuous but whose misfortunes come not from great vice but from some error, like *Oedipus* (xiii. 1453ᵃ7). For unity of plot we must compare the epics with *Oedipus* (xxvi. 1462ᵇ2). Only this work is appealed to at all the crucial points; we may assume that the critic kept it close in view.

### THE KIND OF UNITY IN "OEDIPUS": COMPOUNDED PLOT

The plot that carries through, continuously and completely, is a combination of the characters, their deliberative thought

1. Chap. i, p. 16.

and characteristic reflections, and their action. Aristotle makes the action pre-eminent, but we shall see that in this play, more than in almost any other, there is no need to distinguish among the parts of the plot; for the various characters can be explained as moments of the continuous action.

This continuous action itself, however, is not "one" but composed of two actions: he solves the oracle and he finds out who he is. I intend to lay great stress on this "compounding of the plot," a kind of new beginning from something finished, but a beginning at a much deeper level of involvement. For not only in this play, but in many others, it is the compounding that unbalances the characters and leads to the moments of greatest passion; and this expresses an important human experience that we must discuss.

The continuous action of *Oedipus* is also "complex"; it has discovery and reversal, as Aristotle says. Or, as we shall prefer to put it, it is plaited (πεπλέγμενος) of a hidden strand and an apparent strand, and the tragic excitement is their relative motion. That is, the continuous plot of *Oedipus* is compounded of two actions and is complex in both components.

### SERIOUSNESS IS A RELATION BETWEEN AGENTS AND ACTION

The play is serious because the vital fortunes of Oedipus, Jocasta, the Thebans, etc., turn on the solution of the oracle and the discovery who Oedipus is, and these characters allow themselves to be concerned with nothing but this vitally important action. Let us explore this relation in some detail.

1. The incidents whose probable sequence is the solution (the decision to consult the oracle, the statement of the oracle, the proclamation, the quarrels with Teiresias and Creon, the dialogue with Jocasta, the message from Corinth, Jocasta's exit, the interrogation of the Herdsman) and the solution itself with its consequences (Jocasta hanged, Oedipus blind

and going into exile, and Creon king)—these are "essentially" related to the diction, thoughts, and choices that make up the characters. By "essential" I mean the following: (*a*) The incidents are probable from the whole of the character, exhausting its implications to such a degree that, given a certain turn of the action, the character is destroyed, like Jocasta, or altered throughout, like Oedipus blind and dethroned. (*b*) "Probable from the whole character" means that as the traits of character are presented they imply one another to form a simpler whole more concentratedly and directly involved in the main action; not as in a comedy, where the traits embarrass one another and make the action more scattered. (*c*) Thus, further, there is no probability in the characters for an alternative to the action, but all alternatives are increasingly restricted to its demands, as Oedipus cannot drop the investigation to go off and wage a war—as might happen in an epic poem—nor can he find some other means to stop the plague the way a comic confidence man drops one scheme and tries another. From this comes the sense of doom in plays like *Oedipus*.

2. With respect to the incidents seriousness means: (*a*) If an incident occurs that seems to bear no relation to the action, like the entrance of the Messenger from Corinth, at once it is fatally bound up with it—otherwise it would not involve the characters who are seriously concerned only with the action; it would not get into the play. (*b*) Consequently, in plays like *Oedipus* there are few incidents, just as there are few characters, for in the crisis of action these are all that are relevant. (In a different setup, e.g., in Kafka's "Burrow," each of a long chain of incidents can be serious, a single false step would destroy the beast; this gives an effect of great strain rather than tragic passion. Usually, when a man is in many actions, not all are fatal.)

3. With respect to the characters seriousness means: they

are combined only of parts that move the action. Their gnomic thoughts are few and directly relevant; they do not philosophize or sentimentalize. Their feelings are very powerful, like Jocasta's suicide, yet we do not much know what the characters would feel, or again what they would choose, in other accidents of life. The characters are serious in a different sense from the "well-rounded" characters of a character study, for example, Prince Hal.

4. (*a*) On the other hand, the action of *Oedipus* is almost completely explicable in terms of the single character of Oedipus; for he is not only the protagonist of the complex plot but also the antagonist. This sharply distinguishes this from other complex tragedies, like *Macbeth* or *Agamemnon,* and it determines in a special sense the fact that the discovery brings on the reversal. (*b*) And, again, since the character and action of Oedipus are so close, and the other characters move nothing but the action, it follows that they must be analyzable as foils of Oedipus. I hope to show that they exhaustively represent the separate components of his combined character, and their appearances and disappearances are the working-out of his action.

5. Lastly, the same close unity that exists between action and character (and its deliberative thought) exists between these and the ethical or philosophic thought that appears in the choruses and in the resolution of the play.

### THE POSSIBILITY OF FORMAL DEFINITIONS

Let us bear in mind under what condition a formal definition like the above adds up to what we really mean by "seriousness." Consider if we took some abstract combination like XOX and made it stand for character and followed it, according to the above rules, to an essential "catastrophe"; this would not be serious. But in fact we are dealing with a theatrical experience, in which we are interested, our feelings are engaged, and the situations are "lifelike," as I tried to explain above.[2] Then we can speak of the essential combination as creating a sense of doom, an effect of strain, etc. Midway between these would be, for instance, the experience of the combination in the end play of a chess game. And in music, although the elements seem to be abstract, the formal combinations are emotions because our feelings are engaged.

What is here said of the formal definition of serious applies to the following definitions of fear, pity, joy, ridiculous, etc.

### THE MEANING OF THE COMPOUNDED ACTION

*Oedipus* has a complex plot: the hero makes a discovery. But, if we look in the play, we find that Oedipus makes two major discoveries, of which only the second is a fatal reversal. By line 800 he must know that he is the slayer of Laius; therefore in a technical sense the oracle has been solved and the action *on which he embarked* is at an end. Yet the play goes on. It is the second discovery, who he is and in what situation he is, that destroys Jocasta and ruins Oedipus. What is implied by this compounding?

1. The plague is caused not by an unlucky casual encounter but by parricide and incest. And with respect to a man's fate, even the most important business of the city means something only when it comes close to home. He starts an inquiry out of kingly benevolence; he risks discovering who *he* is. Further, the solution of the oracle, the discovery of the murderer, leaves Oedipus and Jocasta a loophole, to disregard the oracle; this is their ὕβρις as we shall see. Their ὕβρις would prevent the plot from compounding.

2. The reversal and the resolution of the play have to do with the second action, not the beginning. We see not a

2. Chap. i, p. 8.

repentant murderer but a man who saw what he should not and now blind. We see the Theban refound and his own children now Κάδρον τοῦ πάλαι γεά τροφή, the new generation of Cadmus of old. And the other great incident of the resolution, Oedipus' advice to the children and the final chorus, looks back directly to the ὕβρις whose relation to these discoveries we must explore.

3. And, if we look at the "means of discovery" in the two cases (*Poetics* xvi), we see a remarkable sequence. The discovery in the first action is through a memory. Jocasta had mentioned a place where three roads meet (l. 730); such a means is too slight to bring on a reversal. The second discovery is through all the incidents and therefore can be a reversal. But consider the use made of the memory. (Let us mention the subtilty whereby at this stage Oedipus notices how the description of Laius in l. 742 tallies with his traveler at the fork, but he *fails* to notice the remark, "He was not much unlike you in form"!) Through the memory not only does Oedipus learn that he is the murderer but suddenly he recalls the *entire* situation of that time—and at once he is constrained to his great narrative, ἐμοὶ πατὴρ μὲν Πολύβος, "My father was Polybus of Corinth"—and this, by tragic irony, makes probable the entrance of the Messenger. From this point on he is distraught; he is no longer the benevolent nor the irate tyrant engaged in civic business.

The oracle is then the beginning of the action in a special sense. I define: *A plot is compounded when the completion of one action leads to another action that puts the beginning in another light, so that the first action as a whole becomes a new beginning.* The serious character of the first beginning is found to be at stake in another way.

This structural feature of compounding is a frequent and basically important moment of ordinary experience. It occurs, for instance, in a psychotherapy: a man is describing some everyday problem, when suddenly he becomes aware that he is always like that and that something deeper is involved; at once he begins to protest, to rationalize, to become anxious, to say it's of no importance (like Jocasta). Or politically: a man sets out to remedy a petty abuse and suddenly finds that he has a quite different attitude (and program) with regard to the social institutions as a whole.

In *Romeo and Juliet* we see another kind of compounding, the "tragedy of a comedy," as an Italian critic has said. What occurs is that a conflict of love and clan becomes, by the completion of the love, the profound tragedy of adolescent sexuality. Compounding may go also in the comic direction, as in *Le Médecin malgré lui;* Sganarelle's comic battle with his wife plunges him into a much more comic plot.

## THEORY OF THE COMPLEX PLOT

### APPARENT AND HIDDEN PLOT

The complex plot, or plot with discovery and reversal, is necessarily multiple or has two or more strands of incidents running concomitantly. Aristotle does not explain why the plot is called "plaited," but the demonstration would run as follows.

The characters are concerned only with the sequence of the action; thus any discovery must be either without previous probability or made probable by a relatively independent sequence. Again, the characters would not cause their own sudden downfall; therefore, they must be subject to another set of forces, etc. In most cases this multiplicity is the conflict of *protagonist* and *antagonist,* as Brutus and Antony. But we then are confronted with the following problem: if the two strands of the plot are moved by quite different characters or groups, how is a *serious* reversal probable, namely, one where the fall follows essentially from the character? This serious unity is attained when the protagonist partly or unconsciously fights on the side of the antagonist, like Brutus, or despairs of himself, like Macbeth. In *Oedipus* we have the extreme case that there is no distinct antagonist.

(The opposite extreme of improbable construction is melodrama. Melodrama is the convergence of multiple serious plots in an accidental juncture, as the villain attacks the heroine, the Indians raid the village, and the hero arrives with the soldiers.)

1. One way of regarding *Oedipus,* then, is as the attempt of the king to find an antagonist responsible for the troubles that have begun to oppress him. He exhausts the possibilities of the main characters, first Teiresias for money, then Creon for ambition, then Jocasta, who is too proud to let him discover his lowly birth (ll. 1070, 1078); but note how his problem has changed between Creon and Jocasta, for the plot has compounded.

2. But the countersequence is nothing but his ancient doom, appearing in plague, oracle, the words of a seer, forebodings, memory, agony of soul, unexpected good news, and eyewitness testimony.

3. Since Oedipus is his own antagonist, there is no time between the discovery and the reversal. To know is to be ruined. But this is the hero of knowing, who solved the riddle of the Sphinx. This is the limiting case of unity in structures where the discovery leads to the reversal.

4. Obviously in a structure of this kind tragic irony will be a frequent and almost usual diction, since both strands of the plot are occurring at the same time.

Let us call the self-conscious activity of the protagonist the "apparent plot" and the other strand the "hidden plot." In other types of tragedy we have "plot" and "counterplot." In

*Oedipus* there is an interesting difference in the *manner* of the two plot strands. The apparent plot, in the nature of the case, monopolizes the spectacle; it proceeds in proper temporal sequence as the succession of the episodes, and it is acted. The hidden plot, on the other hand, has no temporal order: the oracle concerns the present cause, Teiresias' prediction is for the future, the memory is of the past, etc. Now let us define: *Discovery is the emergence of the hidden plot, to occupy the acted stage and to become part of the unity of time. Reversal is the destruction of the apparent plot and the succession of the hidden plot.* It is the new role of the hero.

### COMPLEX CHARACTER: GOODNESS AND FRAILTY

From these considerations we come at once to a new differentiation of the serious character, for, given an important specification of action and the explanation of seriousness as a relation, we must expect a new trait for Oedipus. This is the tragic error and the disposition to it, or tragic frailty (*Poetics* xiii).

Aristotle demonstrates the need in the complex plot for a complex protagonist, a man good and erring at once, by showing that none other will cause the tragic effect of pity and fear. This is to argue finally, in terms of purpose. Formally we can also relate complex plot, tragic error, and pity and fear, but let us argue the other way round, as follows: The two plot strands are motivated by two groups of characteristics, but a crossing and reversal of the strands in the discovery and reversal is a part in common between the characteristics; that is, the apparent protagonist, to be brought low, must be vulnerable to the other plot (or partly agent of the other plot) as well as agent of his own, etc. Then we can define: *The goodness of the protagonist is the seriousness of the apparent plot. Frailty is the possibility of emergence of the hidden plot.*

It seems clear that Aristotle must have in mind this poetical meaning as well as an ethical meaning, for Medea is a "good" protagonist. Further we see why only the necessary baseness is assigned to the protagonist. (Let us return shortly to the connection between complexity, frailty, and pity and fear.)

### THE CHARACTER OF OEDIPUS: GOODNESS, FRAILTY, TRAGIC INFATUATION

Of what is the character of Oedipus composed?

1. *Goodness.*—He is the paternal tyrant, benevolent, prudent, recognizing the identity of the people and himself (ll. 58 ff., 132 ff.). This character, presented to us from the first words and recurring in the diction and tone until it is a well-marked attitude, motivates the mission to the oracle, the proclamation, the summoning of Teiresias.

2. *Frailty.*—But he is the doomed Oedipus, fleeing from the ancient prophesy. This characteristic, mover of the hidden plot, is at first undeveloped; but, as its plot more and more emerges, it infects the kingly character up to the reckless breakdown of lines 1076 ff., to which we must return.

3. *Tragic infatuation.*—Also, however, Sophocles gives us the boastful, self-confident, proud, and angry tyrant. It is as this tyrant, not the benevolent king, that Oedipus does not know himself. Consider the very first speeches of the play. (Note that in the beginning, where there is as yet no action in which to imply character by choices, it is implied by tone, rhythm, choice of words, what a man says about himself, the attitude of the others toward him.) Oedipus says (ll. 6–8):

> ἀγὼ δικαιῶν μὴ παρ' ἀγγέλων
> ἄλλων ἀκούειν αὐτὸς ὧδ' ἐλήλυθα
> ὁ πᾶσι κλεινὸς 'Οιδίπους καλούμενος

"*I,* judging right to hear not through messengers, have come *myself,* renowned Oedipus, as I'm called." (Or "so-called

Oedipus"! but every word is heavy with Sophoclean irony.) Or again (l. 65): "'Not as one asleep do you rouse me." Or later to Teiresias (ll. 396 ff.): "But I, know-nothing Oedipus, stopped her; conquering her by my wit, untaught by birds." This is, of course, just the characteristic sureness of the man who could not know himself. Then, just as the previous traits express each strand of the plot, this trait directly implies the complexity itself. It will require messengers.

The self-sureness of Oedipus is also his ὕβρις against the gods. This is sharply pointed out at the very beginning by the Priest of Zeus (ll. 31 ff.): "I do not judge you a god, but first of men . . . in dealing with the gods." And this connection is also the implication, it seems to me, of the disputed second stasimon of the chorus (ll. 863 ff.): "There are sublime laws of which Olympus alone is the father: no mortal nature got them. . . . ὕβρις breeds a Tyrant. . . . Already they are setting aside the oracles." For Jocasta has just made light of the oracles, and Oedipus will himself do so in the moment of his triumph (ll. 964 ff.). Again Teiresias says (l. 413): "You have sight and see not in what evil you are . . . ," because Oedipus had boasted of seeing (l. 375). The seer's blindness implies the arrogance and spiritual blindness of mere eyesight.

But, we must say, this third characteristic does not make probable the discovery and reversal; it operates, indeed, to prevent the discovery. So let us in general define: *Tragic infatuation is the continuance of the complexity of the complex serious plot.* It is that which counteracts the serious intention of the good protagonist.

### TRAGIC INFATUATION AND COMPOUND PLOT

Here too, then, there is a peculiar elaborateness in *Oedipus* beyond what the generic complex tragedy of Aristotle would call for, just as in the compounding of the problem of the oracle to the problem of who Oedipus is. Are these two peculiarities related?

Clearly so. It is the compounding to the deeper problem that is the crucial step toward ultimately removing the infatuation, which consists not in Oedipus' ignorance (his frailty as doomed) but in his attitude. It is the ancient oracle (ll. 945–49) that is now destroying the king's confidence; and his brief triumph (in l. 971) is not in his innocence of the murder but over all oracles, in the manner of Jocasta.

(In tragedies without infatuation the goodness is simply involved in the complexity increasingly and lapses as the discovery approaches.)

In *Oedipus* the deepening of the problem undermines the infatuation, and the hidden plot increasingly emerges.

Lastly, in this context, let me comment on Aristotle's remark about the "improbability outside the play" in *Oedipus* (xv. $1454^b5$), namely, that it is improbable that Oedipus should be ignorant of the circumstances of Laius' death. In the first place, I doubt that the poet would have considered this "outside the play," as Aristotle charitably assumes, for he makes the king rebuke the Thebans for not having hunted down the murderer; the king has kept Jocasta in ignorance of his own past, so he has to narrate it, etc. But, on the view that we have been advancing, this very "improbability" becomes wonderfully probable. Oedipus doesn't know because he didn't want to know. He has a characteristic which opposes just such information, either to receive it or to give it. This *wilful* ignorance is the basis of his infatuated security.

It is pointless to say that such feelings are unconscious and thus not assigned by the poet, for clearly we are meant to understand the anger against Creon and Teiresias, not at the value that Oedipus gives to it, but as a projection of his own uneasiness. And, if (still within the play) we look at Sophocles' understanding of his hero, we find that it is just this man who long ago fled from the ancient oracle.

### COMPLEX PLOT

#### APPROACHING STRANDS, TRAGIC RECKLESSNESS

What happens in the complex plot as the strands approach? Consider the climactic speech, lines 1076–85; it is just after Jocasta has made her exit within to her death, and just before the dance-song (*hyporcheme*) and the decisive interrogation of the Herdsman. Oedipus cries out *ὁποῖα χρῄζει ῥηγνύτω*: "Burst forth whatever must: I, though it be mean, shall and will know my origin! Jocasta perhaps . . . is ashamed of my lowly birth. But I think of myself as the child of Chance, giver of good, and I shall not be dishonored. *That* mother begot me! the months my kinsmen have made me small and great." It is a beautiful speech.

When the serious protagonist can say, "Let anything at all occur!" he has lost his identity with his role in the apparent plot, and he has not yet discovered his other role in the hidden plot. Then indeed he is the child of Chance. The character that was unbalanced, unbased, by the compounding, has now broken down by too strong involvement in the complexity; and the breakdown of character is passion. Then, for plays very like *Oedipus,* we might define: *Tragic recklessness is the breakdown of character at the moment before the discovery.*

Where arrogance is absent, this might take the form of despair or self-disbelief; so in *Macbeth,* after Lady Macbeth, the genius of his ambition has died, the King says, "Tomorrow and tomorrow and tomorrow." (To make the analogy to *Oedipus,* we could say that Macbeth's frailty is his murderous vice; his infatuation is that he borrows strength from his wife.)

In general, whenever the plot strands approach each other,

the emotion of the deranged character increases in intensity. In a tragedy of will and intention this emotion is the disintegration of goodness; it consists of doubts, forebodings, recklessness, etc.

### REVERSAL

The reappearance of Oedipus blind and the lament he shares with the Chorus are already part of the ending or resolution; publicity and appropriate grief belong to endings, for they are redintegrative (as we shall discuss below).

So the reversal in *Oedipus* exists most simply in the region of the Narrative of the Messenger-from-within (Exangelos).

(Let me incidentally call attention to the character of the Messenger and to the distinction between the Messenger from Corinth and the Messenger-from-within-the-Palace. The Messenger from Corinth is a means of discovery, an incident in the emergence of the hidden plot: he therefore has character traits and generates incidents; for instance, he wants to relieve Oedipus' fears. But the Exangelos narrates to the audience what the situation is; he reports the deed, the battle; so he has only the normal-serious thoughts and feelings appropriate to his story.)

Why is the reversal here narrated rather than acted? It will not suffice to say, in the neoclassic style, that we exclude what is too horrible to say or what is incredible when seen; for what is emotionally tolerable or theatrically credible depends on the background probability that has been established. The opening of the scene in *Agamemnon* is horrible but artistic; the blinding of Gloster in *King Lear* is a part of—*King Lear*. *Lear* is composed of many violent motions, and these prepare this other one. But *Oedipus* is without abrupt overt action, though continually tending toward it (e.g., in the quarrels). It might be argued, however, that just the contrast of sudden violence might express the sudden internal collapse. I think this would be another play; for in the play as we have it the sequence of the whole is not toward what Oedipus performs and suffers but toward what he becomes, the blinded exile with a mysterious promise. The contrast is spectacular between the king of the proclamation and the reappearance of the ruined man; and it is *this* contrast that would be lost if there were a scene of violence. As it is, the narration makes the spectacle probable and does not diminish it. (I should apply exactly similar reasoning to the narrative in Act V of *The Winter's Tale,* which saves the spectacle for the glorious statue scene.)

The reflective summary at the end of the narrative (ll. 1280–85), "These evils have fallen on both . . . not one disaster is lacking," marks the ending of the complex action, for not one disaster is lacking. The next moment (ll. 1289 ff.) inaugurates a redintegration: sympathy and exile.

### PITY AND FEAR

With the discovery, the apparent plot and the character of the protagonist as its agent are destroyed, and the emerged situation succeeds. These are the moments of maximum fear and pity (*Poetics* xiii). Because the characters are "like ourselves," we fear when they are destroyed.

So we may define: *Fear is the destruction of the apparent plot and its agent.*

Likewise, pity will result from the contemplation of the protagonist in his new role, considering what he was; or, as Aristotle puts it, from the contemplation of undeserved misfortune, considering his goodness.

*Pity is the succession of the hidden to the apparent plot.*

The anticipation of these relations throughout the play is also fearful and pitiful. A relation is "anticipated" when it is presented with alternatives, which in a tragic play are then canceled out. The anticipatory tragic feeling might be called anxiety.

(It should be clear that for other structures of plot, for instance, simple plot, we have to define these emotions in a different way; so for the scene of suffering in *Philoctetes,* analyzed later. But it seems to me that there is also a different nuance of feeling in such other cases.)

We have thus explained the relation among Pity and Fear, the Tragic Hero, and the Complex Plot.

### RESOLUTION AND ENDING

Where the over-all structure is a complex plot, as in *Oedipus,* the resolution of the complexity, in the way we must now discuss, is the ending. (In other structures, e.g., *Philoctetes,* a miracle play, the resolution is not merely the ending.)

There must be incidents in the resolution. For the apparent hero, with his goodness, has been merely destroyed, not otherwise integrated in the new situation—there are thus still possibilities of combination, though few and necessary, and these make up the incidents of the resolution. Further, pity is a disproportion of feeling, but the play cannot end until the experience is complete. Further, the reversal is the moment of greatest formal motion, but ending is a kind of rest, etc.

### RESOLUTION: CATHARSIS AND PENALTY

Aristotle says nothing about the resolution of the play. I should like to argue that resolution is the formal expression of the "catharsis" of such emotions as pity and fear, to which Aristotle assigns no explanation but a name.

There are, of course, a number of famous theories of the catharsis; it seems to me that they are compatible with one another and with the one here proposed. Catharsis, it has been said, is the using-up of the emotion, a purging of the soul. Or it is the intellectual purifying of the emotions from their animal energy. Or, even, it is a rising above such emotions as the protagonist accepts (rises above) his evil fate.

Let us define: *The catharsis or resolution is the redintegration of the destroyed plot elements in the situation after the reversal.* Thus it has elements of recapitulation, correction, and ending. The probability for the new combinations goes back often to the earliest episodes, as in *Oedipus.*

The principal formality of the resolution is the penalty. Penalty is the specific contrary of frailty, appearing as an effect of it; adding the penalty to the character allows the serious elements of the destroyed character to act again in the situation after the reversal.

In Shakespearean tragedy the penalty is death specified by the manner of the death, in the particular action of death or the accompanying speech of the dying or the survivors; for example, the brave fight of Richard II against Exton revives the honor of the deposed king, or Antony eulogizes Brutus. In *Oedipus* Oedipus blind is specifically contrary to the wilful ignorance and arrogance with regard to Teiresias and the oracles: then he saw and saw not, now he cannot see and sees; also he saw what he should not have seen. Further, the act of blinding was done willingly (ll. 1331, 1371 ff.), unlike his frailty as a doomed man. And blind, he can, in the great recollection of lines 1375 ff., review all his past that was previously blank to him: his children, Thebes, Cithaeron, Polybus, and Corinth, the three roads, Laius, and Jocasta. It would be even better if he could not hear it! "Sweet for the mind to dwell outside of evils."

## PHILOSOPHY IS THE THOUGHT OF THE RESOLUTION

The relation between error and penalty is given in the thoughts of the resolution.

Let us distinguish three types of thought in the complex plot. During the complexity the thoughts of the characters are mostly deliberative or persuasive, to advance or retard the plot. So Oedipus, to advance the discovery, as he thinks, declares that kingship has bred envious thoughts in Creon (ll. 380–85). Jocasta, to retard it, declares that Chance rules all; we should live fearlessly as best we can (ll. 977–79). Besides these, in the complexity, there are also the reactive sentimental reflections or outbursts of frailty and infatuation; these occur especially with less active heroes, like Richard II or Hamlet. All these make up the characteristic thought of tragedy.

In the resolution, for the most part, the characters do not express what they want but what they have become and what is the case. These thoughts look like the commonplaces of philosophy; but I think it casts more light to define in the reverse way: *Philosophy is the characteristic thought of the resolution.* (And the thought of those in the play who are not involved in the complexity.) So Oedipus advises his daughters to live in the right measure (l. 1513); and the Chorus throughout speaks the sentiments of the ending, defense of the gods, condemnation of arrogance. (The hesitations of the Chorus lie not in the sentiment but in the application to the present case.) Likewise, the principles and other traits of Creon, as in his defense (ll. 583 ff.) and in his behavior during the quarrel, belong to the ending; he is free from involvement in the complexity and can therefore play the role of active agent of the resolution.

If we define "philosophy" as we have done—not that the poets borrow from the philosophers but that the working-out of poetical plots gives one kind of primitive evidence to philosophy—we can see why books of both ancient and modern philosophy abound in quotations from the poets. And, indeed, this is what we experience in life in general: it is not the special content of a proposition that makes it philosophical, but that it is the thought relevant in a special situation, when the experience is whole and completed, having been passionally involved. So Bosanquet somewhere says that the marks of the philosophical are to be central and concrete. And then we can see why the middle reflections of the Chorus are not truly philosophical: they are abstractly true enough, but they still need proof in the present case.

### SERIOUS, TRAGIC, AND NORMAL

From the above considerations we can come to the following definitions: Tragic characters are those involved essentially in the complexity. Nontragic characters are essentially involved in the plot as a whole rather than in its complexity; let us call these "normal-serious." Normal-serious characters are not reversed, but they are often essential in the resolution. Creon is actively normal-serious, the Chorus reflectively so. Teiresias is a very interesting formality. Since he is already a foil for Oedipus as Oedipus-reversed, it is not convenient to class him with Creon; rather, he is normal-tragic. And Oedipus in the resolution might be called "tragic-normal." Jocasta is only tragic.

In *Oedipus* the thoughts holding sway in the resolution are the accepted social norm of the more serious kind; they are not paradoxes. Thereby further speculation is allayed, and the play can end. Where heterodox opinions are to prevail in the end, as often in Euripides, the whole is likely to be much more dialectical, to make the ending seem necessary.

Lastly, let us consider also the more assuaging parts of the resolution: the satisfactions of the hero in being rid of his frailty, here ignorance of his identity. Oedipus proves to be not such a husband as he thought, but nevertheless a father, and so the small girls are brought on. Further, the sympathy of the Chorus and Creon, made probable by his own benevolence, assuages. Another point, which it is difficult to weigh, is that now he is a Theban. On the one hand, we must take as very important the astounding dance-song of the Chorus (ll. 1086 ff.) occurring right after the reckless exit. "Tomorrow," they sing and dance, "Oedipus will belong to Cithaeron, and the Moon will be full!" (I do not think that poetic daring can go much further than this song.) And we must remember the reverent manner in which, throughout, Oedipus speaks of "the offspring of Labdacus and Polydorus, of earlier Cadmus and Agenor of old" (l. 267). Yet, on the other hand, the measure of this satisfaction is—exile. Most important of all, however, is just the satisfaction of passing from ignorance to knowledge, for this is a serious character and the hero who knows answers. Lastly, Oedipus speaks of a strange expectation (l. 1456): "I should not have been saved alive, except for some amazing woe to come."

### CONCLUSION

This is what I have to say about the plot of *Oedipus,* the mutual implication of action-character-thought that carries through from the beginning to the end. It is a compounded complex plot with a hero surviving in the resolution.

Concerning the diction and spectacle, let me make only a few remarks, simply because there is too much to cope with (and about the music and acting I do not know anything). Because they are not parts of the plot, there is no simple overall formulation in which to sum them up. On the other hand, they imply something and move the plot at every instant; and the climactic effects of the whole, as well as the pervasive earnestness of the whole, are in the diction and spectacle. This can be shown by the fact that excerpted speeches (e.g., Oedipus' reckless outburst or his narrative, "My father was Polybus") can be regarded as lyric poems—they are the flowers of which the rest is the plant. There is a profound truth in

Aristotle's claim that the action is the most important thing, for we are moved in the big over-all motions of the plot. Yet the actual release of feeling occurs in the briefer passages of lyric poetry or portentous or affecting spectacle, like Jocasta's exit or the reappearance of the King.

### TOPICS OF SPECTACLE FOR PLAYS LIKE "OEDIPUS"

1. These are plays for a large theater with mask and buskin and a declamatory delivery. The characters are drawn in simple lines; I trust that it is clear that this does not exclude the most refined subtilty in their drawing. The basic tempo is probably fairly slow. The blocking of the action and the other visual composition of characters and chorus are formal and simply proportioned, though perhaps not necessarily symmetrical.

2. There are very few actors and a more numerous chorus. In the blocking the effect of a representative (and ultimately a sacrificial) action must be kept. (A central altar.)

3. The scene is the outside of a palace, with an entrance into it, probably central. This scene is essentially functional for the plot. It is within that Oedipus broods; and it is within that first Jocasta and then Oedipus rush at the climax. The Messenger from Corinth comes from outside; the Exangelos comes from within; and Oedipus reappears, changed, from within. Such a scene can always imply the overt and hidden action of plays like *Oedipus*.

4. There are episodes of action and intervals of choral song, and these divisions are the various moments of the complex plot. The parodos occurs after the oracle; it is the end of the beginning. The dance-song occurs directly before the reversal, brief and rapid, giving an amazing color but not allowing the motion to subside. The last stasimon occurs directly after the reversal; it is the end of the middle. The exodus and the kommos of lamentation are the ending.

5. Again, given few actors, the entrances and exits are powerfully expressive; this is so in all the Greek plays and is also beautifully studied by Racine. Often the plot is so handled that the mere appearance of the wished-for or feared character is a thunderbolt, and the subsequent speeches can be all pure feeling. So in *Oedipus,* the exit of Jocasta, followed by a pause of silence. (This seems to me to be the meaning of σιωπή in l. 1075, rather than the "reticence" of the translations.)

### TOPICS OF DICTION FOR PLAYS LIKE "OEDIPUS"

1. The dialogue in these plays is in regular verses, fairly long. This again isolates the experience from the ordinary and makes the basic tempo fairly slow. The iambic meter, on the other hand (taking the remark of *Poetics* xxii at its face value), is "like" ordinary speech. The same setting apart from the ordinary and poetic imitation of the ordinary applies to the so-called "tragic dialect," the choice of poetic words and constructions, and the imagery. The style in *Oedipus* has a certain austere richness: the use of imagery and poetical construction is spare; yet the literal words have fundamental feeling and environment, "children," "earth," "fear," and continual local reference.

2. The metrical verse in plays allows the ear easily to compare and contrast the length of various speeches, as the conflict of thought and will in argument is expressed in stychomyth (verse against verse), or the heat of excitement by the transition from one verse to half-verse exchanges—as in the interrogation of the Herdsman (ll. 1173 ff.), where the subsequent broadening-out to the two four-verse paragraphs is poignantly expressive of the end of argument and the beginning of reflection and sorrow. The character of Oedipus is implied by his use of long and very short speeches: the long speeches are either benevolent or boastful (or both mixed), but he is

prone to angry and hasty exchanges. The longest speeches of all are the set narratives of this theatrical convention (as of the French): they must be studied and delivered as complete wholes in order not to pall.

3. There are special rhythms for special effects, for example, in *Oedipus* the broadening-out into tetrameters is the ending (ll. 1515 *ad fin.*). More lyrical or song rhythms express passion, as in the laments. The alteration from the basic iambic trimeters is the essential thing, and we should conceive of the difference as heightened by music.

4. Tragic irony is a pervasive diction in this kind of complex plot. Toward the beginning the irony is more pointedly hostile against the self-confident protagonist; toward the reversal, it becomes more pitiful and fearful. In principle there is no irony in the resolution.

## [ *Analysis of the "Deus ex Machina" in "Philoctetes"* ]

### PLAYS LIKE "PHILOCTETES" IN THE "POETICS"

If, like Aristotle, we apply to plays like *Philoctetes* the formal structure won from *Oedipus,* we must conclude that they are failures. "The dénouement does not rise out of the plot itself, but depends on a stage-artifice" (*Poetics* xv. $1454^{b}1$), here the appearance of Hercules *ex machina.* And to produce tragic emotions by "spectacle rather than the structure of the incidents," as here the passion of Philoctetes, is inartistic: "those who made use of the spectacle to put before us what is merely monstrous and not productive of fear, are wholly out of touch with tragedy" (xiv. $1453^{b}1$). Further, such plays are defective because they have a happy ending and "nobody kills anybody" (xiii. $1453^{a}37$).

Such a method is obviously absurd; it is a beautiful example of what the philosopher jeers at elsewhere as "coming to errors by means of demonstration." The experience of *Philoctetes* goes from the beginning to the end and looses tears; it must have some structure or other.

The error of the *Poetics* is to put in the foreground the complex plot, here plot and counterplot: the scheme to abduct Philoctetes and his unerring bow, and the contrary effort of Philoctetes to go home. But, if we think of this as the main structure, the characters are not even serious (as defined above).[3] In the crisis Neoptolemus simply gives up the scheme and agrees to something else; and, as Philoctetes is presented, his desire to get home is only a small part of his need, it is not the essential thing, to be rid of his wound. Yet it is a serious play. What *is* serious for these characters? It is for Neoptolemus to be himself and fulfil himself, the honest young man thirsting for glory, and for Philoctetes to become whole. This, as it is handled, they cannot possibly achieve, and yet they achieve it.

Supposing we keep in the foreground what actually happens: that the appearance of Hercules is wonderfully moving and is somehow prepared. The structure of probability that we have to explain is *how an impasse becomes a miracle.* If there is such a structure, the *deus ex machina* is not a "stage artifice" but the specific property of such a plot. Our problem in this analysis is to show why the god appears at a certain moment in the plot.

### SUFFERING

A character suffers when he is in a vitally destructive incident. This may be brought on by himself, as in *Oedipus;* or it may be brought on by some antagonist, the protagonist being laid open to it by his frailty. Or it may belong to the character to suffer from the beginning, as in the second epi-

3. P. 28.

sode in *Philoctetes.* The cruel disappointment of Philoctetes is caused by the scheme of Neoptolemus and Odysseus, but his physical pain is from the beginning.

We must also distinguish the suffering of Philoctetes from that of, say, Prometheus. Both suffer from the beginning, but Prometheus' suffering is the necessary consequence of his active defiance: he is still moving it, and his antagonist is moving it. The suffering of Philoctetes is at an impasse; it changes the plot by affecting Neoptolemus, but no change in the plot can affect it.

It is clear why such suffering can reasonably be considered a part of the spectacle, as Aristotle calls it. In principle it is there from the beginning and continuously; it is not in the temporal plot. And its working on the stage does not depend on the handling of the incidents but on the power of the acting, a part of spectacle.

### COMPASSION AND PRAYER

The probable effect of suffering like Philoctetes' is to arouse compassion in Neoptolemus (and in the audience). At the risk of going into psychological subtilties, I must here sharply distinguish such compassion from pity, as the pity in *Oedipus.* Pity is for one's self; it is accompanied by tears for one's self; thus the motion of one's experience in the plot comes, at the moment of breakdown and disproportion, to pity.[4] (And so the psychologists say that much weeping for the misfortunes of others is masochism.) But compassion is a steady will to remedy the distress; it is a refusal to accept it, much less to weep for it.

This steady will (felt in the audience) appears in the plot as the change in Neoptolemus. He gives up the lying scheme to abduct Philoctetes at the moment of its success. He will

4. Above, p. 41.

rather do the best he can for the suffering hero. Unfortunately this cannot be enough. This means that in the theatrical experience, set in motion in the plot, there is a kind of reserve of steady compassionate will for the apparently impossible. Weakly this would be a wish; strongly, as here, it is a prayer. Prayer is the reserve or gratuitous motion in a steady will for the impossible. It is a source of probability.

The compassion of Neoptolemus is, however, importantly effectual in the human plot, for it changes the character of Philoctetes, though not his pain. For he has been presented as impious: "No evil thing has been known to perish, the gods take care of such" (ll. 446 ff.). Further, his suffering had made him vindictive: "May the same happen to them!—Agamemnon and Odysseus" (ll. 275, 1113–15).

#### SACRIFICE IS A GRATUITOUS ELEMENT

Further, Neoptolemus' sacrifice provides a powerful gratuitous motion toward some impossible event. For he gives up not only his impious scheme but also his innocent ambition and the legitimate desire of the Greeks against Troy, without forethought or hope of any return. (In the experience of the audience this is dissatisfaction or "poetic injustice.")

In short, in both plot strands there are strong forces to complete the experience happily, the compassion for Philoctetes and the generous ambition of the young man. But as the plot is handled there cannot be a happy outcome. The resolving outcome in such a case let us call a miracle.

#### HINDRANCE AND MIRACLE

Why, however, should such an outcome occur at one moment in the plot rather than another? Because the hindrances have been removed. The miracle follows not directly from the action but from the removal, by the action, of the hindrances. That which hinders or retards the miracle is the infatuation in plays of this kind,[5] and it is in specific contrast to the principle of the miracle. Here it is the impiety and bitterness of Philoctetes and the uncharacteristic lies of the son of Achilles. But by the end of the human plot these vices have been allayed.

When the human plot has neutralized the retarding factors, Hercules proclaims the opposite principles: "First I'll tell my own chance: suffering and going through so many labors to the end, I have immortal grace, as you see; know well that you must endure this, from such labors to get a glorious life" (ll. 1418 ff.). This is the resolution of the gratuitous pain and the vice of bitterness. "Keep this in mind when you lay waste the land, to be pious toward the gods; for father Zeus holds all else second; piety dies not with mortal men; it is immortal if they live or die." Here is the resolution of the gratuitous sacrifice and the vice of impious lies.

So far, then, we can distinguish the following formal elements: the gratuitous forces, the sin, the atonement, and the miracle. Sin is the retardation of the miracle; atonement is the destruction in the human plot of the sin.

But with this much introduction let us start afresh and briefly discuss the plot of *Philoctetes* as a whole.

### "PHILOCTETES" AS A COMPLEX PLOT

The human part of *Philoctetes* is a complex tragedy of plot and counterplot: the stratagem of Odysseus and Neoptolemus to abduct Philoctetes against the desire of Philoctetes to get home off the island. On the part of Philoctetes, the discovery is of the opposing scheme, and the reversal is his despair up to the cry φονᾷ φονᾷ νοός ἤδη . . . ἔτ' οὐδέν εἰμι: "On death! on death is set my heart . . . now am I nothing" (ll. 1209 ff.).

5. Cf. above, p. 37.

But this very despair brings about the reversal in the plot of Neoptolemus. The plot of Neoptolemus is a passage from the stratagem of Odysseus to compassion for Philoctetes. The probability for the change is in his character: he is piously averse to the lie and physically courageous, filial, and the generous own son of Achilles; and it is also in the character of Philoctetes, the suffering friend of Achilles and Ajax. The character of the young man is warm simple nature to which is added the sophistication of Odysseus aiming at victory by any means and an abiding habit of guile. Neoptolemus, then, is the complex tragic hero, with incompatible actions to perform and only temporarily compatible traits. In the crisis of natural feeling his character breaks down, he disowns the Odyssean stratagem, and he agrees to carry out honestly the promise made as a lie. (The fact that Odysseus is a coward makes it all the more probable that the Achillean youth must disown him.) We feel pity for Neoptolemus, as we did for Philoctetes deceived.

In the complex plot like *Oedipus* this would be the beginning of the ending and also the resolution. Here it cannot be the ending, for there are the persisting possibilities of combination in the gratuitous sacrifice of the youth, the gratuitous pain of Philoctetes, and the legitimate desire (encouraged by oracles) of the Greeks against Troy. To complete the experience, there must be more incidents. Yet, on the other hand, the *complex action has come to a full close.* For example, there were three ways to take Philoctetes, by guile, by force, and by persuasion. All three have now been exhausted, frustrated by the character of Neoptolemus, for he will not lie or use force, and he cannot successfully persuade.

### IMPASSE, GRATUITOUS ELEMENTS, MIRACLE

We then have the following state of affairs: (*a*) the complete exhaustion of the possibilities of action inherent in the characters; (*b*) elements of further motion in the characters that cannot be activated; and (*c*) the destruction of the sin in the human action.

Let us define: *An impasse is an action so handled as to "end" before the exhaustion of the possibilities. Gratuitous elements are the probability for action in an impasse.* In this play we feel the sense of impasse in the close connection of Philoctetes' stubbornness and his justification; and of Neoptolemus' desire for glory and his sense of shame.

We can now answer fully the question we started from: how an impasse becomes a miracle and at what moment.

*The miracle follows the impasse, it follows the gratuitous elements, and it follows the atonement of the sin;* and we have seen how these are related.

In its suddenness the miracle follows on the impasse. In its incidents it completes the gratuitous needs and is the specific contrary of the sins. These considerations explain the Agent of the Miracle. He is not subject to the impasse, because he is of a different kind from the characters; he has a different kind of power or authority. Here he is a demigod. And his spectacular "descent from above" expresses the fact that what limits the persons on the stage will not limit him. And to this agent are assigned the traits of grace and atonement.

### EMOTIONS OF THE MIRACLE

*Despair is the completion of a serious impasse.* It is the feeling that grips us when we know our vital need cannot be achieved. (Distinguish this from rage, when we perceive not the necessity but the obstacle.)

*Conversion is the alteration of the characters of an impasse so that they can act in the miracle.*

*Joy is the succession of action to inaction.*

*Wonder is the succession of the extraordinary action.*

In *Philoctetes* the most beautiful thing, it seems to me, is the transition from joy to joyful wonder. For the situation, before the miracle, when Neoptolemus returns with the bow, is already relieving and joyful to the suffering hero; this is as if miraculous to him, though it is not a miracle in the course of the plot, since we have witnessed the progress of the change in Neoptolemus. Nothing is basically solved, yet the scene becomes busy and begins to breathe. What the poem says is, "Relent of the scheme you don't believe in, and relax your bitter despair, let the blood flow, take a breath, even this much is a pleasure; and then will occur something extraordinary." The miracle itself, when it occurs, is cheerful, not ecstatic or painful, as, for example, in *Hagar and Ishmael;* it is a miracle of nature, wonderfully expressed in freely varying anapests.

### REMARKS ON THE FEELING, SPECTACLE, AND DICTION

If we compare *Philoctetes* with *Oedipus,* we see that it is much less tragically serious, less concentrated; but this means, put positively, that it is looser, the background of underlying nature—in the characters and in the scene—is more present and can break through. There is much more color and variety. The narrative of Neoptolemus and the Merchant win an interest to themselves as circumstantial lies, darkly comic. The description of Philoctetes' life on the island has romantic as well as tragic interest. The physical passion of Philoctetes is a dark picture beautifully framed in the response of the young man. There is scenery instead of the palace front of the pure complex plot; the volcano, the cave, the rugged shore —everything that implies the natural rather than the deliberate in the situation of Philoctetes and that works on the natural in Neoptolemus. Further, the tragic concentration in the plot and counterplot is continually relieved by the poignant but pleasurable evocation of Achilles and the mutual sympathy of the actors. (Odysseus is the foil of pure deliberate guile.) In brief, the emphasis is on what the characters spontaneously feel in contrast to (and despite) what their intentions are.

My point is not that the action is less serious than *Oedipus* but that the seriousness, the essential wholeness of the characters in the plot, is in the looseness of spontaneous background and intentional foreground, allowing for a miracle of nature.

Correspondingly, *Philoctetes* is highly colored in diction. The busying scene leading into the miracle is given in the sharp marchlike excitement of trochee tetrameters, the same meter as the broadening-out march at the end of *Oedipus,* but here irregularly divided between the speakers about to leave for Oeta (ll. 1402 ff.); and then it gives way to the wonderfully easy anapests of the god. Or contrast the anxious haste of the light consonants of lines 468 ff. (cf. ll. 484 ff.), when Philoctetes begs to be taken along, with the relief of the balanced exclamations and profuse etas in lines 530–31, when he thinks they have consented; or again with the woe of Neoptolemus' heavy repetitions in lines 759–61, during Philoctetes' passion. Also the outcries of the sufferer are colorfully studied: the gasping phrases of the first onset (ll. 742–50), the longer panting and groans of the bleeding (ll. 782–800), the Chorus's sweet vowels of sleep (ll. 827–32). The boyish embarrassment of Neoptolemus is beautifully given in his persistent inability to speak (as ll. 805 ff., 895 ff.). Tragic irony is not absent (e.g., l. 628), but it is not pervasive.

### GENERAL REMARKS ON IMPASSE AND MIRACLE

I hope it is clear that the moment we have been analyzing, the passage from impasse to miracle, is a special moment of quite ordinary experience; it does not depend on any framework of religion, mythology, or allegory. For instance, it is a frequent, and much sought for, incident in any psychotherapy: when the patient understands that he cannot will it and relaxes the grip on himself (his "character-neurosis"), and then suddenly there is a new creative possibility.

In general, the extreme of impasse is death, for this the human actors cannot remedy. The Passion Play is the typical miracle on this theme. A famous miracle in which death is thwarted is the *Alcestis* of Euripides, where the god is this same Hercules. This work differs in important ways from *Philoctetes.* It is much nearer to the comic. Hercules imitates a drunkard; he appears first in the human plot and performs nonmiraculous acts, so that it is partly the gratitude of the guest as well as the gratuitous desire of the husband and the gratuitous loyalty of Alcestis that lead to the miraculous action.

An interesting handling of the impasse of death is *The Winter's Tale.* Here time, repentance, springtime, and young love miraculously revive the queen; but, since she is not "really" dead but immobilized as a statue, there is no need to bring a god on the scene, and the miracle play turns into a "romance" (genre of 1610). Generically speaking, we could differentiate these plays in terms of the relation of the seriousness of the impasse and the divinity of the miracle. In the Passion Play we require an invisible god; in *Philoctetes* a visible one; in *Alcestis* one partly human; in *The Winter's Tale* the work of an artist. Further, more or less importance may be given to the conversion of the characters. In *Philoctetes* the conversion is the relaxing of stubbornness; but in *Hagar and Ishmael* the youth becomes a "new man," and we then have a character miracle or conversion play rather than a miracle of action.

## [ *Philosophic Thought in "Richard II"* ]

### THOUGHT IN TRAGIC PLAYS

We saw that in plays like *Oedipus* (and such other experiences of life) philosophy can be profitably regarded as the thought of the resolution; it is what the characters think when they are free of the complexity in the plot. As such, it is not working in the plot from the beginning; but of course a steady concern for getting *to* the truth belongs to the characters from the beginning, for they are serious. They, and we, get there by acting things out, including their erroneous thought.

In plays where the characters are less ideal than in *Oedipus,* what they think is less essential. On the other hand, in many so-called "problem plays," it is the dialectic of the thoughts that is moving the action, and the characters are drawn largely as those who might think or represent certain thoughts; for instance, we might be most concerned with the characters' social status; and the extreme of this type is the expressionistic drama of, say, Toller, where the persons are universal terms.

Frequently in the plays of Shakespeare, and throughout the English history plays, we have another situation again. There is a philosophic thought presented from the beginning and appearing, in its various stages of demonstration, throughout the plot, as if moving the plot; meantime there are characters involved in a complex plot and moving the plot. There is only one action, not two parallel actions, but the action is doubly determined, by the theory and by the serious characters. The interesting artistic problem is how, in the one action with characters responsible and serious and really moving the plot, to present the double determination.

What is conveyed in such a structure, of course, is the sense of being not only a free individual but a figure of history. The philosophic thought of the resolution, after the complexity, is naturally the original theory itself: the character knows his historical role.

Here let me make a few remarks about *Richard II,* a simple play but with several formal peculiarities. In the next chapter we shall deal with the sequel in *Henry IV*.

### THE COMPLEX PLOT IN "RICHARD II"

The play is the deposing and death of King Richard. Richard, his queen, and retinue are the protagonist of the plot; Henry Bolingbroke, Northumberland, etc., are the antagonist. The chief discovery occurs in Act III, scene 2, when Richard finds himself deserted and powerless and his enemy powerful. The consequent reversal is verbally marked in the following scene when Richard cries, "Down, down I come; like glistering Phaeton." (It is characteristic of Richard that he verbally deposes himself ahead of the action.) The full-blown reversal is the deposition, a scene of passion, extremely pitiful.

As a complex action, it is not very fearful. As a character, Richard is weak, imprudent, and especially politically fainéant —so not much goodness is destroyed. As a tragic *agent,* he is almost not serious. But Shakespeare compensates for this by assigning to him extraordinary powers to react sentimentally to the complex events moved by others: great eloquence and a readiness to suffer and weep; he is one of Shakespeare's giants of sentiment, in the line of Hamlet.[6] His fall is not so much fearful as his succeeding plight is pitiful; he becomes serious in adversity.

*After* the complex plot, when Richard has become serious, he understands himself as an historical figure: "I wasted time, and now doth time waste me," and he valorously resists the assassins. This makes very clear the double determination of the historical plot, for it means that as a man Richard is good

6. Cf. below, chap. iv, p. 166.

but not as a king. Unfortunately the tragedy of Richard as a serious man does not have enough magnitude, and this afterthought scene is not powerful.

Bolingbroke, the agent of the counterplot, has just the opposite traits, and these make probable his success. He is politically adept and decisive and seizes the occasion. Yet he is not a figure of resolution and cannot satisfactorily occupy the stage and make an *end,* when Richard is dead, for he does not counterbalance the pitiful virtues of Richard with commensurate virtues of his own. A kind of attempt is made to humanize him, in the clemency to Aumerle and the banishment of Exton; but these incidents again seem like afterthoughts and lack power (the whole fifth act is feeble, to my taste). It is better, I shall argue, to consider that the play does *not* end; it calls for an historical sequel in which the memory of "Richard, that sweet lovely rose" (*I Henry IV,* 1, 3), will find a champion.

### THE THEORY FROM THE BEGINNING

But, besides these characters moving the plot, we are presented from the beginning (by various means that we shall discuss) with an elaborate theory of the Wars of the Roses. The theory runs somewhat as follows: One must not break the succession of history either by dallying in the present and retarding the future (this is Richard's frailty) or by haste that prevents the past from growing into the future (the error of Richard with regard to Gaunt's estate and of Henry with regard to the Crown). The result of such a break in history is revolt of man and nature, rebellious citizens, and crops damage by unseasonable weather.

This theory, it is clear, judges against both plot strands and means that both are subject to destruction. But, since in this play only Richard is destroyed, we must expect further incidents in a sequel.

In Richard's plot he comes to realize his historical error, and his personal action can come to a close. But Henry has not yet grown to this realization—not perhaps until *II Henry IV* (IV, 4). By the end of *Richard II* there is a certain completeness in Richard's personality, but not in Henry's The resolution is partial.

The whole plot is framed and judged by the previous generation; *they* have the resolving thought, that is, therefore, in a sense, literally presented from the beginning. The two chief oldsters are Gaunt and York. Gaunt does not lift "an angry arm" against Richard for Gloster's death, but he says, "God's is the quarrel"; but Gaunt's death is the immediate occasion for *both* Richard and Henry to err, Richard by usurping Henry's rights as heir, Henry by rebelling against the successive king. Gaunt, then, can be regarded as the thought of the resolution that prevents the complexity; and his death at once precipitates the complexity. (As the philosophers have said, if men were wise and happy, there wouldn't be any history.)

York's character, on the other hand, frames and explains the plot by showing how the previous generation, the true thought, survives among men lost in the tragic error: in pointing out the error, he is strong, but in action he is even comically weak. He remembers a time when he would have been strong in action. Given a different age (no doubt the Tudors), he could play the role of agent of the resolution, like Creon in *Oedipus,* and bring the plot to a close.

### THE STRUCTURE OF TRAGIC HISTORIES OF THIS KIND

We can now define cyclical tragic histories like *Richard II.* They are overdetermined complex actions, determined by the characters and by some relatively independent cause, such as a theory of history or a set of social causes; the seriousness is given by the combination of the two determinants. The characters are destroyed by the history but suffer and are pitiful as persons. There are two kinds of discovery: the discovery of the personal plight and the disclosure of the general causes; and these causes survive into the sequel.

I feel I must draw, here, a difficult but important distinction. *Macbeth* is not a tragic history, though it has an historical setting and the actions are the kind that have historical importance (whether or not the setting is "true" or fantastic, and whether or not the actions are history or mythology, is not to the point). *Macbeth* is not history because there is no strong expression of noncharacteristic historic forces in the plot; therefore, the hero's tragedy does not follow importantly from his being historically inadequate to those forces not moved by himself (again, whether or not the historical forces, e.g., in *Richard II,* are true history is beside the point). Now let us consider *Julius Caesar.* It seems to me that the first part, the death of Caesar, is simply tragedy; but that this compounds into a tragic history, in which Brutus is an "historically inadequate protagonist," unable to cope with Caesarism, which survives. (The long, long sequel was written by Gibbon.)

Perhaps we can grasp the idea of tragic history if we recall the Elizabethan times in which these plays were written. In the politics of those days the agents were, as at all times, personalities; they had characters and private lives. At the same time they were "tragically" involved in the politics, for a false step was a matter of life or death or of disgrace and banishment: failure was not simply a matter of retirement. So the statesman's fate was essentially a combination of the consequences of his character and also of political forces over which he had a precarious control or no control at all. And we must think too of the attitude that the audience brought to the experience of these plays: the perturbations in their own lives depended on just the personal disasters of these families as well as on their political wisdom and error.

### THE THEORY IN THE ACTION: SYSTEM OF IMAGES

How does the theory, the independent cause, appear in the action of the characters?

We have already mentioned the characters, Gaunt and York, who exemplify the true theory; and the significance of Gaunt's death, permitting the complexity, and of York's impotence. Further, the speeches of these characters, not caught in the complexity, explain the true theory. This applies also to Carlisle when he speaks prophetically. Or again, of course, to the thoughts of Richard in the resolution, for the thought of the resolution is philosophy. Also a special scene, the garden scene, is given over to stating the theory.

But let us now discuss a method that is characteristically Shakespearean: this is to present a line of thought by an independent development of the system of imagery. Put formally: when several characters independently and throughout the play employ the same system of images, the diction becomes an independent part of the plot implying a thought, action, etc., whatever is the principle of the system. For it is not in character for different characters to use the same images.

The system of images in *Richard II* comprises: the sun, its darkening by clouds, day and night, thieves at night, storms on land and sea, seasonable and unseasonable weather, floods, sea and land, land flourishing and land flooded, brine and balm, silver water, tears, steel swords and golden crowns as crops, gardens pruned and unpruned, nettles and serpents, meteors, sunset and Phaeton, graves and testaments, clocks and music.

The principle of this system is obviously some such theory of due and undue succession as explained above:[7] time, order, the right season, and their derangements.

As an example of the direct implication of action and thought by the imagery, let us go through the beautiful scene of Richard's landing in Wales (III, 2). The rough sea threatens in the first lines but is contradicted by Richard's dear earth, his child, which for the native king will flourish but to rebels will yield snakes. (We remember back to Gaunt's apostrophe to England, the precious stone in the sea, the other Eden, now leased out and become a pelting farm.) Rough water, says Richard, cannot wash away the balm of a king; the rebels are lifting steel against gold; the king is the returning sun, the night thieves skulk away. At this moment Salisbury enters with a speech about clouds and a day too late. And Scroop speaks of a stormy day out of season, a flood like tears, and hard bright steel. Then Richard declares that his friends are the snakes and that his land is nothing but a little grave. It's Richard's night and Bolingbroke's fair day.

There is here a complete reversal in the imagery. But through this reversal, Richard comes to a resolution: the king is after all nothing but a man, and he says,

> That power I have, discharge; and let them go
> To ear the land that hath some hope to grow,
> For I have none.

But Bolingbroke too is threatened with the same reversal in the imagery, though it does not come on him in this play. At the moment of Richard's reversal, his day is "fair";

7. P. 61.

but he is nevertheless sowing ten thousand bloody crowns and watering the grass with blood; the testament that he opens is bleeding war (III, 3, and again Carlisle's speech, IV, 1). In the very last speech of the play King Henry himself perceives this and says:

> Lords, I protest, my soul is full of woe,
> That blood should sprinkle me to make me grow.

He is still "growing"; his image is not yet reversed but is clearly deeply involved in complexity. And this carries over to the opening speeches of *I Henry IV,* where Henry hopes that the soil will drink no more blood and is even then confronted with a new rebellion.

## [ *General Remarks on Epic Plots* ]

### EPICS AND EPICAL ACTIONS

The remarks on epic poetry in the *Poetics* are quite unsatisfactory. They are made by analogy with complex tragedy and from a surprisingly poor induction from the *Iliad* and *Odyssey.* In the peculiar contest between Epic and Tragedy (xxvi), tragedy, and especially *Oedipus,* wins the palm because it can attain the "end" (namely, the end of plays like *Oedipus*) with less space and time and fewer words, and it has a tighter unity. The analysis of the epic poems themselves seeks to show the tragic unity of the action and then explains the remainder of the poems as "episodes . . . to relieve the uniformity of the narrative" (xviii. 1459$^a$30); the action of the *Odyssey* is essentially the slaying of the suitors; the rest is episode (xvii. 1455$^b$16 ff.). This is not a profitable approach.

Here let us start afresh with a little collection of epical actions, find what they have in common, and draw a kind of generalized scheme of the epic plot. This will be merely a discussion of genre[8] and not the structure of any actual experience.

Consider a few poems that are called "epics" or actions that are called "epical." The deeds of purgative heroes, like Beowulf or Hercules, are epic; and also donative heroes, like Prometheus; battles against odds, like *Roland* or *Malden;* wars with individual heroes, like the *Iliad.* Real voyages are epical, like the *Odyssey* or the *Lusiad.* Also allegorical voyages through difficult terrain, like the *Commedia.* Also the initiation of great enterprises, as the *Aeneid* is a voyage with difficulties and temptations, and a war, to found a city. The laying of the Atlantic cable, the winning of the West, Sherman's march to the sea, would all be called "epical"; and, in general, many battles and triumphs over nature.

### PERFORMING EXPLOITS

#### DISTINCTION FROM TRAGEDY

These are all heroes or heroic groups performing exploits, great, important, and admirable actions accompanied by difficulty and danger. Poems with such actions must be called "serious."

But first let us distinguish between the seriousness of an epic exploit and of a tragic action. The tragic action is serious because it is essential to the integration or breakdown of the character—we noted the breakdown in *Oedipus,* the integration in *Philoctetes.* If the action turns out well, he becomes himself or finds his identity; if it turns out badly, he changes. In this sense the episode of Dido in the *Aeneid* is tragic for Dido and Aeneas; and the action of Achilles is tragic throughout the *Iliad,* except precisely when he is fighting.

It is not this relation that makes an epic exploit serious and essential, but because it is something important and necessary,

8. Above, chap. i, p. 18.

that must be done, in itself. What concerns many people is important; what has lasting and useful consequences; what is divinely ordained; etc. It is true that (*a*) the hero must perform the exploit and that (*b*) he is threatened with destruction in performing it; but it is just these two that in the epic exploit are not the same, whereas in the tragedy what the hero must do is to be threatened with destruction.

*a*) The exploit and the character are externally, though essentially, related. The exploit must be done because it is necessary. The hero must perform it because he can, he has the requisite virtue; and it is his task, otherwise he is not acting out his habit.

*b*) The difficulty and danger of the exploit are, of course, vital threats to the hero, as Aeneas may be sunk in Aeolus' waves or be lost in Hell. But it is not these risks that are his concern; they are merely incidental to the founding of Rome. Or Roland takes the risk, faces the danger, as his task; but his exploit is not in what he is threatened with but in what he does, saving the army.

The distinction may be put formally as follows: Tragic action and passion involve character change; the epic exploit follows from the character as fixed: some habitual virtue. Thus the actions in epic are more external to the character and may win more interest in themselves, just as the hero may have a tragic or romantic plot that is not directly essential to his exploit. In the *Iliad* strong bonds of probability connect Achilles' tragic plot and his exploit, but both are allowed independent development. The same is true in the *Aeneid* of Aeneas' relations to Dido and to Anchises, which are tragically essential, yet are importantly connected with his exploit.

#### DISTINCTION FROM "EPIC NOVELS"

Further, the epic hero *performs* the exploits. They belong to his nature to do, and he does them. In this the *Aeneid* differs from an "epic novel" like *War and Peace,* where there are battles and other epic incidents, but such major characters as Prince André respond sentimentally to them rather than perform them. (The meaning of "sentimental" will be explored in chapter iv.) It is not in the Prince's nature, as such, to be in these incidents.

To be sure, Aeneas himself is not a very active hero; his exploits are often fatalities that he bears with a pious fortitude, his chief virtue. And a very large part of the beauty of the *Aeneid* is its sentimentality, the Virgilian reflectiveness and melancholy.

### MEANING OF EPIC SERIOUSNESS

Since the exploits follow from an habitual virtue, the same hero can perform more than one exploit (which would be impossible of a tragic action); and he can even, because the plot is narrated rather than presented, be engaged in more than one at the same time, as Aeneas, seeking his *antiqua mater* Italy, pauses to conduct the funeral games for Anchises. (Of course he must pay this honor before he goes to mother-Italy, just as he must descend to propitiate the *inferos* when he first lands. His ritual is not very different from that in the Creed.)

Seriousness means some or all of the following relations: each of the exploits flows from the essential virtue of the hero, as from the piety of Aeneas; thus he cannot omit the performance and may be involved in danger. He is threatened with the destruction of his life and purpose if he is not successful in the exploit. But further—and this is a capital point for epic poetry and explains much about the plotting—the exploit is vicariously essential to him as a member of a group, the group, namely, to whom the exploit is objectively important. By "vicariously essential" I mean the essential relation not of a man and his antagonist but of a representative and the group he represents. Thus Oedipus is a representative hero in unriddling the Sphinx, for the solution of the riddle is vital to the Thebans; but he is a tragic hero when the oracle turns against himself.

### THE EPIC HERO

The epic hero is thus always a double role: the person (with his virtue) and the representative of the group to whom the exploit is important. In either of these roles there may be a frailty laying him open to dangers and reversals; Aeneas the Trojan is frail, the object of Juno's wrath, but the pious Aeneas is not. (This is what makes him a savior hero rather than a tragic epic hero like Achilles, who is frail in both roles.) Again, there may be an important plot between the two roles, as where Achilles sits in his tent and the Greek ships are burned, or, contrariwise, where the sailors of Columbus want to turn back, but Columbus drives them to their own glory.

In general, since the performance of the exploit is important because of the group rather than the person, the man may be destroyed by his frailty, like Roland, and yet the group be saved by the virtue of its representative.

Again, because of the essential relevance of the group, episodes may occur in which the hero himself does not appear at all, as Lausus and Mezentius, part of the war. (This episode is also a character foil to Aeneas and Pallas.)

It might be useful, in considering the double role of the epic hero, to refer back to what was said above about the hero of tragic history, who is both a tragic character and a figure of history.[9]

### THE EPIC PLOT IS EPISODIC

The action must of course have a beginning, middle, and ending, otherwise it would not be one poem. Yet, from what

9. Cf. above, p. 63.

has just been said, the hero can finish an exploit and his habitual virtue survive for another, and within limits the other characters may perform independent exploits, for the group may have other representatives. All these considerations point to the following type of plot: an episodic plot in which the episodes are partial actions of the one action.

The over-all action of the existing poems lend themselves to this arrangement. A voyage home may include many adventures, a siege many battles, and founding a city the overcoming of many difficulties. In the handling, two contrary problems arise. On the one hand, the unity of the over-all action must not be lost. In some stories (e.g., a voyage) there is an obvious progression, but in others the order must be made clear, as why to descend to the underworld upon landing in Italy. On the other hand, the greatness of the individual exploits must not be lost; they must not be underwritten to hasten to the end, or they will not be epic. The whole must not fall apart into an "episodic plot"; yet each episode must not be pusillanimous.

A fine arrangement is for the episodes to lead up to a tragic episode, as in *Roland,* the *Odyssey, Götterdämmerung,* for at the same time this achieves the goal and destroys or completes the hero. (Or likewise a miraculous episode, a wedding, or any other finale.)

In the *Iliad* the tragic conflict, moved by Achilles' wrath, persists through most of the poem; yet meantime the epic exploits are performed by other representatives until the death of Patroclus brings back the virtuous Achilles—yet with a cognate frailty, for he exchanges wrath for ruthlessness. This general pattern of a personal story against a background of epic incident is even usual in the historical novels, from *War and Peace* to *Ben Hur;* but in such cases, as we have said, the personal actors do not perform the epic incidents, or at least not as champions.

Again, where in an epic novel the responses of Prince André to the great events may be very numerous, in the epic poem it is the events themselves that are greatly presented; and, if these are great, they cannot be infinite. So formally: The epic plot contains not one or very many but a few great incidents.

### THE EPIC EPISODE

An epic episode differs from a tragic episode (what we call an act of the play) in being relatively self-contained, so that even a new hero may be introduced for the exploit, as Lausus or Glaucon, if he is a representative champion. "Relatively self-contained" would have to be analyzed for each case in the whole of the particular poem. Frequently it means that the beginning of the episode grows out of the main action, as the meeting of Glaucon and Diomed flows from the battle yet is the beginning of their conversation; and the same with the ending, as they return to the battle (which they have made so pathetic).

Most of the episodes are active exploits; but some may be great descriptions, etc., as the Building of Carthage or the Storm, or the Catalogue of the Ships.

### THE HERO OF THE EPISODIC PLOT

We have mentioned the hero's habitual virtue and his being representative of a group, and these motivate an episodic epic plot, for he may perform several exploits, and the group may have other champions. Let us go a little further into this.

The hero's virtue is specific to the kind of exploit, as Aeneas is pious to transfer the Penates. Now the "goodness" of a tragic hero is not specific; it means simply that he is serious and will cope with the problem. But of course it is, in a special sense, his *own* problem; the tragic character is responsible for his plight. But the epic hero need not be responsible for the existence of his task but only for its performance; he overcomes difficulties either imposed from outside altogether or brought on by the guilt of his group; and he may receive outside aid, usually from a god (though not in the respect in which he is virtuous—the fatal bird in Aeneas' flight with Turnus is not too impressive). These things give occasions to introduce historical causes and divine destiny from the beginning.

Since he must persist in crises from outside, the hero cannot be passionate; his passion is weaker than his habit (except in the tragic episode). Obviously it is impossible to construct a passionate episodic plot with unity, since the character is changed and the passion is purged once and for all. But this restriction does not apply to sentiment, which, like the sadness of the *Iliad* or the melancholy of the *Aeneid,* may pervade the whole; and it is really the expression of the Narrator.

The hero may be a single man, like Aeneas, or, as in the *Iliad,* rival groups: the Greeks and the Trojans. In the latter case, the group itself has a character; in the *Iliad* it is wonderfully drawn, the adventuring soldiers quarreling over their booty, against the people of the city, including wives and children.

To sum up with an example: Roughly the plot of the *Aeneid* is that Juno retards the founding of Rome with difficulties which are met by the heroic virtues of Aeneas—patience for the retarding, courage for the difficulties, and piety for the main action. As a man, the hero is virtuous; as a Trojan, he is frail, but he makes up for their frailty by his virtues, until Juno relents. (In the *Iliad* it is the other way, for the Greeks suffer by their leaders.)

### EPIC EMOTIONS: THE NARRATOR

What are the emotions of an epic plot as an experience? The destructive and tragic episodes are fearful, pitiful, and resolving, not too unlike the tragic plots we have been discussing.

But with regard to the exploits, the epic part, it seems to me that again we must take into account the doubleness that comes from the more external relation between the hero and the action.

1. The feeling of performing an exploit is pride, as if to say, "One of us is doing this." Unlike the tragic feelings, pride can be cumulative from episode to episode. It is even likely that it is best felt when there are several episodes, for then it is securely grounded in an habitual expectation, as a father says of his son, or a son says of his father, "See! I told you so; that's how he always does. Look at *him!*" Also, this is not the kind of feeling that requires discharge or catharsis; we may carry it away with us.

(Psychologically, the feeling of epic pride seems to be precisely the means of expansively showing off by belonging to the pride group; for this avoids, on the one hand, the feeling of envy of the exploit of the "other" and, on the other hand, the fear of castration in showing off one's self in a possibly hostile company. In epic pride it is *we* who display our prowess.)

2. The feeling of the exploit performed is importance, as if to say, "This is a necessary or great thing for us." An exploit is what is, so to speak, objectively important. By "objectively" I mean what belongs to our habitual physiological, civic, or religious needs rather than to our personal crisis. If there is not this underlying sense of importance, there cannot be the pride. We are proud of our friend who saves someone from drowning, because life-saving is important.

Of course the important and the proud-making are historically relative. To slay a dragon is important when there are dragons but romantic when there are none. Tragic themes are also historically relative, of course, as adultery was serious in England but comic in France; but somewhere in the psyche there are always the contrary evaluations, and the play can evoke one or the other. But with epic themes it is a question whether it is not indispensable for them to be grounded in "our" history or institutional mythology; for what is a great, extrinsic, merely fictional action? This raises the question of "suspension of disbelief"; and I think it is best handled by the following consideration.

3. These exploits are narrated. In the art experience in which the plot is the sequence of our foreground attention, the background is always the presence of the Narrator; we are listening to or reading the story. And it is the attitude, conviction, selection, and emphasis of the Narrator that implies the importance of the exploits. (Let us call this attitude, etc., of the Narrator simply the "narrator"; later, in the third analysis in chapter iii and throughout chapter iv, we shall explore the narrator part as a structural part of the plot.)

Aristotle praises Homer for speaking little in his own person but rather being always the imitator; "he brings in forthwith a man or woman or some other character, no one of them characterless" (xxiv. 1460$^a$5 ff.). This is very sound in principle, when in fact the imitation is part of the important life-experience of the audience;[10] that is, when the exploits are important exploits "for us." But with the lapse of history we find that the aesthetic experience has turned inside out: it is because of Homer, his style and attitude, that those exploits are still exploits; he proves their human worth. Even from antiquity this has been recognized; the difference between Achilles and other heroes of history is simply that "they have no Homer and are dead." And when we come to a modern "epic" writer like Milton, almost in his own time and certainly

10. Cf. above, chap. i, p. 8.

in ours it is that a Milton tells it that makes his myth important.

In brief, the question of credibility, to repeat this, depends not on our willingness to suspend disbelief but on the ongoing art experience itself: in narrative works it is the narrator who convinces, and in principle we ought to be able to demonstrate this in the details of the work. A talking horse does not make sense, but Homer makes sense of Achilles' talking horse, and "Homer" is a certain rhythm, diction, selection, and arrangement of episodes.

### THE NARRATIVE MANNER AND THE EPISODIC PLOT

Speaking of the narrative manner, Aristotle says (xxiv. 1459$^{b}$24–25): "In a play one cannot represent an action with a number of parts going on simultaneously . . . but in epic poetry the narrative manner makes it possible to describe a number of simultaneous incidents; and these, if germane to the subject, increase the body of the poem . . . there is room for episodes of diverse kinds."

Strictly speaking, what he says about plays is false. By cross-cutting the scenes, as Shakespeare and most moderns do, the playwright can present simultaneous actions: we know simultaneously about Lady Macduff in her castle, Malcolm in England, and Macbeth in his castle. Yet, more deeply, every such interruption of the unity of place and time, whether by pulling the curtain or emptying the stage and rebeginning, strongly implies the author and takes us into the narrative manner. In our fourth chapter we shall try to define formally "dramatic manner" and "narrative manner" and shall explore the meaning of unity of time and place.

Obviously the narrative manner is capital in preserving the unity of the main action through the relatively independent episodes of the episodic plot. The narrator gives continuity, either explicitly by explanatory statements of the relation of the episodes (e.g., "Et iam finis erat, cum Iuppiter despiciens," etc.), or implicitly by his tone and attitude, rising and falling with the incidents but not to such extremes as the actors, so that the whole is kept in attention. In plays like *Oedipus* such a problem of continuity does not exist, for the action and time coincide (the action tragically speeded up), and the time coincides precisely with the actual flow of the speeches. The epic action is usually much longer than the time of narrating. Sometimes it has the same serial order as the flow of the words; at other times, as in the *Odyssey* or the *Aeneid,* there are incidents that flash back in time; and the narrator must make this clear.

### THE EPIC DICTION OF THE NARRATOR

Speeches have the characteristic diction of the speakers in the situation. Here, too—as in not rising and falling to the same extremes in describing the action—a certain tone of the narrator makes all the speeches somewhat more alike than they would be in a tragic play. And even more so when the narrator is speaking in his own person. (*Except,* of course, when there is a special plot of the narrator that appears as he narrates the various incidents, like Milton's apostrophe to Light.)

To say what is important, overt, and an exploit, the epic style is in various modifications grand and earnest, vivid, reserved, realistic and objective. Thus, to use contrasts, ballad is simple, epic is grand; novel is sentimental, epic is objective; romance is fantastic, epic realistic; in drama the speech becomes the acton, in epic something is reserved for the whole narrative. Homer is "rapid, simple, clear, and noble," says Matthew Arnold; Virgil is solemn, elegant, and pathetic; Dante is portentous and minute. Further, the meters in the existing poems are grand: they are hexameters, assonantal *laisses, terza rima,* the blank-verse paragraph. Dryden rather curiously notices this in his Preface to *Annus mirabilis* when he objects to couplets as too brief and chooses pentameter quatrains, as if four lines were twice as grand as two. (Yet his *Aeneis,* in couplets, is not meaner than Virgil but a little too salty and vigorous.) Again, epic poems find place for impressive enumerations like the Catalogue of the Ships or the list of Fallen Angels; for repeated lines and epithets; descriptions of ritual actions; formal similes; and formal proemiums and invocations. All these things belong to the narrator and imply the importance of the exploit.

## [ *Conclusion* ]

In this chapter we have said something about four kinds of serious plots, chosen for their variety and importance. The variety is shown by the fact that in exploring the seriousness of each kind, the essential relation of agent and action, we have had to bring in ever new basic formal notions, such as Impasse, God, and Miracle; or Figure of History and Thought from the beginning; or Episodic Plot, Group Representative, Importance of the Exploit. But I should like to lay stress here on the importance of these literary kinds by recalling how each one is a special moment of ordinary experience, occurring not only in the experience of art works but also in the experience of everyday. So we have been speaking, in turn, about insightful memory; relaxing one's grip so the creative forces can flow; the sense of one's self in history; and pride in the group. My point here is that literature is, not an imitation of life, but a good spell of life, in conditions set by the medium.

Only in the case of *Oedipus* have I worked out an analysis of more or less the whole plot. This is because the complex plot is a combination that appears in almost every elaborate work in some form or other (somewhat like sonata or canon or rondo in music). In the other works I have just mentioned the parts that were somewhat like *Oedipus* and pointed up rather the parts that were decidedly different. In discussing the epics, I devoted the space entirely to the idea of the genre itself, because I do not know of a good attempt on the subject.

Lastly, these have been discussions of the plot, with only a few suggestions about the diction and the narrator.

[CHAPTER III]

# Comic Plots

LET US TAKE COMEDY, AGAIN, AS A RELATION, A "DEFLATABLE accidental connection," among the parts. Consider a farce: again and again the intrigue is reversed, and the intentions of the agents come to naught; yet we do not feel pity or fear, but we laugh. We do not feel it tragically because the actions are "of no account," the agents are "not seriously involved" or are "completely worthless anyway," and they do not win our sympathy; we do not suffer. So Aristotle (in *Poetics* v) puts the laughable in the class of the deformed whether of behavior (ἄισχος, disgraceful, ugly) or thought (ἁμάρτημα, error). Yet not every deformity is laughable, for Oedipus is certainly in error and, by Greek standards, Philoctetes' wound would be disgraceful; but only such cases as are "painless and harmless" (ἀνώδυνον καὶ οὐ φθαρτικόν). Kant, similarly, says that laughter is an expectation that comes to "absolutely naught"; he must mean while we ourselves remain secure in our faculties; what is comically destroyed is not like us. (So, for Kant, comedy is the direct contrary of the sublime, where it is our intellectual faculties that break down.)

Psychologically, in this comedy of Aristotle and Kant, the positive feeling is malicious pleasure in the destruction and the flooding release from the strain of attending to an improbable or trivial connection and contemptuously dismissing it. But we may also find an underlying ground of laughter in what is left after the destruction and the dismissal; this is pointed to in the theories of comedy of, for instance, Bergson and Freud. For Bergson the complicated and mechanical are destroyed; the simple vitality explosively asserts itself. For Freud it is the inhibited more infantile drives that return—laughter is a kind of freeing from embarrassment. Thus, pervasively under the deflatable accidental connections of comedy there is an abiding simpler attitude: infantile animality, lubricity, malice, etc.; and at the end there is often a philosophical (abiding) thought springing from the same source—for example, "Good food is better than battles" (*The Acharnians*). Most popularly the ending of comic plays is a wedding, but this usually means that a nondeflatable romantic strand has been a part of the plot, and the whole is not pure comedy but a mixed genre, arousing sympathy and apprehension as well as laughter.[1]

There are two special difficulties, which did not arise for serious plays, in writing out the structure of a comedy in a book like this. In a serious plot, where everything converges to the same meaning, it does not much matter if we notice small details of acting, inflection, timing; but it is of course just these things that set off the loudest laughter in comedy, when the tiniest touch deflates the biggest balloon. Thus our criticism may quite accurately lay bare the rough structure of what is happening, yet leave the reader in the dark as to why it is funny, for that must be seen and heard in detail performed by a good comedian. Samuel Johnson pointed this out by saying that tragedies may be read in books but that comedies must be experienced on the stage. The second difficulty of exposition comes from the fact that the pervasive underlying drives I have mentioned, that are the energy of loud laughter, cannot be too directly presented, for that would

1. Cf. below, p. 100.

freeze the embarrassment; they exist allusively in the play and dormantly in the audience.

As the chief example for this chapter, I have chosen *The Alchemist,* because among English plays Ben Jonson's are the purest comic actions, as pure deflation, and *The Alchemist* is the most fully worked out, so we can touch on the most points. (Further, a structural analysis of a comedy by Jonson brings out with striking clarity the peculiar delight of this poet, unfunny but very glorious.) In *I Henry IV* we have a remarkable combination of the comic and serious, both kept fairly pure, in a framework that is neither serious nor comic, resulting in a work of immense formal magnitude. Finally, I chose *Mac Flecknoe* as an example where the mixing kinds are not kept pure, in order to be able to discuss the narrator as a part of the poem and to draw an important distinction between "natural" implications among the parts and "sophisticated" ones, as in *Mac Flecknoe.*

## [*"The Alchemist": Comic Intrigue*]

### DOUBLENESS OF COMIC CHARACTERS

In the last chapter we started from "seriousness" as an essential relation between the character and his action; let us now explore the relation between a base character and his action. This is "comic" when the intrigue can be reversed or even be deflated (come to nothing), and still the character is not destroyed; yet the intrigue is the intrigue *of* the character in the sense that in part it follows from him and follows from a part of him. This is what I mean by an "accidental" connection. It will be seen at once that a character of comedy has two aspects: that which is destroyed and that which survives in, let us say, "normalcy." Most of the possibilities of this comic relation occur in *The Alchemist.*

1. The character may be composed simply of a comic trait

necessary for the intrigue and of the normal trait of being a man, as when a man persists in a single illusion and then awakes from it. When a play is made mainly of such characters, we have a comedy of situation, and we sympathize with the persons in their return to normalcy. In broader kinds of farce such a character is a straight man, brought into the comedy by his accidental connection with the broader comedians and afterward of no further interest.

2. On the contrary, the disposition to comic intrigues, whether as a butt or as an initiator, may be strongly developed, so that, even after the deflation, the mask survives as a name of ridicule. We think of the mask and not the normal man. These are the humors, and the Jonsonian comedy is mainly comedy of humors, as here the simpleton Abel, Sir Epicure Mammon, the stormy Kastril, the materialistic Puritan.

3. Or not only the comic but also the normal may be strongly developed, as when the deflation of the intrigue purges the normal man of an error or humor. So Surly comes to recognize in himself that "same foolish vice of honesty." Honesty and the need to expose rogues, these are of course humors among the Jonsonian Lovewits and Truewits. For Jonson the flawless normal man is urbane; he knows his way around. But we can see how this same combination of the comic and normal may easily verge on the tragic, as in *Le Misanthrope,* where the disposition to a comic intrigue is really a tragic flaw for a man who is not urbanely normal but serious.

4. On the contrary again, what seems to be a merely comical disposition, such as gluttony, knavery, deviltry, may be so apt for any eventuality that it survives every deflation and proves in the end to be a lively way of normal life. Let us call these traits Wits, like Face, Falstaff (at the end of the first part of *Henry IV*), Figaro, Scapin, or Schweik. In rela-

tion to these witty knaves, the other characters are dupes and butts.

5. Or it may be the normal or even heroic part of the character that is most developed and that, in detachment, permits or enjoys or profits by the comedy, like Lovewit or Prince Hal or even Theseus in *A Midsummer Night's Dream*. This is the Urbane.

6. A completely deflatable trait is a Buffoon. Mostly this would occur in passing.

### BUFFOONERY AND THE UNDERLYING DRIVES

Comic traits are base because they generate superficial or accidental relations that in the end do not make any difference. But they are not completely absurd, because they generate determinate probable intrigues. A character completely absurd could enter at any time, and from him anything could be expected; he would be the object merely of indifference or contempt.

Yet, since the comic intrigue is combined of the accidental relations of accidental relations, when the combination reaches the utmost limits of accidentality, all the comic characters and their actions tend to become ad libitum, at sea. There is a pervasive buffoonery. Consider Kastril, for example: at the climax he might do or say anything.[2]

What is it, at such a moment, that makes the comedy most delicious and not merely contemptible, since it is apparently so devoid of sense? Obviously it is the emergence of the more elementary but *by no means formless* underlying drives, wanton destructiveness and animal lubricity. Compared with the intricacy of the plot, this underlying part is a dim background, everywhere suggested in the incidents, gestures, language, in-

2. Compare this moment of general buffoonery with the "tragic recklessness" of the complex protagonist, above, chap. ii, p. 39.

nuendo, but never given a plot. But, when the plot itself turns to chaos, this part abides and makes sense. A comedy where all "human values" are absolutely deflated proves to be a fertility ritual of the highest human value.

So we shall see that the normalcy that survives the explosion of the comedy, as a resolution, is not the normalcy of everyday but is a lively normalcy, man in a wanton mood. The comic and normal parts of the comic characters are integrally related for this lively function.

## COMIC INTRIGUE

### EXPANSION

The combination of incidents probable from the wits, dupes, and humors is, as a whole, the comic intrigue. And it is immediately evident that such an intrigue, unlike the serious plot, is more than the acting-out of the characters, for some comic events befall the characters not as they choose or as is in their disposition but simply because, with quite other ends in view, they have entered the situation. Since the situation is accidentally related to some, it can be accidentally related to others, and, by a compounding of accidents, characters who originally have nothing to do with one another are thrown together. Thus, Surly comes disguised as the amorous Don; Dol, the appropriate bawd, is occupied elsewhere; the Don must have some woman, and Dame Pliant, who has come on other business, happens to be the only other woman; so Surly is thrown with Dame Pliant. Here indeed we have a case not merely of comic probability but of comic necessity (for it depends on the exhaustion of the possibilities), yet it is absurd. In extreme cases mere juxtaposition is a sufficient generator of comic incidents, as in the famous tradition of multioccupied closets.

Such an intrigue is naturally divergent and expansive, freely introducing new complications, whereas the tragic plot converges to remove just the complexity that it has. Thus one might diagram the action of *The Alchemist* as a kind of expanding balloon. In general, as the strands of action are more numerous, the unity among them all becomes more accidental to each—the characters become more distracted, the pace more dizzy, the probability more heady and tenuous. (This explains why melodrama, the climactic coming-together of many serious plots—the attack of the Indians, the attempt on the heroine, the coming of the soldiers from the post—is likely to become uproariously funny.)

### PROBABILITY AND REVERSAL

The strands of a comic action may cross by normal probability, as when a character plans to do something and does it. Or by a comic probability: the characters are thrown into new, unmeant, and still more accidental situations that they have to cope with. Then the comedy is heightened if these new situations surprisingly provoke new traits of characters that have a comic compatibility with the previous traits and intentions. Thus, disappointed at the explosion of the stone, Sir Epicure is provoked to the remorseful outcry, "O my voluptuous mind! I am justly punished" (IV, 5).

This is a comic reversal. But we must make an important distinction. The new situation may be one of continuing comedy or of the return to normalcy (deflation to absolutely naught). Unlike the reversals of tragedy, comic reversals are not brought on by discoveries; rather, they compound the errors. Tragic reversals are apprehensive and fearful, but these heighten daring and bewilderment, or the daring to be bewildered.

In this context we may make a further distinction of the characters in plays like *The Alchemist*. The humors and dupes are subject to continual comic reversals; but the Alchemist himself is the agent of reversals. He knows what is going on; therefore, he is not reversed; he is, however, exposed in the general deflation to normalcy. But Face and Lovewit, the witty and the urbane, are not subject to the deflation either.

Obviously it is the hallmark of Jonsonian comedy to fill out this whole line: humors, knaves, wits, and the urbane. Jonson gives us a hierarchy of malicious intelligence. In *The Alchemist* the hierarchy is kept neat, and the effect is pleasant throughout; Lovewit, the urbane, is not involved in the comedy as an agent, and so he may pleasantly profit from the spoils set free by laughter, namely, sex and an heiress. But perhaps *Volpone* is more profoundly Jonsonian: the Fox is both onlooker and agent; he lusts in the malicious intelligence itself, not in the profits: "Oh more than if I had enjoyed the wench: the pleasure of all womankind's not like it." This is cruel.

(Correspondingly, in Jonson's comedies the underlying suggestiveness is rarely very warm. There is plenty of lubricity but little pornographic excitement. A typical verse: "For she must milk his epididymus." We have the remarkable case of great comedy that is not funny; we are not invited to let go to belly laughter.)

### LICENSE AND DEFLATION

Ordinarily we expect normal thoughts and feelings to be effective causes, for mistakes and misunderstandings to right themselves, etc. Thus, special comic conditions are prerequisite for comic probability, the compounding of accidents and errors. In a sense every humor provides such conditions. Mammon wills to believe anything that will make him rich, Dame Pliant wants any husband, and the gull wants to be gulled. (And, philosophically considered, no special conditions are required for comic complication; the ordinary illusions of people are obviously self-compounding. To a disinterested view, life is at least as comic and serious as it is "normal.")

Often, however, the poet provides a special comic license to compound errors, in a special place and for a limited time. One is licensed to be mad on St. John's Day or to play tricks on April Fools'. Wine and the party spirit give a license for dirty jokes. In *The Alchemist* the master of the house is away, and this gives a license; the comic complication depends on the erroneous belief that he will be gone for a fortnight. Then we may simply define for plays like *The Alchemist:* Normalcy is the part of the play after the revoking of the comic license (return of Lovewit at the end of Act IV). The reversal to normalcy is the deflation. (Revoking the license is, of course, analogous to discovery and the deflation to the tragic reversal.)

Many comedies are not deflated to normalcy. *The Clouds,* for example, ends with the establishment of the Cloud-Cuckoo Utopia; what need for a deflation? *The Acharnians* is not deflated for the opposite reason; the proposition of the end is witty and true. Comedies that can end undeflated have a peculiar heady glory (and socially are more aphrodisiac).

On the other hand, sentimental comedies, those in which we sympathize with the romantic couple (socially, a vicarious outlet), require the removal of the comic conditions, the revoking of license, in order that the lovers may be no longer anxious. In such cases there is often a comic miracle to clear up the difficulties. This may be a windfall, like the inheritance that falls to Léandre in *Le Médecin malgré lui* and nullifies the old man's objection to the marriage (for his humor is stubborn; he could not be made urbane). A windfall is the removal of comic conditions that are not deflatable; and there are likely to be such stubborn conditions in sentimental comedies because the sympathetic (noncomic) lovers are not likely to be involved for only comic reasons—they would avoid merely comic complication and go off by themselves. The structure, the gratuitous probability, of such windfalls is analogous to the *deus ex machina:* the comic complication has come to a threatening impasse, but the lovers are deserving of better than deflation, etc.

The formal comic license issued and revoked by Jonson is characteristic of his art: he is the controlling comic master who will neither allow a sympathetic plot strand nor, on the other hand, let the comic malice release a libido that carries everything before it.

### THE BEGINNING

We may now speak of the beginning, the middle, and the ending.

The beginning is the comic license and the agents who generate the intrigue, not subject to comic reversals but subject to revoking of the license. In *The Alchemist,* Act I, scene 1, could be regarded as a sufficient beginning: the trio who generate the intrigue, the dupes they practice on, the likelihood of a later disruption within the trio because of their quarrels and rivalry (making probable the deflation), and the possible return of the master of the house (revoking the license). The rest follows from this.

But comedy is expansive, and it may be said also that each new humor introduces new comic conditions. Thus in a comedy of this type the effect depends not on a distinction between the beginning and the middle but rather on the continual expansion of the possibilities of accident. This is different from tragedies like *Oedipus,* where each new entrance (e.g., the Messenger from Corinth) eliminates an alternative in the converging plot strands.

### THE MIDDLE

In the middle the intrigue is enlarged (1) by the introduction of new humors (start of Acts II and III) and (2) by the combination of the previous combinations. The new humors are introduced with a certain probability from what has preceded, as Tribulation enters because he has lead roofing to sell to Sir Epicure for projection; yet each humor has peculiarities that serve as starting places for new trails.

But what principle, then, determines the magnitude of a play so enlarged? For the principle of tragedy, "just what is necessary to produce the reversal," has no place here. Why should not the balloon expand indefinitely, introducing ever new humors and their complications? This question may be answered by two related considerations drawn from the limits of the comic intrigue in itself and from the relation of the intrigue to normalcy.

First, the compounding of accidents cannot be indefinitely comic; after a while it reaches the random or trivial. This occurs when the potentiality of the humors to operate in new reversals has been exhausted. If new humors are introduced with which the previous humors can no longer react, we would no longer have one play. Thus, the plight of Surly when the bellicose Kastril turns on him as the cheat is near the limit; it is only because Kastril has been developed as such a buffoon that this climax of buffoonery is sensible. And that Ananias should now turn on the Spanish fiend with his ruff of pride and his idolatrous breeches is simply wondrous. The next moment would be absurd, but Jonson, of course, allows no next moment. (We might think of a sequence of expansion somewhat as follows: the comic, the buffoon, the absurd, the trivial.)

Second, the probable return of normalcy sets a limit to the comic expansion. But this is integrally probable from what is happening to the intrigue; for we must remember that all the characters have a normal component, and, as the intrigue becomes too tenuous and absurd, the characters must return to normalcy, for otherwise they would be destroyed completely: they would be madmen and not characters of comedy. Thus, we must expect Surly to call the police; but the police and the crowd have not been handled at all, so they need not now be dupes. Another aspect of this is that the comic expansion begins to touch themes that by convention are only normal; thus Jonson cannot allow the chastity of Dame Pliant to be actually comic but only to threaten to be so; so in the comic crisis at the end of Act IV we are near the deflation. Again, from previous to the expansion, there is the probability of the return of normalcy: Lovewit must return, for the possibility was mentioned in the beginning; the license is for a limited time and place. To give another example, at the beginning of *A Midsummer Night's Dream* we are told that "Four nights will quickly dream away the time [of waiting]"; but these nights pass in due course, and then the dreamlike probability is over. And, as with the limited time, so with the place: when the madness becomes so violent that it overflows among the neighbors, there is a deflation. Thus in *Les Précieuses ridicules* the spectacular motion, noise, and crowding of the dance (scene 12) is a sufficient inflation and makes probable the entry of the irate suitors with their sticks.

### THE ENDING: COMIC FEELINGS

The deflation of the comic intrigue is the beginning of the ending. The humors are destroyed. The incidents of the ending comprise the salvaging of what survives in normalcy.

Let us choose this turning point in the plot to discuss the kinds of laughter. (The kinds of comic laughter fit in the spectrum between the giggling of embarrassment on one extreme and the gurgling of animal satisfaction on the other.)

The deflation of the humors is malicious laughter, energized by released destructiveness and made safe by contempt or indifference. The succession of the normal persons to the humors is the belly laughter of the released underlying drives. And the resolution is a kind of happy smiling and chuckling.

We have argued above[3] that the audience identifies not with this or that particular character but with the world of the work as a whole, a space and time and drama. In discussing the feelings of comedy, it is essential to bear this in mind. With tragedy, everything centers in the end in the protagonist, so that what is felt for him is not far from what is felt during the work. But with comedy, no such thing.

Malicious laughter is roused in a titillating or embarrassed way by the forethought of the reversals; it is roused restrainedly by every reversal; and it is aroused unrestrainedly at the deflation or reduction of the comedy to absolutely nought. This is the moment of greatest absurdity: "All goes up in fume." Obviously this laughter is not identification with what is deflated; usually it is explained as a laughter of superiority (identification with the author?), that we are *not* that; it is base, we are superior. But I think the case is simpler; it is that we *are,* we are left, even in the dangerous activity of mocking, destroying, childishly laying about us. No superiority or contempt need be inferred; when it is strongly present, the comedy passes over into satire and invective. The energy of ordinarily suppressed destructiveness bursts out laughing. It is as though the base intrigue that we have been following has become a burden, and we are glad to annihilate it.

But then why have we involved ourselves in it from the beginning? It is because of the suggestion of the more ele-

3. Chap. i, p. 4.

mentary animal drives that accompanies the intrigue of base aims and vices. We do not identify with the characters, knaves, and humors, but we identify with their world, which is after all compact of simple childish wants. At the deflation the comic characters are destroyed; they carry off with them the shame and the base imputation. But the point is that what is left is not nothing, but normal persons, we ourselves—nobody has been hurt. Then comes the loud laughter of the released instincts that have all along been suggested; we have allowed ourselves successfully to be seduced. Toward this end the comic reversals and the absorption in the increasingly absurd are capital, for they surprise and distract us, and we find ourselves out further than we intended to go, or even than we knew. We are astonished to be laughing from our bellies. There is no sense to it; it is never "so funny as all that"; but that's just the point.

### JONSON'S COMIC FEELINGS

Jonson is extremely malicious (and satiric), but he is weak in deep laughter. There is not enough suggestiveness. He presents gluttony but little gusto, and lechery but almost no pornography; only the scatological part is strongly felt, and this expresses itself not so much in excretion as in hostility. (Compare the good nature of a really dirty comedy like *Ubu.*)

On the other hand, Jonson, especially in *The Alchemist,* is glorious in the smiling and chuckling of the resolution, the satisfaction of the cat that has lapped up the cream. We are left with a normalcy that is lively indeed. For other poets liveliness means mainly a wedding, and Jonson nods in this direction by assigning the pretty rich girl to Lovewit: it is the prize of urbanity; there is no romantic nonsense. But what he is mainly concerned with is that poetic justice be given to intelligence and skill, and he works this out in the nicest detail.

Face gets off free. In the beginning, Face and Subtile seemed almost formally identical; but, as the intrigue progresses, we find Face infinitely various, while Subtile is handled more and more as an expert in one line; therefore, Subtile is deflatable, but Face is not. (So in Gogol's "Gamblers" the master-cardsharp is taken by the all-round crooks.) Face is a wit; he can operate in normalcy, where normalcy belongs to a Lovewit, not a Surly who has the vice of honesty. Subtile is not punished, for he was so skilful. The surprising adequacy to normal conditions of what seemed to be a deflatable trait (knavery) is glorious. Glory is the survival, and reward, of a comic trait in the resolution. Glory is the discovery that a deflatable talent is a wit.

I have said that the officers and the crowd are not handled as dupes. Yet surely there is a sense in which they, and a fortiori the normal Sir Epicure and Surly, are made ridiculous by Lovewit and Face. But this is the comic world of everyday, not of accident. Herein one may get "Happiness . . . though with some small strain of his own candour" (V, 5, l. 483). We may take this as the comic thought of the resolution; it is a philosophical truth. (Note that the poet has to apologize for it, for it is not quite the morality of the audience.)

### CHARACTERS AS ASPECTS OF THE PLOT

In a rough way the characters are introduced as foils: the intrigue is expanded by the interplay of contraries. Dapper and Drugger are dupes, the simpleton and the fool; they make no long speeches. Sir Epicure and Tribulation, the contrary vices, are heroic humors; they make long speeches; and, in the mutual dealing between lust and puritanism, each is secretly subject to the vice of the other. The foil between the friends, Sir Epicure and Surly, expresses an important structural moment, the humorous-normal; it is a probability within the intrigue for the ultimate deflation. Surly and Lovewit, again, are foils in that both aspire for the normal prize, the rich marriage; here the lively-normal or urbane has succession over the humorous-normal. Lastly, Face and the Alchemist are foils. Subtile is the comic genius who gives his name to this particular intrigue, but Face is a wit who can survive for any Jonsonian sequel. Thus Face and Lovewit, the witty and the urbane, are universal characters, not involved in a particular intrigue; and this is expressed by having these two appear together before the curtain (V, 5, ll. 484 *ad fin.*). They can address the audience directly, since they are no longer "in" the play.

The humors are "unsympathetic"; that is, they are completely deflatable without reconstitution. Thus the comedy of humors tends to be a little cruel; and where the humor is involved with a person's happiness and station, as in *Volpone* or in *Le Misanthrope, L'Avare,* and *Tartuffe,* we pass easily from comedy to tragic satire, from the heroic humor to the tragic flaw. The comic talents, the knaves or shrewd fools, on the other hand, are in a certain sense "like the audience"; they have a cleverness that anyone might wish for himself. Thus their deflation calls for such reconstitution as is possible in normalcy. (We might say this formally as follows: The fact that these talents survive so many comic reversals creates a presumption of permanence also in the deflation, which is the last reversal; whereas the fact that the humors are always being reversed implies that they will be reversed out of existence.)

### SPECTACLE

Spectacular disguises and hiding places imply a comic intrigue, accidental connections. In serious plays the disguises are for the most part natural, deep-going traits, as that Orestes does not recognize Iphigenia because of the lapse of time. And hiding places are not serious, because it is not the local place of the actor but his character and thought that must save or destroy him. A disguise on the scene, for instance Surly as the Don, presents us with two traits at once; it is the foretaste of a comic reversal. And, in general, the ability to assume different disguises is a comic talent; it sets intrigues in motion. To be named "Face" is to be a universal wit and to survive. In the setting of *The Alchemist* there are many rooms, from each one of which threatens to emerge a fatal secret, and, of course, Dapper is waiting in the privy.

Further, the spectacle of many persons engaged in heterogeneous occupations is comic; it promises accidental connections. So the Don is pleasure-bound, the Alchemist busy with his retorts, Dol as the Queen of Faerie is waving her wand, Face has his medals, and the carriers are bringing on the leaden roofs of the churches of the elect. Out of this potpourri the disguised actors frequently make asides and out-of-character grimaces, which may be in some other character or "real" and out of the play, normalcy. But the "reality" of the actor is itself comic in the ideality of the theater.

By means of spectacle there are quick reversals and deflations, unmaskings. To be hit with a soft pie is a quick reversal of superficial dignity. When the intrigue is thickly starred with such spectacular reversals, not much prepared, we have the effect of slapstick.

On the other hand, a very effective expression of normalcy is the presence of the normal crowd as opposed to the comic company, for the anonymous crowd is not a humor. Bergson remarks on this well when he says that monstrosities develop in private and are destroyed by publicity. The crowd is active and vociferous but homogeneous and anonymous; it is lively and normal. The crowded comic company is active, vociferous, and heterogeneous. And, following the convention of Roman comedy, we see in *The Alchemist* the contrast of Inside the House, where there is comic license, and Outside, normalcy pounding at the door.

The Time, nearly continuous with the drama, is exhilaratingly crowded. The relation between continuous time and the comedy of juxtaposition is obvious, for where there are many actions, and all of them must be carried on at once, accidental relations are inevitable. Jonson makes good use also of the neoclassical acts, the entrances and curtains: the end of Act I, scene 1, is the end of the formal beginning; Act II, scene 1, and Act III, scene 1, introduce the major heroic humors; and Act V, scene 1, is the entrance of the normal crowd, lively and noisy enough to avoid a letdown after the climax.

### DICTION

The dramatic irony of comedy is jokes. In serious plays ironic speech makes even the sparse lines of the plot more fatally simple; but jokes fly off in every direction, and each one is a reversal of thought and a deflation of intention. Slapstick is the multitudinous and unprepared deflation of comic appearance, jokes of comic thought. So the feeling of the whole becomes heady and unpredictable. (But, if once the jokes become predictable, the whole falls like a wet cake.)

In an important class of cases it is pointless to distinguish comic thought from comic diction, namely, where laughter is roused by the deflation of sense to sound, as in puns. Speech is sound significant by convention; the comedian breaks the convention. Puns are usually trivial (e.g., Drugger's "angels" are also coins), but Jonson is a master of the sophisms that turn on form of sentences rather than the composition of meanings, what sounds like sense (e.g., Face on Dapper's birth caul: "How! swear by your fac, and in a thing so known unto the Doctor? how shall he then believe you i' the other matter?"). The matter-of-fact tone, the wild absurdity, the careful logic; it is a kind of fun that is as rich as can be, and yet we are not invited to let go but to keep pent up and finally mellowing within us the philosophic wine of how ridiculous the world is. Then a whole character may be deflated to a sound, as we are assured that Dapper is no "chiaus."

The scientific arguments of a Subtile or a Sganarelle are, of course, the same comedy of sophisms. But Molière on the physicians is not savorous but sharp (it is mere folly); he turns the comedy outward in persistent satire; whereas the learned Jonson savors and dreams of learned men, and it is mere folly.

The reduction of character and plot to sound is very marked in those plays (not *The Alchemist*) that employ elaborate comic rhythms; for example, in *The Archarnians* the cretics of the Chorus are so warlike and striking that the soldiers become singers and chorus boys. Gilbert and Sullivan are English masters in this kind and also in the patter songs of individuals.

In general, when the rhythm is kept subordinate to the thought and action, regular rhythm dignifies and ennobles. A simple smooth rhythm that does not call attention to itself makes the speech serious; iambic rhythm elevates colloquial speech. The tack that Jonson takes, however, is to handle the iambics roughly, to bring the music *down* to colloquial speech, and this is a comic diction. Compare an excited moment in *Oedipus* with one in *The Alchemist:* in the tragedy the verse is climactically cut to hemistichs, but in the comedy to six speeches to a pentameter (e.g., I, 1, l. 107). Naturally the audience cannot hear such a meter, but that too is one of

Jonson's learned jokes. Also, the crowded heterogeneous scene fits with broken rhythms.

We must not overlook the long speeches in *The Alchemist,* those that most directly give the heroic humors. They are of the lineage of Horace and Martial and just as good. Thus, the marvelous characteristic rhapsodies of Sir Epicure: "Come on, sir. Now you set your foot on shore . . ." (II, 1, ll. 1 ff.); "I will have all my beds blown up, not stuft . . ." (II, 2, ll. 145 ff.); "We'll therefore go with all, my girl, and live / In a free state . . ." (IV, 1, ll. 156 ff.); or Tribulation's "The children of perdition are oft-times / Made instruments . . ." (III, 1, ll. 15 ff.). These, with their compactness of idea and firm march of sound, are truly heroic. They are laughable, not part by part but as wholes; this is epic comedy. At the other extreme the dupes do not express themselves at all, as if speech were too grand for them, but the adaptable Face speaks up for them: " 'Slight, I bring you no cheating Clim-o'-the-Cloughs . . ." (I, 2, ll. 244 ff.), or "This is my friend Abel, an honest fellow . . ." (I, 3, ll. 396 ff.).

Insults and obscenity belong to comedy, both for their malice and to create the suggestive atmosphere of the deep laughter. In the first seven lines of *The Alchemist* we have farting, shitting, and pissing; and we proceed thence to uncomplimentary personal remarks. (I have previously suggested that the cruel use of the excretory is the characteristic libido of Jonson.)

The so-called speech of low characters and any other emphasis on individual tricks of speech (e.g., the dialect of Lucas in *Le Médecin malgré lui*) may or may not be comic, depending on the structure. If the thought, and especially the sentiment, is strongly developed, as in Wordsworth, then the speech appears as a halting attempt to be serious with inadequate means, and the effect is pathetic; but if, by the emphasis, the character is reduced to the mere eccentric use of words, the effect is comic. The particular Jonsonian mixture of base speech and Marlovian high rhetoric is quite his own. He does not mean it to be bombastic and satiric, and it is not; it is not comic but simply strange, the soaring dreams of a gross animal body (indeed, the daring comparison that comes to mind is *L'Après-midi d'un faune!*). And this gross beauty, again, he involves with a matter-of-fact naturalism and an acutely intelligent appraisal of the types of the town.

Finally, there is a good deal of actual "topical reference": to the actual statute of sorcery, to a real highwayman, a current "Persian" incident, etc. Such random actual reference tends to trivialize tragedy, reducing it to the level of news, "his tragedy has become a *fait divers*"—unless, of course, there is one great unified reference to an important current event, in which case the tragedy becomes a kind of tract for the times. In comedies like *The Alchemist,* however, the references to actuality provide a ballast, a comic normalcy of reality continuous with the normalcy of the humors. Such comedy verges into social satire. (Quite different is the effort to use the topical reference as a joke, like a radio comedian; the laughter is then often embarrassed, for the audience is unwilling to deflate the actual world to nought.)

### A NOTE ON SENTIMENTAL COMEDY

As a form of experiencing—as in the Rorschach analysis of apperception—a comic intrigue is a structure of "wholes" and "small details." As in seeing together two wholes of characters-and-their-intentions some small detail suddenly assumes prominence and compels a reorganization; and the new structure is again reversed by a small detail; and so on, until we become heady and expect anything whatever to occur. Concretely, we have seen, every such comic reversal is grounded in resentment, malice, and lubricity; and in the sudden change these are released with increasing laughter and glory.

Comic experience is universal, yet it is quite extraordinary. It requires, on the one hand, a considerable intellectuality, to make sudden connections through small details rather than through the large parts; thus small children have no comic sense; they take everything seriously and cannot abstract. Yet, on the other hand, it requires a tolerance of the underlying forbidden drives. Comedy is the art of hyperintelligent monkeys, and Jonson was apt for it.

In the average person, however, such a form of experience is likely to rouse anxiety. Comedy in which both the intellectual and the animal elements are strongly developed is rare in literature. Far more common, as pure comedy, are farces, slapsticks, strings of gags, where no large whole is developed and not much of the ordinary world is destroyed. And the most popular kind of whole play is sentimental comedy, a mixture of a comic intrigue with a sympathetic love story; this is the so-called "New Comedy" (e.g., of Terence), a kind of descendant of the Old Comedy tamed and of the tragedy-with-a-happy-ending.

In sentimental comedy the romantic plot persists from the beginning to the end; it is not deflated. The romantic plot is not noncomic in the sense of being merely normal (outside the comic license); the love story excites an independent interest, with feelings of desire, anxiety, fulfilment; it gives the audience something to latch on to. This sympathetic line, with which the audience can identify, is crossed by the malicious and resentful accidents of the comic intrigue—and the whole is an accurate imitation of the insecurities of adolescent sexuality.

The poetic structure of the sympathetic plot, a persisting desire delayed by hindrances, is the subject matter of the next chapter—I shall call these plots of "sentiment" rather than of passion or laughter. In this place let us touch merely on some possible relations of such a sympathetic plot to the comic intrigue. The sentimental characters who are not characters of comedy are *ingénus.* For instance, there may be a humor, an irate father, whose comedy retards the sentimental fulfilment; but some comic agent, a wit, a clever servant, deflates the humor and ends the retardation. The retarding is the occasion for sentimental episodes, hesitations, wishes, love scenes, and these are the interesting plot of the *ingénus.*

More deep-going is the plot in which the retarding comic conditions are not comic but conventionally normal, as there is between the families a difference of wealth or birth rather than humorous pride or anger. When this normal hindrance is flouted by desire, a comic intrigue is generated: then the lovers' guilt and the parents' humors are penalized by comic reversals; but a miracle, a windfall, an inheritance, a gypsy's tale, solves the whole, deserved by a wit. Here the hero is not merely *ingénu,* for he is flouting the convention as well as experiencing the sentiment.

Or the sentimental characters may be also humorous, as the lovers in *A Midsummer Night's Dream* are disposed to infatuations; their comic reversals purge their errors, until it becomes clear what is their real desire. (More trivially, the lovers become comically involved by some misunderstanding rather than by their humors.)

The sentimental hero may himself be a wit and deflate the irate father, as Léandre in *Le Médecin malgré lui;* obviously this involves a more thoroughgoing destruction of the ordinary world and has more comic magnitude, more malice, and more release of laughter. A very urbane variant of this is where the sentimental hero is both the humor and the wit: he creates complexities and also solves them, as in *The Importance of Being Earnest* (we bring our troubles on ourselves, but "the only way to overcome temptation is to succumb to it").

## [ *Structure of "I Henry IV": Serious and Comic* ]

### MIXTURE OF ETHICAL KINDS

In the last chapter we discussed serious plots; in this chapter we are discussing comic plots; in the next chapter we shall discuss sentimental (novelistic) plots. But these "ethical kinds" are frequently mixed in a single work, as the sentimental comedies mix a sentimental plot in a comic intrigue. Let us briefly consider abstractly the possibilities of such mixtures.

The main comic and serious unities (or comic and sentimental or serious and sentimental) may be developed pure and independently, alternately in different scenes, and then brought together. This allows each kind to become large; the problem is then how to achieve unity in the scene of mixture. In *I Henry IV* great serious and comic magnitudes are brought together in only one climactic scene (V, 4); but there they are triumphantly unified. In sentimental comedies or seriosentimental stories, the mixture is less difficult, for contretemps and difficulties are expected for young love, if only the lovers do not become too ridiculous for continuing sympathy or so endangered that there must be purgation of fear and a change of character.

Mixtures of pure parts do not require any special Attitude of the Author, directing the reading, when to laugh and when to weep. The author is "simply imitating," and the audience accepts the imitation at face value as its experience. Let us call these "natural mixtures." But there are also "sophisticated mixtures" of the different kinds, where the serious and comic, or the sentimental and the comic, are kept in continual fusion, with an effect of oddity, mockery, sarcasm, spoofing. Thus, in a work like *Mac Flecknoe* (discussed below), there is a sophisticated mixture of the serious and comic that we are directed to read in one direction, with an effect of mockery; but in his "naïve" poems Wordsworth mixes the comic and the sentimental and directs us to read in the opposite direction, with an effect of pathos. In such works the Narrator's Attitude is always apparent and is part of the formal structure of the whole.

Irony and wit are spontaneous mixtures of the serious with the serious and the comic with the comic; they do not require a deliberate attitude. But, if they are carried on beyond the feeling already in the context, they become sophisticated, often with frigid effect.

Still another possibility of natural mixture is where one kind succeeds to another. We shall see in the next chapter that this occurs in most novels: the sentimental is fulfilled and passes over into the serious or the comic. *Romeo and Juliet* is an excellent example of the comic passing into the tragic; in the first half there is a preponderance of comedy but almost no comedy in the rest. The sentimental comedy progresses to its conclusion in a marriage and even a night of love, but meanwhile it has turned into a tragedy; and this compounded structure is a profound exploration of the sexuality of early adolescence: the kids get involved in a lively way, but then they cannot cope. *The Merchant of Venice* tries the other way, to compound a sentimental comedy out of a tragedy, but less successfully, for the sacrifice clouds the scene. In *I Henry IV* the serious and comic are not compounded, one out of the other, but are mixed complexly, as crossing strands, and their conjunction is the resolution of the play. In what structure is such a resolution possible? As a whole, *I Henry IV* is one of the largest poems in our language, not second but equal to *Lear* and *Hamlet.*

### HOTSPUR'S PLOT

Regarded as an action, *Henry IV* is woven of three main strands each of which is complex in itself: (1) Hotspur's conspiracy; (2) the comedies of Falstaff; and (3) the relations of the King and the Prince.

At the end of *Richard II* we saw[4] that Henry was laid open to further conspiracies; the plot and its imagery were not resolved—so we called the play part of a cycle. In the opening lines of *Henry IV,* as in the closing lines of *Richard,* the King's desire is still an atoning pilgrimage; but, when the plot is finally resolved, his atoning Jerusalem will in fact be his death (*II Henry IV,* IV, 4).

The conspirators take up arms in the name of the deposed Richard and because of the previous incidents: Bolingbroke had revolted beyond his original justification, and he had turned on those who helped him rise. It is clear that these reasons, of Hotspur and Worcester, are not compatible. The conspiracy does not have a moral integrity that can survive into the resolution. Further, the conspirators have a major political frailty, feudal separatism. The national traits of the Welshman, the Scotsman, and the Northumbrian are strongly handled; each is made interesting and sympathetic in itself, but, therefore, together they are almost comic as a conspiracy. And thus the pretendant Mortimer, who would be the unifier, is handled as a secondary figure, like Arthur in *King John.*

Now, as a serious character, Hotspur is brave in war and eager for the reputation of bravery, Honor. This combination is involved in a double complexity. First, it is tragically fatal in that it leads to hasty commitments and unprepared battle (IV, 3; cf. the behavior of Brutus in *Julius Caesar,* IV, 3). Second, Hotspur is a comic humor, as in the conspiracy in Act I, the

4. Above, chap. ii, p. 66.

scene with Kate in Act II, in Wales in Act III, and in his quick envy of Hal:

> No more, no more; worse than the sun in March,
> This praise doth nourish agues [IV, 1].

And so the Prince, who, as we shall see, is a figure of resolution with respect to both the serious and the comic actions, and therefore speaks philosophically (not as a character) in both, judges Percy to be comic and mentions him in a breath with Francis the Drawer (II, 4).

It is Hotspur's humor that lays him open to a reversal into the comic action. But after his death, of course, his honor is purged of its comic part, and the Prince then speaks the lines, "Fare thee well, great heart."

### FALSTAFF

Falstaff has enormous humors, heroic ability as a comic agent, and (during this play) a triumphant wit, and these imply one another. The liar who lays himself open to reversals can turn the laugh by a new invention, and he can successfully impose a counterfeit in the resolution. The drinker of sack makes money out of the enlistment, and yet he survives on the field, because to be a sensual man is a viable way of life, whereas honor is not flesh but air. Falstaff is thus a remarkable formal invention, a humor that survives the comic intrigue; it is not only Falstaff's inventiveness and philosophy that survive but along with them his tun of flesh.

He is given great formal magnitude not only in spectacle, character, and intrigue but also in diction and thought; and not only in the comic thought that is reversed and deflated (as Instinct and the True Prince) but also in lively philosophy, the thought of the comic resolution. Such are the soliloquies of Act V: "Well, 'tis no matter; honour pricks me on . . ."; "Sir

Walter Blunt:—there's honour for you . . ."; and " 'Sblood, 'twas time to counterfeit." The fact that these speeches are soliloquies proves them philosophical and not humorous, for Sir John is not one to fool himself (conversely, Hamlet's soliloquies are not philosophical but sentimental). By such thoughts, Falstaff is able to survive. They are truths. What do they mean in the structure of the play? As Hal is the foil of Hotspur serious and too serious, Falstaff is the foil of Hotspur comic. Falstaff's honor against Hotspur's honor. And even Falstaff's politics against Hotspur's politics; for, when Hal comes on Hotspur's body, he says:

> When that this body did contain a spirit,
> A kingdom for it was too small a bound;
> But now two paces of the vilest earth
> Is room enough

And when he sees Falstaff's body, he says:

> What, old acquaintance! could not all this flesh
> Keep in a little life?

—except that Falstaff is still alive! "The better part of valor *is* discretion." And the reputation of valor so desired by Hotspur is won, with Hal's license, by Falstaff. "Nothing confutes me but eyes, and nobody sees me." The ethical reversal is absolute: the comic becomes the essential and the essential the counterfeit. "I am no counterfeit," says Sir John: "to die is to be a counterfeit; for he is but the counterfeit of a man who hath not the life of a man; but to counterfeit dying, when a man thereby liveth, is to be no counterfeit, but the true and perfect image of life indeed." So Falstaff carries Percy off. It is not the whole truth, to be sure, for the final values are given in Hal's plot; but the place of Hal in the structure as a whole is such, we shall see, that he must give the license for this wonderful comedy. At the end of the First Part it is still time for Sir John to be in favor, and this is because Hal is still the Prince and his relation to the King is ambiguous.

The conjunction of Falstaff and Percy, the comic and the serious plots, is glorious and pitiful. The death of Percy is not very fearful (he has been handled too humorously), but his fate is exceptionally pitiful; and so much the greater is the glory of Falstaff's witty triumph.

### HAL'S NONINVOLVEMENT

Carefully Hal is protected from any comic involvement that might deflate him. (He is not allowed even the profits of a normal wit, like Lovewit, for he is the Prince.) It is Poins and Poins's scheme that relate him to the robbery; it is the thieves and not the honest men whom he robs. His role is thus formally very peculiar: he takes part in the same incidents as Falstaff, and he vies with him in diction; everywhere he manifests a wit and sets going the reversals wherein Falstaff shows his virtuosity; at the same time he is only a straight man, not essentially a character of comedy. He is like Face rather than Lovewit in that he participates; but, like Lovewit rather than Face, he is never in danger of reversal; he has "the receipt of Fern-seed, he walks invisible." So for Face at the end we feel glory, as here for Falstaff. Not for Hal; he was in no danger, and he wins no reward.

In the other part, Hal is not involved in the complexity of the serious plot either. First, he does not share either the political frailty of the conspirators or the personal frailty of Hotspur, nor again the opposite frailty, cowardice or lack of martial skill. That is, he is not a proper antagonist to Hotspur, for he does not conquer him through his weakness (e.g., if Hal were presented as politic and prudent). Hotspur's proper antagonists are Falstaff for his humor and the King for his tragic flaw.

But, second, and more deeply important, Hal is not involved in the frailty of King Henry, which has laid him open to rebellions; and it is this consideration that takes us to the heart of the play.

### THE PRINCE AND THE KING

The two parts of *Henry IV* treat of the manner of succession of Henry V to Henry IV. In *I Henry IV* the Prince proves to have a worth that the King, necessarily judging erroneously because of his own character, could not properly estimate. In *II Henry IV* the Prince succeeds to the throne.

Now we saw in *Richard II* how the succession of Henry IV involved a tragic mistake. At the end of *II Henry IV* the King comes to admit this:

> God knows, my son,
> By what by-paths and indirect crook'd ways
> I met this crown; and I myself know well
> How troublesome it sat upon my head:
> To thee it shall descend with better quiet. . . .
> For all the soil of the achievement goes
> With me into the earth. . . .
> And I had many living to upbraid
> My gain of it by their assistances;
> Which daily grew to quarrel. . . .
> For all my reign hath been but as a scene
> Acting that argument: and now my death
> Changes the mode; for what in me was purchas'd,
> Falls upon thee in a more fairer sort;
> So thou the garland wear'st successively [IV, 4].

This, at the end of *II Henry IV,* is the resolution of the historical tragedy, in serious normalcy.

Quite different is the King's thought in *I Henry IV*. Here he compares Hal to Richard, who lost out; and he compares Hotspur, whom he would have Hal emulate, to Bolingbroke, who won (III, 2; I, 1). As Richard wasted his time and frequented the many, so now Hal; and as busy and warlike as was Bolingbroke, so now Hotspur. (And, just because this view is erroneous, it is the burden of King Falstaff's homily in the extempore play [II, 4]: Hal is wasting his youth.) But this is precisely the necessary error of the infatuated King who would have his son commit the same error as himself. But Henry V is being prepared for us as the nearly perfect king; his play is to be not a tragedy but an epic. Therefore, Hal must not be involved in the complexity of Richard versus Bolingbroke. And this is accomplished by the formula: Be Richard as Prince and Henry as King. Henry is in error, and the ironical triumph of Falstaff over Hotspur proves it; but, when Hal becomes king, Falstaff must fall. (Politically, indeed, just the opposite of Henry's judgment is true, for Hotspur is like the feudal Richard who called on the legions of angels to fight for the King's name, whereas Hal is like the Bolingbroke who "doffed his bonnet to an oyster-wench.")

In his first soliloquy the Prince tells us what he is about: "I know you all, and will awhile uphold. . . ." Like Richard, he compares himself to the sun smothered by clouds; the difference is that he is the Prince and not the responsible King; he will break through those clouds. But the complete statement of what the Prince is doing is given in the lines: "I have sounded the very base string of humility. . . . I am now of all humours that have showed themselves humours since the old days of goodman Adam to the pupil age of this present twelve o'clock at midnight." He is forming himself anew to be a man (without flaw), and from midnight on we get nearer to the sunrise. And this is indeed the philosophical explanation that emerges in the resolving scene of the cycle (*II Henry IV,* IV, 4); says Warwick:

> The prince but studies his companions
> Like a strange tongue . . .
> will in the perfectness of time
> Cast off his followers; and their memory
> Shall as a pattern or a measure live,
> By which his grace must mete the lives of others,
> Turning past evils to advantages.

(Alas! if I may digress a moment. Once he has unmade the flaws of old Adam, Prince Hal turns out, aesthetically, to be only—*Henry V,* whose love scenes are contemptible, and even the epic has undergone a touch of frost.)

We are concerned with the education of the true prince, to make the perfect king. The success of the education is announced at once in *Henry V* (I, 1): Canterbury calls him the universal wit, combiner of theory and practice; and Ely points out that somehow his past courses are the cause of his present perfection. The sounder of all humors becomes the universal wit.

But in *I Henry IV* just what the Prince must not do is to become involved in the intrigue of the court, like Hotspur and Prince John. It is the life of Henry IV that is sacrificed to the flaw in the succession. Once the rebellion is crushed, Henry is stricken and dies. Henry V can then wear the garland successively.

The nice problem of the blameless succession of the Prince to the King is, more generally, the problem of the succession of any son to any father. This is made amply clear. In *I Henry IV* Falstaff speaks (I, 2) of "resolution thus fobbed as it is with the rusty curb of old father antic the Law." (I think that this passage gives the correct psychoanalysis of the similar syntax in *Hamlet,* "sicklied o'er with the pale cast of thought," after the father is murdered.) There is a persistent rumor that Hal wants to do away with not only father the Law but with his own father the King; and this rumor climaxes in the magnificent stealing of the crown when Henry IV is on his deathbed,

> Is he so hasty that he doth suppose
> My sleep my death? . . .
> For this the foolish over-careful fathers
> Have broke their sleep with thoughts.

No one has written so simply about these bitter facts. But, by his rebellious wild oats, Hal has avoided at least this crime. And lo! when he becomes Henry V, he at once says to the Chief Justice (*II Henry IV,* V, 2):

> You shall be as a father to my youth . . .
> That the great body of our state may go
> In equal rank with the best-govern'd nation.

(And, to digress again, it is false; for on this premise—Falstaff banished—the supreme art rapidly begins to lapse. I think we see here one of the limits of the limitless poet.)

### PRINCE HAL IN THE STRUCTURE OF THE PLOT

What, then, is the role of the Prince? (1) His essential role is in the act of succession. (2) Therefore, he is not tragically handled in the tragic action or comically in the comic. This is his aloofness from the plot. (3) But at the same time he participates importantly in both these actions, because (4), by so doing, he carries on his essential action, the forming of Henry V.

Actively participant yet neither comic nor tragic, this is the rather cold effect of the Prince's role; but confronting his father he is more sympathetic. Yet again, to participate actively in actions as widely divergent as the comic and serious in these plays, is to be an all-round or universal rather than a merely epic character; and this arouses an humane interest of its own, the romance of education.

Regarding the first and second parts of *Henry IV* as Hal's play, we have the development to full power of the universal active hero; *Henry V* will then portray his exploits. The plays are a kind of educational romance treated epically in a few exploits rather than psychologically and novelistically (like *Émile* or *Wilhelm Meister*). At the same time the plays are in the cycle of *Richard II* to *Henry V,* and as such they are the historical tragedy of Henry IV and *his* succession. It is only in a structure of such formal magnitude that we can unify so many different genres—tragedy, comedy, education, and history; the atonement for a broken succession, the judgment on bygone political and moral ideas, the development of the national rather than the feudal monarch.

We could consider *Henry IV* as a social history: the unification of the nation presented in incidents widely differing socially and politically: the royal and feudal courts, the town and tavern, the countryside, public and domestic life, the various ethnic types; and all these explored in a convenient story. But in the end the analysis would come to the same thing, for the story expresses the causal social relationships of the various milieux, as Shakespeare conceived them; the plot is a theory of history, and the chief agents are representatives of their groups.

### SYSTEM OF IMAGERY

The imagery is less richly developed than in *Richard II,* for there is more outward action and variety of milieux. The same system of imagery occurs, but more sparsely. In Act I, scene 1, King Henry speaks of the thirsty soil and blood; well-ordered planets are contrasted with wild meteors (I, 1; V, 1); Hal is the Sun that will break through the clouds in due time (I, 2); to Henry he is the too-frequent Sun (III, 2); to Hotspur, the too-early Sun (IV, 1); to Vernon, the Sun of May (IV, 1).

There is an interesting addition, the Moon. This is Falstaff:

"Let us be Diana's foresters," says Sir John, "gentlemen of the shade, minions of the moon" (I, 2). Are we to think that the Moon is the counterfeit light that yet shines? Now note the persistent inquiry: "What time is it?" In Act I, scene 2, it is night; at the beginning of Act II, scene 4, it is midnight, and all the humors of mankind have been explored; at the end of Act II, scene 4, after the announcement of the rebellion, it is "good-morrow, is it not?" And thus we progress from the Moon's reign to the Sun's.

### PROSE AND VERSE

Lastly, let us make a few remarks on the diction. Since this play is prima facie "half verse and half prose," and since we have already had something to say about the expression of plot and character in metric verses, let us here notice especially the expressiveness of the ametric rhythms.

1. In this play I do not find any "pure prose." By "pure prose" I mean the neutralizing of the character and feeling of rhythm and harmony. Pure prose might, for instance, convey information without calling much attention to the expression; or it might set off a characteristic rhythm and tone by contrast. By "neutralize" I do not mean, of course, to make the motion and sound absolutely inexpressive, but inexpressive in the context; for instance, the Duke's speech in *Othello* (I, 3), "The Turk with a most mighty preparation . . . ," would be dignified anywhere, but in the place its dignity is relatively neutral (completely expected), and the prose prevents the war from stealing attention from the wedding, and it makes the dignity of the Duke a neutral background for the magniloquence of the Moor.

2. The rhythm of the soliloquy of Hotspur reading the letter (II, 3) expresses his character, and the feeling of such a character, becoming involved in his tragic action: rapidly

mounting ire and snap decision; the phrases are short and breathless, the thought is broken by exclamations, tangential interpolations, and repetitions. The letter itself, on the contrary, is rapid but straightforward; and because it seems to be all thought and no feeling it becomes, in the circumstances, not neutral but characteristically chilly.

3. The so-called "prose of low characters," for example, the amorphous rhythm of the carriers at the beginning of Act II—and, in general, of the minor clowns who read no lines but puns (cf. *Romeo and Juliet,* IV, 5)—this is often a flat realism, a kind of background spectacle against which the comic action develops; it is not itself part of the plot. The clowns would have to be discussed for each case. Mistress Quickly, of course, is not rhythmless but a proper humor.

4. We must distinguish also the lively normal prose of the wit and the ametric rhythm of the humor. The wit's speech, for example, Hal's narrative, "With three or four loggerheads amongst three or fourscore hogsheads . . ." (II, 4), is spirited (i.e., rapid, easy, various); it is the speech of lively normalcy and, as such, is expressive of character not in the intrigue but detached.

5. On the contrary, the characteristic speech of a humor, for example, Falstaff's great speech, "A plague of all cowards . . . ," is highly rhythmic, much more so than would be possible with a regular meter. It requires long pauses, sudden emphases, muttering in the beard. This "prose" is at almost as great a remove from pure prose as the outcries of a Scene of Suffering. The humorous blank verse of Hotspur in the last part of Act I, scene 3, combines these effects with a rich bombast.

6. Falstaff has also the rhythms of a comic agent, as well as of a humor, as the impressment speech (IV, 2) and the speeches on honor. Here the ease and spirit are like Hal's lively

normalcy, but there is also character and therefore greater magnitude: these thoughts express Falstaff's essential plot.

7. Besides, there are dictions in this comedy that, rather than merely implying character and action, are themselves comic episodes. They are bravura passages aimed to bring down the house just by being spoken. Such are the tirade on Bardolph's nose, Hal's description of Falstaff in the extempore play, and the exchanges of comparative epithets. This is a kind of word play for the sake of the words that we hear from six-year-olds who are first getting the feeling of deliberate speech. We have above mentioned a similar effect of diction raised to a comic episode in the patter of elaborate meters.

8. Let us notice also the blank verse in the comic parts. First, the soliloquy of Hal at the end of Act I, scene 2, "I know you all," is a pat expression of the contrast between Hal's assumed and his essential roles; it is the earnest blank verse of his serious plot.

9. Very interesting is the snatch of conversation between Hal and the Sheriff at the end of Act IV, scene 4. Here Hal is in the comedy so far as he is shielding it, appearing serious in order to shield it, and yet being himself more than he is when in the comedy, so he speaks in a rhythmless blank verse, without character, but with embarrassment and briefly, to get rid of the other man.

10. At the end of Act III there is a martial shift to blank verse. Hal's lines are transitional to true earnest. Falstaff's couplet is the comic interpretation of nobility, just as in his blank verse in the first part of the extempore play. Such comic nobility is itself a humor, as in the case of Ancient Pistol; but of course Falstaff is aware of what he is saying (it is part of a larger whole), whereas Pistol, with his Caesars and cannibals, is mere folly.

## [ *Structure of "Mac Flecknoe"* ]

### SPECIAL TOPICS IN POEMS LIKE "MAC FLECKNOE"

Let us turn to another combination of the serious and comic, a parody; this is a "sophisticated" mixture, whereby "sophistication" I mean systematic interference with the ordinary implications of some part—interference with what is naturally or conventionally expected—so that the whole must be seen in a certain light, read in a certain direction. In "natural" mixtures, like *Henry IV,* the parts are allowed their ordinary implications.[5] Obviously, where there is systematic interference, the hand of the author is always in evidence, so it is necessary to consider an author's part, the narrator, as part of the plot. (By the "narrator," of course, I mean something in the poem, not the man the author.) Not all poems with an important narrator part are sophisticated; for example, the epic attitude is always important; in the panegyrics of Pindar the attitude of the narrator is even the main source of excitement; and in poems of feeling, lyrical poems, there is in the nature of the case no distinction between the narration and the action. (Lyrical poems are discussed at length in chapter v.) Satires, however, are all sophisticated.

On the other hand, not all sophisticated poems are comic. Naturalism, for instance, is a style sophisticated through and through with a sociological intention; and, as we have said, Wordsworth's naïve poems, that mix the base and the sentimental or the base and the serious, are sophisticated with an effect of pathos (where he hits it off) or of burlesque (where he fails). Generally, in any poem where the comic and serious, or other ethical kinds, are mixed continually, there is required the systematic interference of the narrator to direct the reading.

*Mac Flecknoe* is an invective by parody. As an invective, it

5. Cf. above, p. 104.

combines a specific narrator's attitude, contempt, with an object, Dulness or Shadwell. As a parody, it mocks by sophisticatedly telling a base incident in an epic manner. Invectives that proceed by parody of an epic action have gotten the name of "Varronian satires." (Besides these there are Mock Epics, like *Le Lutrin, The Rape of the Lock,* or the *Battle of the Frogs and Mice,* that also employ parody but are not directly invectives.)

### THE NARRATOR'S ATTITUDE

In poems where the action is the organizing part, character is implied in the action, either as choices or as motives that generate incidents. But we have also noticed that character is implied in another way, namely, by the sameness in a series of characteristic rhythms, thoughts, etc., whose unity is not the fact that one moment leads to another in the motion of an argument, a mounting rhythm, an intrigue, but just in that all the series have some common characteristic. Thus, a series of regular blank verses implies a character. So an attitude or habitual feeling, as distinct from a passion or a sentiment, is implied by the sameness in a series of similar images, tones, or rhetorical figures.

At the start of any work, where nothing is yet in motion, it is this method of sameness that is used to establish character, to give grounds of probability for what follows. Thus we get to know Face and Subtile by the scurrilous exchange of the beginning of Act I, scene 1. In poems of action, however, the sequence of the plot soon takes primacy, and the characters become characters of the action. But where, as in *Mac Flecknoe,* the major parts are precisely the attitude and character, the poet may persist in the method of sameness-through-a-series; he may combine even a series of similar actions to give character, as in *Don Quixote*. Consider "Sporus" in the *Epistle to Dr. Arbuthnot:*

> Let Sporus tremble.—What? that thing of silk,
> Sporus, that mere white curd of ass's milk!
> Satire of sense, alas! can Sporus feel?
> Who breaks a butterfly upon a wheel?
> —Yet let me flap this bug with gilded wings,
> This painted child of dirt that stinks and stings;
> Whose buzz the witty and the fair annoys,
> Yet wit ne'er tastes, and beauty ne'er enjoys. . . .

Here the forward motion, the conversational gambit, is quite specious; the whole is a series of name-callings; and it has great power.

In *Mac Flecknoe* the invective is a series of deflating epigrams. Shadwell, the object, is repeatedly let down, his character is "sinking while declaiming"; the contempt of the narrator is the virtuoso use of a great variety of literary gestures with the one identical point. The nice selection of the meaning of a word serves for a comic reversal—"Mature in dulness from his tender years," "never deviates into sense," "his goodly fabric fills the eye, . . . designed for thoughtless majesty." Dryden is a master also of the broad fun of incongruous naturalism:

> Methinks I see the new Arion sail,
> The lute still trembling underneath thy nail. . . .
> About thy boat the little fishes throng
> As at the morning toast that floats along.

And of course the parody itself, the base heroic, has the same identical point.

Any literary gesture that attracts attention to itself implies the narrator; and a similar series of such gestures is the narrator's attitude. In the epigrams here we see the comic object and the poking of fun at it. This is an essential difference between satire and comedy, for in satire no identification with the humorous character is allowed; we are dissociated from it all the way by the narrator's attitude.

An epigram is a mutual implication of a diction and a proposition. Putting together the proposition generates a structure of words that attracts attention to itself, and this structure proves also to imply the proposition. There is an effect of surprise and glory, though not necessarily of laughter; for example, the definitions of mathematicians are, to my taste, frequently epigrammatic, especially when the surprise is strong and we ask, "How is that again?" (For instance, Russell's: "A cardinal number is a class of classes similar to a given class.") There is laughter when the new tight structure maliciously destroys the vaguer connotations. Epigrams in which the diction is strong are generally comic, because we normally expect thought to express character, motive, etc., but here the thought is deflated to diction. The comedy is urbane if the thought is also very strong, as in Dr. Johnson or Wilde. In *Mac Flecknoe,* mostly, we do not find a very urbane or philosophical comedy; it is a rough invective; it calls names and makes ridiculous. The aptness of epigrams for satire, and of rhymes and rhymed couplets for epigram, is obvious.

Dryden lets Shadwell down with every kind of deflation. He introduces him among words, ideas, actions of false elevation, then drops him. Most simply in a phrase, "lambent dulness." Or in a verse, "Thoughtless as monarch oaks that shade the plain." Or in a couplet where the first verse is noble, the second base. Or in a pair of couplets, the first, for example, describing Hannibal's the second Shadwell's oath. Flecknoe, meanwhile, is ridiculed simply by having him espouse the base part of each point. The Varronian parody is a similar letting-down: throughout we are given connotations of Virgil, but the locale of the nursery for actors. And the over-all story framework, Crowning a Successor, is again the same; it starts with the indisputable premise that "All human things are subject to decay" and terminates with "Down they sent the yet declaiming bard" through a prepared trap. There is a variety of approaches, and the one endlessly repeated low conclusion: stupid, dull, dunce, thoughtless, vanished mind, foggy, damp, senseless, tautologous, Irish, Shadwell.

Toward the end, there is a motion of the narrator toward a more philosophical attitude, Jonson's excellence in nature and art; and this, if it were persisted in, would change the tone of the satire from invective to something more serious, perhaps indignation, or even a kind of terror, as in the remarkable ending of *The Dunciad*.

### SOPHISTICATION

Let us go back again to the notion of sophistication. The poem has mixed ethical kinds, serious diction and action, and base character and thought, but the reading is directed so that the effect is comic.

Since every part in a poem is expressive,[6] the serious elements in a mixed poem would usually deepen the whole, for example, bring out serious aspects of the comedy, as in *Henry IV*, or as a noble rhythm will dignify a sentimental comedy. But in burlesques, travesties, mock epics, Varronian satires, etc., the reverse is the case, for the attitude of the telling makes the serious heighten the comic. How this occurs is intuitively obvious, yet it is worth spelling out, because the devices of sophistication have wide bearings, not only for satire.

1. The serious parts are persistently isolated; their natural implications are inhibited, and they are not allowed to have consequences. But the comic parts are allowed free association and expansion. The serious cannot influence the comic; therefore, since there it is, it must heighten it by contrast. In such conditions the serious must seem exaggerated and liable to deflation. Such an effect of burlesque may occur unintentional-

6. Cf. above, chap. i, p. 16.

ly, as when bad actors can make the audience weep with laughter at the death of Desdemona.

Correspondingly, however, it may be the base parts that are inhibited among the serious or the sentimental parts. We have mentioned Wordsworth as doing this; in a poem like "The Idiot Boy" he inhibits the comic implications of the character and vocabulary and so reinforces his own narrator's plot (feeling); the effect is naïve and pathetic. In contemporary writing this method is much overworked; for example, in a typical southern novel the base rhapsody of the poor critter is interspersed with religious references to the Blood of the Lamb; but, since such references cannot, by nature or convention, be isolated and inconsequential, the whole achieves a cheaply bought pathos. Given exactly the same mixture, Swift would take care to deflate the religious reference and achieve a blazing sarcasm; or Anatole France involves the religious references in an ambiguous irony and makes a gentler satire.

2. The reading of the ethical mixture may be directed also by the handling of the hierarchy of parts, depending on the expectation of this ordering in similar nonsophisticated works. Thus, we ordinarily take meaning as ordinal over rhythm; we take the action and its locale as ordinal over the similes and other figures of speech; and the conclusion over the beginning. So when we read "Thoughtless as monarch oaks that shade the plain," we laugh; yet the line is a noble one, and with another handling we might be teased into a solemn feeling. (One can almost fancy it as a line of William Cullen Bryant.) So the references to Virgil are only figures of speech; the base real action determines the reading. And the end of the epigram is what counts. This is a fairly simple-minded satire, aiming at broad effects.

Suppose the direction is reversed, however, and the action is grand but the thoughts and language base. Then, if the whole is still handled to be comic, we might have the urbanity of the *Amphitryons* or the savage calumny of a debunking.

But of course the sophisticated derangement of the hierarchy of parts need not be comic. In much naturalism, for instance, we are made to dwell on details of the locale (e.g., the price and state of repair of the curtains in the room in which the romantic episode is occurring); the effect is sociology, with its attendant feelings—for example, Chekhov's "It is shameful the way we live."

3. Lastly, reading is directed quite simply by the narrator's telling us how to take the mixture. For example, an orator tells us by his manner, "Laugh at this" or "Don't laugh; the poor devil is dying." Or the narrator may comment on the meaning in so many words. Or, as in *Mac Flecknoe,* he may make his attitude perfectly evident and irresistible.

In principle, where the major parts are allowed their natural implications and the narrator calls no further attention to himself, we would not mention the narrator. Aristotle praises Homer for not being a character in his poems. But indeed such an absent narrator is rare, if he exists at all. Certainly the Homer described by Matthew Arnold (rapid, simple, etc.) is a very present narrator who directs us how to take the world of his heroes, which could equally plausibly, in another telling, be shockingly primitive, horribly cruel, romantically legendary, etc. So Virgil's melancholy inhibits the grandeur of historical Rome, whereas Milton gives grandeur to a fantasy. And perhaps the somewhat excessively mordant irony of Sophocles makes even *Oedipus* pessimistic a little beyond its plot. To be paradoxical, if we consider the giant classics of our tradition, how personal, odd, sophisticated, and little "classical" they are! Good petty works are more likely to be "classical," regular, natural, and without a distinguishable part of the narrator.

### STORY FRAMEWORK

Let us ask about the beginning, the middle, and the ending of *Mac Flecknoe*. There is a problem that we have not encountered in discussing poems of action. For, since action, acting, and speech are all temporal, the flow of words and scenes can be made to give the temporal unity of the action. We saw in *The Alchemist,* for instance, how this "unity of time" helped produce the comic crowding of the heterogeneous intrigue, whereas in *Oedipus* it heightened the intensity of the single action. But invectives like *Mac Flecknoe* are organized chiefly by the attitude and the object; these are habitual and are not primarily temporal like action or feeling. They are given not in a probable sequence but in the sameness in a similar series of pointed epigrams. How then to determine the beginning, middle, and ending?

1. One method is character exploration. The character (either Shadwell or the narrator) could be given dialectically in contrasting aspects and successive depths; and the innermost is the end. For example, in "She Was a Phantom of Delight" there is a series of similar stanzas, but we start from the outward phantom that "first . . . gleamed upon my sight," and we proceed to the "very pulse of the machine"; this gives sequence to the character, and the exploring itself is a psychological action of the narrator. (The chief literary example of such an action of psychological exploration is *À la Recherche du temps perdu* taken as a whole.) In Dryden's poem there are traces of an exploration of the declaiming dulness: we start from the hero's natural aptitude both physical and mental and move toward his achievements past and future; the injunction

> Leave writing plays, and choose for thy command
> Some peaceful province in Acrostic Land.
> There thou may'st wings display and altars raise
> And torture one poor word ten thousand ways—

this is quite climactic in its way. And in the narrator, correspondingly, the contrast with Jonson, the perfect comic writer, belongs near the end, as the most serious strain of the poem.

2. A common sequence in invective satires is argument for a thesis. The order is then statement, evidence, and conclusion. We reach the end when the case is proved.

3. But certainly in *Mac Flecknoe* the chief sequence is given by the action, and the ending is the Trap. Yet this could hardly be called a plot. There is no interesting probability or expectation; we do not care especially what happens next. The poem is kept going by the virtuosity of the narrator. Thus it is profitable to introduce the notion of a story framework. A framework is any part with a temporal order that offers convenient occasions for parts (attitude, character, idea) that do not have a temporal order. For instance, the dialogue form for presenting a nondialectical proposition is a framework; so is the epistolary form of most "heroical epistles"; so is the description of a landscape in a lyric of mood. Consider a fairly common case of the last: describing the landscape in some plausible sequence, the poet develops his mood, explores its aspects; then the mood heightens to a feeling, of which the landscape may be a symbolic object, and this is the ending.

Generally, the framework is ethically similar to the more important parts, comic for comic, sentimental for sentimental, etc., for otherwise it would attract undue attention to itself. Also, the sequence of the framework (e.g., the friendship of the sender and the receiver of the epistle) is merely plausible or not too implausible; it is not probable, for then it becomes interesting in its own right and is not a framework. The framework is simple, multiple or otherwise impressive in the occasions that it offers to make points, and it itself is a point.

The trap at the end of *Mac Flecknoe* is the same point as the letting-down everywhere else (there is an identical ending to Byron's "Vision of Judgment"). This ending has a certain comic probability just because of its suddenness and triviality—to break off, without a climax or summation, is quite pat. Thus, at the end of Seneca's satire (if we have a whole text), Claudius rapidly becomes a Sisyphus of the dice box and a Law Clerk, and that's that.

[CHAPTER IV]

# Novelistic Plots

NOVELS OF THE SENTIMENTAL KIND ARE SEQUENCES OF OCCAsions for sentiment, leading to abiding attitudes or active commitments. Unlike serious poems, the actions of the persons do not essentially engage them; that is, formally, the persons have a scope and career greater than these particular actions; the persons respond to the events rather than being completely in them. And yet, unlike comedies of deflation, these actions and other occasions of response do make a difference; the responses add up; disposition is fixed into character. In analyzing the structure of a sentimental sequence, therefore, we must look for two things. First, the principle of the adding-up, to the fixing of character, including the predisposition of the persons to such a career. But, second—and this is what is almost always overlooked in the analysis of novels—we must explain the retardation, why it is that the persons are not more seriously committed to the actions, for this also is something positive and dynamic (just as, in psychology, laziness, apathy, distraction, etc., prove always to be active counterforces).

Aristotle says (*Poetics* ii): "The agents must be either above our own level of goodness or beneath it or just such as we are." Imitations of the first two are the serious and comic plots. For the third he gives no hint of an analysis (he refers to works of Cleophon, whoever he may be); but these can reasonably be thought of as the objects of our novels of sentiment. For "as we are," the multitude of our daily actions and the events that impinge on us becomes meaningful in our slowly maturing commitments; our actions are dramatic, but they are potentially so and become so (whether we perform serious actions or ossify into comic humors); they are novelistic. The feeling of such portrayals of men as they are is, correspondingly, sympathy. In ancient times sympathetic plots, as contrasted with grievous or laughable ones, existed, as we have said,[1] in the New Comedy and the tragedy-with-a-happy-ending and later in pastoral works; but for the full expansion of such slowly maturing sequences we must look in our long prose novels.

Flaubert's *L'Éducation sentimentale* is a remarkably pure example in that, though having a well-defined action, it remains novelistic; it does not compound into dramatic scenes. There is a full development of sentiment and character-fixation, and yet "nothing happens"; it is very "as we are." On the other hand, I make some remarks about the structure of *Hamlet,* because, as Goethe pointed out, it is a continuous mixture of the sentimental and dramatic and so illustrates both. Lastly, I include a brief analysis of a still more complicated structure, *The Castle.*

## [ *Analysis of "L'Éducation sentimentale"* ]

### SENTIMENT, ATTITUDE, CHARACTER

*L'Éducation sentimentale* is organized most obviously (though not as a whole) around its sentimental hero Frédéric. The chief persons can be understood as parts of Frédéric; and Arnoux, the husband of his chief love, is anti-Frédéric. But the history of France in the novel goes beyond this principle of organization, and its relation to Frédéric is the whole.

Frédéric's sequence is his growth and change of interest to-

1. Cf. chap. iii, p. 101.

ward several objects of desire and the relation of these changes to one another; and the ending is the character-fixation of the hero, such as it is. Let us here distinguish "sentiment," "attitude," "character." Sentiment is the response of a person on a temporary occasion—the response may be a feeling, thought, action, or combination of these. Attitude is his more permanent feeling, opinion, action, commitment or rejection, with regard to the objects. But character is the emerging unity among his attitudes, so that we can speak of character apart from any particular objects. Usually novels of the sentimental kind come to abiding commitments or rejections and the ensuing dramatic actions; but this particular novel is "educational" rather than dramatic in that the resolution consists not in tragic or romantic actions with regard to objects but rather in the fixing of character.

In serious works we speak of "character change," as the character of Oedipus changes at the reversal. In such a change one abiding structure gives way to another related one, because from the beginning the character is seriously involved. In the novelistic "fixing of character," on the other hand, there is a sequence in relatively freely varying responses. (But, of course, as we shall see in discussing *Hamlet,* where there are tragic changes, there is always a loosening of character, and this may come to very extensive sentimental sequences.)

### THE SPECTRUM OF NOVELISTIC GENRES

We have distinguished the novels that come to commitments and serious actions from those sequences that resolve not in the acts but in the fixing of character. Another possibility is to center attention on the acts, with little treatment of the fixing of character: where the persons are merely plausible agents, we have simple adventure stories; and this is of course a very popular genre, for the reader can make the hero fit his own requirements and vicariously enjoy the adventures. Picaresques are adventure stories where the persons are more marked; they are usually comic epics with episodic plots.[2] In epical plots the actions follow more closely from the will of the hero; in adventure stories the occasions for action are given more externally, as in *Treasure Island*. In novels of sentiment the fixation of character may be followed by tragic scenes, as in *The Scarlet Letter* the fixing of the will of the Reverend Dimmesdale leads to the disclosure on the scaffold; or again by marriages, as in *Tom Jones*. In the former case the sentimental development is restricted to a few occasions; throughout we have a more serious tone, for the catastrophe is impending, and the persons are already deeply committed. In the other case there is a good deal of comic deflation along the way.

At the other extreme from adventure stories, the interest is in the sentimentalizing as well as or rather than the actions, as in the novels of Sterne; these are "humorous" in Pirandello's sense of the word. And there are extraordinary giants of sentiment, like Marcel or Tristram or Hamlet.

### THE SENTIMENTAL OCCASION

As a relation, a sentimental occasion has properties somewhat as follows:

1. The occasion—it may be an action performed or suffered, a thought, a landscape experienced, the weather, etc.—need not be essential to the person; yet it has not a comically accidental or again a merely random relation to him, for it belongs to a sequence that, as a whole, will define him. For example, it is merely by the accident of juxtaposition that Frédéric first sees Marie Arnoux, yet the encounter is so handled that we see that it relates to his deep interests.

2. Where the actions are great, we have the epics of chap. ii, p. 67, above.

2. Of course the molding effect of the occasion may be negative, as when an important offer is laid in Frédéric's way by Dambreuse, but he goes off to see Marie instead; then the noneffect of the offer determines his final character: he is the kind of person who has committed himself away from there.

3. There is often a dual probability in the occasion. On the one hand, the occasion is plausibly given by the hero's situation; for example, Frédéric is a law student and therefore has examinations, or he walks the streets of Paris and therefore has sensations of the city. But, on the other hand, his interests are working in the occasion; for example, he neglects his studies because of despondency of love and therefore fails, or he works hard because Marie admires orators and therefore passes; or his anticipation or despair makes him notice the scene excitedly and colors it with joy or gloom. To the extent that the situation giving the occasion is merely plausible (i.e., we are not much interested in that), it is a kind of story framework, as explained above.[3] But, obviously, as the novel proceeds and the hero becomes more strongly concerned with specific objects, we find that both probabilities are sentimental; for example, one sentimental strand provides occasions for another: Frédéric, embracing Rosanette, thinks of Marie.

4. That is, as the development nears the commitments and the fixing of character, the nonessential part is less. The later episodes in many novels are not very different in effect from serious plots; and, vice versa, tragic recklessness and tragic waverings of doubt may be called sentimental, tending to a different fixing of character. An important difference is that the sentiments in tragedy are destructive of the previous character (for he was from the beginning presented as serious), and there are corresponding feelings of pity and fear; but

3. Chap. iii, p. 124.

in the novels we are discussing, there is no such thing, though tragic scenes may follow. In *L'Éducation sentimentale* Flaubert is at pains to weaken the seriousness of even the later scenes, so that the character, whose commitments are entirely negative, becomes fixed by default.

5. The occasions may be indefinitely numerous; and, the farther we are from commitments and rejections, the more freely they are introduced. The extreme case is the hero completely passive to his environment, with no important interests—this is the *tabula rasa* of one school of naturalism. We have the greatest freedom to introduce the occasions, and nothing is ruled out as irrelevant; the sequence that is then developed—the system and deepening of the responses—expresses the structure of the environment.

6. Or, contrariwise, the unified kind of response in a free plurality of occasions gives us the structure of the sentimentalizing. This is common in novels in scenes where the hero occupies a Point of View, as Coverdale in *The Blithedale Romance* sits unobserved in a tree and responds to the landscape and the passers-by. (This device is everywhere in Hawthorne's tales.) In our novel, for instance, Frédéric is at the races with Rosanette, and from the point of view of this stage in his sentimental career he sees Marie, Mme Dambreuse, Deslauriers, and others. We saw that the involvement of an epic hero through his habits rather than himself allowed for a plurality of episodes, though not very many, since the deeds are great. In picaresque epics, where the adventures are more ordinary, the episodes become very numerous; and so, through works like Smollett's, the generic transition to the indefinitely numerous occasions of sentiment is easy. And at the extreme is what might be called the sentimental picaresque, like Sterne's *Sentimental Journey,* founded on the principle of avoiding fixing the character or generating a single action.

THE SENTIMENTAL HERO

1. The sentimental hero must have interests. (This is so even in the case of the *tabula rasa* hero, whose interests are likely to be "simple biological needs.") Most often we are presented with a hero with a propensity for blondes and so forth. Thus, Frédéric is a *rentier* with a quasi-noble background: he will seek out people with money; he will have certain literary, political, and professional interests; he will be smitten by matronly women of Andalusian features; etc. Such interests may conveniently be divided into desires and interests of situation, where the interests of situation provide the plausibility for the occasions for sentiment.

2. But—and this is very important to bear in mind—these interests taken as a whole do not give the hero's character, for he does not act them out to a finish or respond completely in the occasions that they bring about. There are always certain hindrances. Contrast Frédéric or Deslauriers, who are sentimental persons, with Dambreuse, who is presented as a fixed character, the man of affairs (or contrast Rastignac with Vautrin). To say this another way, Dambreuse is hindered by external events, the Revolution, but Frédéric by an internal hindrance. Or to give an example profoundly explored by Flaubert: the radical Sénécal is presented almost throughout as a man of fixed opinions and no other traits, yet in the end we see that his politics have made a *volte-face,* and he is disclosed as an egotist; the foil of Sénécal is the simple sentimentalist Dussardier, who is gradually affirmed in his radical opinions and dies for them.

The internal hindrances to Frédéric's actions are what lay him open to nonessential occasions, when he would otherwise have committed himself; it is these hindrances that must be overcome for him to come to commitments and fixed character. That is, hindrance is the principle of the sentimental expansion, the retardation of action.

In some novels the sentimental hindrance is fairly simple, as in *The Scarlet Letter* Dimmesdale's hindrance is moral cowardice, closely related to his separation from Hester; the interplay of this with his active traits, such as moral self-reliance, results in such makeshifts as his appearance on the scaffold at midnight. But Frédéric is a creature "de toutes les faiblesses," as Flaubert puts it. Besides, his interests themselves are incompatible and hinder one another, nor is this incompatibility unrelated to his "faiblesse."

We must then look for hindrance as well as interest, where interest will be found in the occasion and the response, and hindrance in the incompleteness of the response.

3. Underlying the division of interest and internal hindrance, there is the potential character: let us call this the Sentimental Disposition. This disposition is at length realized in the fixing of character. Often the disposition is explicitly presented in the beginning by the device of synoptic genealogies and accounts of the hero's heredity and education, as in *The Way of All Flesh.*

There are several possibilities of combination. In the simple case of *The Scarlet Letter* the disposition is realized by the removal of the hindrance; in such a case, the hindrance is nothing but a tragic frailty that destroys the hero by making him commit himself too late. In the more intricate case of *Madame Bovary* the realized disposition itself contains a tragic frailty, for bovarysm is not a viable life. In *L'Éducation sentimentale* the situation is still more intricate, to the point of elusiveness: it is perfectly clear that there is a basic disposition underlying Frédéric's weakness, fastidiousness, bovarysm of the object ("par la force de ses rêves, il l'avait posée en dehors des conditions humaines"); if the cause of this basic disposition were touched, the discord between interest and hindrance would be resolved, and there would be commitments. But Flaubert carefully avoids touching it, and the resolution is ironical and negative.

To sum up: The hindrance is the hero's weakness, the incompatibility of his interests, etc. The disposition is the unity of the division between interest and hindrance. The fixing of character is the realizing of the disposition by resolving the division; it generally involves removing the hindrance and transforming and sacrificing some of the interests. But in *L'Éducation sentimentale* the disposition is unexplored and the resolution is uneasy; so that, what the novelist omits, the psychoanalyst is tempted to supply (except that it seems clear that the novelist is quite aware of what he is omitting). And it is just this uneasy resolution that makes Flaubert's book such beautiful realism of ordinary life, in contrast with the dramatic and schematic education of a Rastignac or the psychoanalysis of Marcel. But Flaubert cannot resist strong irony in the ending.

### SENTIMENTAL SEQUENCE: STAGES

A sentimental sequence is composed of occasions in order; the later occasions present the responses of the hero's disposition as already more defined by the previous occasions.

In an epic or picaresque story the external hindrances do not alter the hero's interests, which are therefore his abiding character; his disposition is realized from the beginning. So in adventure stories and sentimental dramas the principal change is in overcoming the hindering forces or succumbing to them. But in sentimental novels both the fulfilment of desire and its hindrance are equally molding, so that the disposition has changed at every later stage.

The sequence may conveniently be divided into successive

stages or sentimental fixations. A stage is often given in a chapter—it may be a little drama or a short story—a working-out of one mode of sentimental response, so that the hero is more defined in the sequel.

Some of the stages in Frédéric's attachment to Marie are the following. In the first chapter of the first part he meets her and is taken with dreams and not very precise longings. He walks out with her and is hopeful and joyous. By the fifth chapter, since he has gotten nowhere and has failed in other sexual attempts, he is in despair. At the beginning of the second part he is disillusioned with her poverty, for he has fallen into an inheritance and has hopes for new pleasures. In the third chapter of the second part he is "the parasite of the house," for she has confided in him, and he has witnessed her quarrels with her husband Arnoux. Then he sacrifices for her his oldest friend, becomes involved in a comic duel, and ruins his career. Then he is through with all that and goes home to Nogent. Then in the sixth chapter, emboldened by his success with Louise, the girl back home, he is able to kiss her at once. Later he is tempted to kill Arnoux.

Such stages of sentimental commitment must by no means be confused with increase in feeling, for the feeling varies from joy to gloom and its strength from indifference to suicidal rage; and even so he becomes more and more committed.

The progress from stage to stage may be due to a change in the object, as when Marie moves and "les passions s'étiolent quand on les dépayse"; more deeply to a change in the hero's behavior toward the object, as Frédéric tires of Rosanette when he has lived with her or is angry with himself and with Marie because he has given money to her husband; or, again, to his development in the other sentimental strands, the change in his disposition, as we shall see at length.

Deepening commitment is usually convergent, the exclusion

of alternatives. The hero may come to realize that many things that he thought essential to his desire, and their absence fatal, really make no difference, for they are removed and the desire persists (his character emerges); so it is with Frédéric and Marie throughout. Or a situation may generate such external consequences, as status, children, etc., that the possibility of free sentimental response is progressively curtailed.

### FRÉDÉRIC'S SENTIMENTAL SEQUENCES: NONAMOROUS

Taken as the story of Frédéric, *L'Éducation sentimentale* combines half-a-dozen sentimental sequences. First, let us distinguish the nonamorous and the amorous sequences.

The chief nonamorous part of Frédéric's disposition is his childhood friendship for Deslauriers. It is Deslauriers who presses him to make use of the financier Dambreuse; who is the friend of the radical Sénécal; and who tries to involve him in the political journal. Frédéric's interests-of-situation are bound up with Deslauriers—his law studies and political ambitions—for they were together at school and together planned a future life. But from the beginning Frédéric and Deslauriers are presented as foils; Frédéric dreams of romance and literature, Deslauriers of metaphysics and economics. And in the resolution, when both are once more alone together in the uneasy fixing of their original dispositions, the summary is: "They had both of them failed, the one who had dreamed of love, the one who had dreamed of power"; and Deslauriers explains it, " 'I had too much logic, you too much sentiment.' " This is the familiar psychology of nineteenth-century novels: the soul consists of sense and sensibility, and (as Flaubert tells us) of the male and the female. The disharmony between them is Frédéric's disposition; but—we return to the same point—the cause of the disharmony is not explored. We are left with a very uneasy resolution: "Then they laid the blame on chance, circumstance, the age in which they were born."

Deslauriers is Frédéric's attempt to cope with the "logical." A second independent nonamorous sequence is his relation with Dussardier, the poor worker, who has "le génie du cœur," genius of the heart. He is the sensibility of Frédéric working in the nonamorous, with a corresponding change of object from Power (Deslauriers) to the Ideal Republic; and Dussardier's foil, in turn, is the hyperlogical Sénécal, who strives for Power Absolute. Dussardier is very important for Frédéric; it is sufficient to break up his pastorale with Rosanette to learn that Dussardier has been wounded; and, conversely, Sénécal is almost the one person whom Frédéric cannot abide. Dussardier and Marie are the only persons admirable and disinterested throughout, the one in the nonamorous, the other in the amorous.

We seem then to have the following hierarchy of importance, or deepening of significance, in the realizing of Frédéric's disposition: The nonamorous with a passionate heart is deeper than sensual love (Rosanette), but not so deep as passionate amour (for Frédéric is willing to blacken Dussardier for the sake of Marie). Likewise, the combination of power and the kind of expedient love offered by Mme Dambreuse, as schemed by Deslauriers from the beginning, is declined in the interest of passionate love even though it is hopeless, or *because* it is hopeless.

Frédéric's nonamorous relations with the other persons, as Pellerin the painter, Hussonet the editor, Regimbart the citizen, are dependent on the independent sequences we have been discussing. Sénécal, to repeat, is Deslauriers in the extreme, logic and power absolute, and as such cannot affect Frédéric directly, but he can slay Dussardier.

In the end, Deslauriers and Frédéric survive: both are

moderate, both are confused; and the grounds of the confusion remain unexplored. Happiness is not possible; it cannot be worked out: that is the philosophic thought.

We have been distinguishing between the nonamorous and the amorous sequences. But, of course, in Flaubert's novels, all the characters are amorous sentimentalists, and there is no sharp distinction. Deslauriers is deeply shaded with jealousy, *amour-propre,* etc.; and the friendship is erotic though not sexual. Consider, by contrast, the psychology of Balzac: reason, reasonable passion, and passion are kept much more distinct. Balzac's books, correspondingly, are ethical and tend to dramatic scenes; Flaubert's are more sentimental and novelistic.

### OCCASIONS FOR THE NONAMOROUS

The occasions for these sequences are Frédéric's law career, his dealings with Dambreuse, the journal, his political ambitions, and the very strongly presented political history. Now we must regard these, especially the political history, in two aspects, first, as occasions for Frédéric's sentimental education; but, second, as a major independent part of the work, the history of those times. The combination of these two things expresses a third thing altogether; to this we shall return later.

As occasions for Frédéric, the form is elegantly simple: all the occasions for nonamorous sentiment are simply anti-occasions for his amours. In the distractions of his love affairs, Frédéric fails an examination and misses business engagements; he flouts his friendship for Deslauriers and uses elsewhere the money he has promised for the journal; he holds the political opinions that pass in the circle of his current love affair or that express spite at his amorous disappointment; he experiences '48 with the joy and excitement of having succeeded with Rosanette, but during this pastorale all the doings of men seem remote to him. When his heart is set on love, as it is always, the political debates at the luncheon that he gives are intolerably boring, and he muffs campaigning for his candidacy. In the interests of love, Frédéric's response to his nonamorous plots is avoidance. Contrariwise, it is only when his love affairs have reached an impasse that he willingly turns to literature, the journal, money, politics; or when he thinks that these reflect or advance his interests of love.

His "real" interests, then, seem to be merely love affairs, and the rest looks like a "story framework." But we must then ask: Why is the hero involved in so many occasions not sought out by his "real" interests? Contrast the case of *Madame Bovary:* the heroine is thrown by accident of birth and marriage into uncongenial surroundings, and the plot is just the sentimental escape from these. But here we have no such case. Frédéric does really desire these nonamorous occasions, only they are weaker than his loves; and, when they prove incompatible to them, they are always sacrified. But of course his loves also are incompatible. An important trait of the character that emerges is not-to-succeed. The proof that Frédéric is "really" interested is that there are stages of awareness, enthusiasm, and indifference in his political interests that are not merely effects of his love plot but reflect palely the passions of Dussardier.

Frédéric's feelings for Deslauriers, Dussardier, and literature draw on sentimental depths in his disposition that are prior to the division of the amorous and the nonamorous; the love plot does not exhaust his sentimental disposition.

### FRÉDÉRIC'S SENTIMENTAL SEQUENCES: AMOROUS

#### ORDER OF INTRODUCTION

There are four main objects of love: Marie Arnoux, the good wife and mother maltreated by her husband; Mme Dambreuse, the elegant and selfish *grande dame;* Rosanette, the lively and stupid kept girl; and Louise Roque, the girl back home who loves him. We must see how these form a system of loves, complementing and interacting with one another.

First, let us notice a structure of the highest importance in this novel, namely, the order in which the various sequences, both amorous and nonamorous, are introduced and resolved.

1. Marie is first met with altogether, and last disposed of in the amorous part. She is the object on which at least the whole love plot is organized. Louise, who occupies a peculiar role because she loves rather than is loved, is brought in next after Marie, in a curiously offhand manner; and she is next to last to be disposed of. Next is Mme Dambreuse, introduced especially through Deslauriers, and she is disposed of before Louise; but she represents a broader synthesis of interests than Rosanette, who is last to be introduced and first to be disposed of.

2. Now Deslauriers is introduced after Marie and after the mention of Louise. He dominates the second chapter as a countertheme, just as Marie dominates the first chapter; he introduces the many nonamorous interests. Yet, after Marie has been disposed of, Deslauriers still persists. What does this mean? The explanation must be that Deslauriers is Frédéric's persistent boyhood, prior to his amours; he is the rival to Frédéric's life with mother, as Flaubert makes explicit; and this disposition outlives the hero's mature interests. But then why, on the contrary, is Marie introduced first? I conclude that Marie must be understood in two ways: first, as Frédéric's chief mature interest, which cannot ultimately survive; but, second, as his most basic and enduring interest, his mother—but this is never explored, for he does not attain to her. (This can, by the way, be shown psychoanalytically with perfect evidence from the text; but what is interesting is how the novelistic structure itself expresses it adequately.)

The antagonism between Marie and Deslauriers is parallel to that between Deslauriers and Mme Moreau, Frédéric's mother, but in the opposite direction, for Frédéric draws away from his mother toward his friend, but from his friend toward his ideal love.

3. What then of Mme Moreau? The fact is that Frédéric's relation to his mother does not enjoy the dignity of a sequence of the plot! She quite simply vanishes from the picture. For instance, it is likely that she dies somewhere toward the end, but it is not mentioned. Frédéric has sentiments for only everything else. But no, she reappears: in the resolution of the plot with Marie, "Frédéric suspected that Mme Arnoux had come to offer herself; and he was taken by a lust stronger than ever, furious, raging. Yet he felt something inexpressible, a repulsion, and as if the fear of incest. . . . She kissed him on the brow—like a mother" (Part III, chap. vi). Thus we can understand why Marie is first and yet apparently not last; why she is superseded by Deslauriers; and why the ending is an uneasy fixity. (We must return, of course, to what it means for Marie to be the wife of Arnoux.)

In this novel, then, the order of introduction of the sentimental objects is the unfolding of the basic disposition, whose fixing is to come about by the sentimental response to these objects. Such a structure has the enormous advantage that the deepest interests are presented in the most emphatic places. Its effect, however, is cyclical rather than climactic. Consider the common alternative structure, where the progressive emergence of the deep interests is given in the progressive introduction of more and more interesting concerns. Such a handling is more likely to end in positive commitments and dramatic action.

### OCCASIONS FOR THE AMOROUS

The objects of love are introduced in nonessential occasions. Frédéric meets Marie on the boat that is taking him home to

Nogent; it is by accident in Part I, chapter iii, that he turns down the street where Arnoux's shop is located; through Hussonet, a chance acquaintance, he tries to reach Marie; but it is when Arnoux receives a trout from Geneva (in I, iv) that he is finally invited. (The retardation of a desired meeting by such accidental preventions allows more experience to cluster around the object before the "crystallization," as Stendhal would say, is in turn brought about by an accident.) Louise is mentioned merely by the way (in I, i), and Frédéric dismisses her name "négligemment," the fate of this relationship throughout. He first sees Mme Dambreuse in the courtyard, when he has come to call on Monsieur. Rosanette is introduced through the elaborate machinery of Arnoux's clandestine affair with her, as, for example, Frédéric breaks her parasol but takes it to be Marie's.

As these persons become more definitely his sentimental objects, however, Frédéric seeks out the occasions in which they are involved; yet, even so, his response in the occasions is not given by his intentions but by his progressively defining disposition. And he persists as a sentimental person to the end, even while his character and attitudes are fixed; so that in the latest pages he is still presented with nonessential occasions, the landscape, the weather, to which he responds.

## AMOROUS SEQUENCES

### FRÉDÉRIC'S SYSTEM OF LOVE

The variety of the amorous sequences (and of course the interplay of the amorous and nonamorous) discloses Frédéric's amorous disposition, especially when his attitudes have reached stages of relative fixity. Thus, in Part III, chapter iii, he comes to see that Rosanette has "un mauvais goût irrémédiable, une incompréhensible paresse, une ignorance de sauvage"; whereas Mme Dambreuse, "celle-là, au moins, l'amusait! Elle savait les intrigues du monde, les mutations d'ambassadeurs, le personnel des couturières." Madame is the great world of power and refinement that he cannot decline in the interest of sensual enjoyment. But by chapter iv he has learned with respect to Madame "la désillusion de ses sens, ce qu'il s'était caché. Il n'en feignait pas moins de grands ardeurs; mais pour les ressentir, il lui fallait évoquer l'image de Rosanette ou de Mme Arnoux." (To be sure, they are not there.)

Rosanette at her best is contrasted with Marie: "l'une folâtre, emportée, divertissante; l'autre grave et presque réligieuse" (II, ii). But at this stage of sentiment, they do not clash but augment one another, Rosanette coming to mind because she is less unattainable, Marie because she is more so.

His sensual antipathy for Mme Dambreuse is also a moral antipathy; he finds, especially after the death of Monsieur (when she is really attainable), that she is selfish, hardhearted, cold: "Elle avait une façon de jouer du piano, correcte et dure. ... Elle était hautaine avec ses gens; ses yeux restaient secs devant les haillons des pauvres"—marriage with such a person is incompatible with Frédéric-Dussardier, "génie du cœur."

It is Marie Arnoux who combines the perfections of both the other women and has also wifely and matronly perfections that they lack (and that, of course, make her absolutely unattainable). Of himself and Marie: "Leurs goûts, leurs jugements étaient les mêmes. Souvent celui des deux qui écoutait l'autre s'écriait, 'Moi aussi!' " She is the ideal; she could truly satisfy the whole Frédéric—except that he cannot possess her. She is a sentimental and not a committed ideal. And Frédéric himself comes to this view (III, vi): "Une autre crainte l'arrêta, celle d'en avoir dégoût plus tard. D'ailleurs, quel embarras ce serait!—et tout à la fois par prudence et pour ne pas dégrader son idéal, il tourna sur ses talons et se mit à faire une cigarette." It is such a beautiful climax.

Marie can satisfy every requirement except that basic need that keeps him a sentimental person rather than a committed character.

The remaining object of love is Louise. She, it seems, is always attainable, for she throws herself at him—which gives him a pleasure "qui n'excédait pas l'ordre des sentiments agréables." She has wealth and animal ardor, but she does not have that touch of beauty that is the property of the unattainable. Even so, when Frédéric is through with all the rest, he longs for his home environment: "il souhaita la fraîcheur de l'herbe, le repos de la province, une vie somnolente passée à l'ombre du toit natal avec des cœurs ingénus" (III, v), and his thought then turns to Louise. Too late! Deslauriers, his boyhood rival, has stolen the prize. (Allow me to speculate: might we not go on to another volume—the love of Frédéric for his best friend's wife, in which he suffers intensely, like Swann, for a woman who is not even his type!)

### IMPASSES

A temporary impasse in one sequence plunges the hero back into another. This principle is operative everywhere in this novel (it is almost a defining property of the sentimental hero with an internal hindrance); but let us mention only a few variations.

In general, a sentimental impasse is the inability of the hero, because of changes in the object or in himself, to sentimentalize along certain lines as new occasions arise. Most often external difficulties cannot create an impasse, for the hero will make sentimental occasions of these very difficulties; the absence of the beloved is a better occasion even than her presence.

In an impasse, the author, or better the hero, can take up some interest previously postponed. When the author's hand is apparent, the effect is somewhat tricky and miraculous, a trivial *deus ex machina,* for we then go back to important accidents at stages of the sequence where the disposition is too fixed for such accidents to occur. But this is largely a matter of handling. The postponed interest is always in abeyance in the hero's mind: for example, Frédéric might have received a letter or an invitation a month ago and put it off because of his love, and now he attends to it just because of spite or deception. An example of the author's hand: When the pastorale with Rosanette at Fontainebleau has come to the stage where "on découvre chez l'autre ou dans soi-même des précipices qui empêchent de poursuivre; on sent qué l'on ne serait pas compris ... aussi les unions complètes sont rares"; suddenly Frédéric reads in the paper that Dussardier has been wounded, and he must return to Paris. Yet here I think the author's hand is by no means tricky but on the contrary an example of remarkable insight; for the situation is one of the dread and confusion of instinct itself, brought on by the possibility of total satisfaction. In such a case one is rescued by a "sublimation," a safer terror; and symbolically it is being wounded on the barricades. Again, during the first series of embarrassments of his relations with Rosanette and Marie, brought on by Arnoux's lies (II, iii), "La situation devenait intolérable"; at once he is distracted by receipt of the 15,000 francs he is to lend to Deslauriers, and he becomes enthusiastic about the journal. Allaying an intolerable conflict releases energy for something else, but the release is of course temporary.

In other cases when Frédéric becomes fed up with a situation that seems to have no future he brusquely turns elsewhere; for example, after the humiliations following on the duel—the articles of Hussonet, the showing of Pellerin's picture, the mockery at the Dambreuses'—he goes back to Nogent. Such a return home requires a very strong impasse. And we may conveniently divide Frédéric's disposition by the change in scene, Paris and Province. In Paris the different interests can interact with a certain rapidity, and there is thus a relative unity of place, whereas Paris and Nogent are true sentimental changes of scene. But of course at Nogent the match with Louise becomes in turn too pressing, and he feels compelled to return to his other life.

An important impasse is Marie's missing the rendezvous: "il se jura de n'avoir plus même un désir"—therefore at once he has his will of Rosanette, the first of his realized satisfactions and the end of Part II. Again it is a case of an allayed conflict releasing new energy. (Earlier this has occurred more partially: his desire for Marie is active but hopeless; he turns where there is hope, and less guilt, to Rosanette. Later, strengthened by his other successes, his hope revives also with respect to Marie.)

The general pattern, thus, is as follows: an impasse in one sequence plunges the hero into another; and the occasions of the other sequence bring the hero to a new stage at which the original sequence is no longer in an impasse.

### CONFLICTS AND REVERSALS

The passage from one sequence to another by impasses that we have been describing is very novelistic, for it is because of his internal hindrances that a sentimental hero cannot finish an action. Success is even more likely than failure to bring him to a pause.

Besides this structure, however, the sentimental sequences cross in conflicts, dramatic scenes, and reversals. This is the familiar complex plot that we have already discussed many times. The multiplicity of the interests produces different plot strands, and these converge and cross.

There are numerous possible combinations. For instance, the other sequences may be viewed sentimentally from the point of view of one sequence, with or without effecting this sequence: as, from the satisfaction of the pastorale with Rosanette (before it becomes too hectic, instinctually dangerous), Frédéric views the Revolution as a small thing; or, on the other hand, in the carriage at the races with Rosanette, the view of Marie, Madame, and Deslauriers produces a confusion in Frédéric, so that he recalls the days "où il enviait l'inexprimable bonheur de se trouver dans une de ces voitures à côté d'une de ces femmes. Il le possedait, ce bonheur-là, et n'en était pas plus joyeux." (This is the formula that Proust employs with such subtilty and grandeur.)

When the strands of interest cross, one may make the other pale or be negated; or they may advance once another, or confuse one another, or threaten to destroy one another. Frédéric negates Deslauriers for fear of belittling himself by introducing this shabby friend at Arnoux's. The beginning of his double life with Rosanette and Marie are like "deux musiques"; or his double life with Rosanette and Madame, compacted of difficulties and lies, is a kind of game; or again, at the great party at the Dambreuses', where Louise and Marie are present, Frédéric is lionized and rides the tide of his first success with Madame yet does not miss the chance to advance with the others. On the other hand, the extreme of confusion is sentimental despair, thoughts of suicide, world-weariness; this might be called a pervasive impasse: "Lasse, plein de désirs contradictoires, et ne sachant plus même ce qu'il voulait, il éprouvait une tristesse démésurée, une envie de mourir."

We may distinguish two kinds of sentimental reversal: that in which the hero, by his disposition alone, loses interest (e.g., Frédéric tires of Rosanette because, once he has succeeded, she is irrelevant to his emerging character) and that in which there is a conflict, and one sequence destroys another. Then suicidal despair may be either a total loss of interest (pervasive impasse) or a mutual destruction of all the interests: breakdown of character. Despair is frequently the prelude to a new sentimental discovery of the self; the hero now thinks he knows what he really wants. When the despair of loss of interest has exhausted all the possibilities of the disposition, we are at the end.

Conflicts and reversals may be either purely sentimental or partly dramatic. They are sentimental when they are a clash of his interests and attitudes; they become dramatic when the objects, the consequences of his interests, conflict. Thus, Rosanette dramatically appears at Arnoux's and destroys Frédéric's *rapprochement* with Marie; or the party at the Dambreuses' is fraught with dramatic anxiety. Now such scenes—and this is why the distinction is worth making—are quite different in feeling from the sentimentality of the rest. They involve a change in the reader's sympathy from simple identification with the hero to taking in the conflicting objects, and this shift is expressed in a shift in the narrative manner that we must discuss later.

Lastly, whenever there is a complex plot and a multiplex hero, there is the possibility of irony. This may involve only the objects, as when Madame and Rosanette unknowingly imitate each other; or, more novelistically, it may involve the attitudes of the hero, as, for example, Frédéric is outraged that Marie should think, mistakenly, that Rosanette is his mistress, though to be sure this is what he wants and is working for.

### OTHER PERSONS AS PARTS OF FRÉDÉRIC'S PLOT

The other persons are either Frédéric's intermediaries or his antagonists. The intermediaries are used by Frédéric to advance his interests, or, his plans miscarrying, they serve to create sentimental conflicts. Frédéric makes an enormous number of attempts of this kind (indeed, just the opposite of Deslauriers's judgment is true: Frédéric is too logical). In the beginning M. Roque is his entry to Dambreuse; he tries to get Hussonet and Regimbart to present him at Marie's. He gets Sénécal a job with Arnoux, hoping to use him as a go-between. He has Pellerin paint the portrait of Rosanette in order to meet her in the afternoons. He sends Hussonet off with the poodle in order to be alone with Rosanette. He abuses Dussardier's reputation to get money for Arnoux from Mme Dambreuse. These schemes uniformly do not pan out: Sénécal goes off to the country; Pellerin's portrait causes nothing but embarrassment; Rosanette goes with M. de Cisy; Mme Dambreuse sees through the Dussardier deception.

Frédéric's sentimental antagonists provide external hindrances to him: Arnoux with Marie; Delmar, M. de Cisy, etc., with Rosanette; Martinon with Madame. These, as a generality, are active characters rather than sentimental persons; they have resources (M. de Cisy's wealth, Delmar's meretricious talent, Martinon's cunning) that assure their success; and they do not have sentimental hindrances. But it is interesting that, except for Arnoux, they are not Frédéric's rivals; this is not a novel of jealousy and triangles; for, once Frédéric has his way, he realizes that this is not what he wants after all.

### ARNOUX AS THE ANTI-FRÉDÉRIC

Arnoux, of course, demands special attention. He is (to my taste) the most realized and original person in the novel. He is the anti-Frédéric: he dogs his steps from the first pages, for he is introduced, nonessentially, even before Marie; and at the end he is still in possession of the ideal, somewhere off in Brittany.

Yet it is difficult to state just what the antagonism between Frédéric and Arnoux consists in. Consider the following points: Just as Frédéric uses, or tries to use, the others, so Arnoux successfully uses him: he must help Arnoux, to keep

Marie in Paris, to save her furniture, to protect her from pain, etc.; likewise he must continually seek out Arnoux to be near Marie. With both Marie and Rosanette, Arnoux has succeeded; therefore, he seems to be active rather than sentimental, as is also clear from his elaborate and questionable business affairs. Yet clearly Arnoux has a full-fledged sentimental life of his own, the cause of his mysterious failures; but what this is, is never disclosed. Frédéric's responses to him run through well-marked stages: he admires him, defends him, mistrusts him, hates him, dreams of killing him. Yet Arnoux's sanguine and sympathetic temperament is such that Frédéric can never take an outright stand against him.

The puzzle of Arnoux's role, then, is this: On the one hand, he is nothing but the key to Marie, Frédéric's deepest interest. On the other hand, he is another Frédéric, introduced even before Marie, and reflecting in a base and practical way the very interests of Frédéric. We may then contrast Deslauriers and Arnoux as foils of Frédéric: Deslauriers is an anti-Frédéric, because he is what Frédéric is not; their interests are divergent. But Arnoux is an anti-Frédéric because he is in a peculiar way what Frédéric is. The psychoanalysis of the situation is evident enough: Arnoux is the father who has the mother—and, just as Marie is idealized, so he is base and practical. Frédéric cannot put him aside; instead he settles for a disastrous split in his disposition, Frédéric and Deslauriers.

### BEGINNING, MIDDLE, ENDING

We may now sufficiently explain the beginning, the middle, and the ending of novels of sentiment.

The beginning is the nonessential introduction of the sentimental objects, whether persons, ideas, or goals of some other kind; for example, the hero of *The Trial* is introduced to his fight for life. Besides, there may be the presentation of the original disposition, heredity, education, etc., as on the first page of *Grit, the Young Boatman of Pine Point.* Or if the disposition is to be presented implicitly, or as it emerges as the unity of responses, the first responses are often handled as typical. Further, there is a day-to-day career that serves as a plausible framework for sentimental occasions, and that may also strongly call attention to itself as part of the disposition, as, for example, the social and economic action of the hero of *An American Tragedy* strongly marks him as well as giving him occasions. Again, as uniformly in Balzac, there may be a description of the physical and moral environment, determining on the one side the occasions and on the other side the limits of possible commitment.

The middle consists of the impasses, reversals, and stages of sentimental fixation. The latter part of the middle is marked by definite rejections and commitments, scenes of suffering and satisfaction, dramatic scenes and reversals, and by deaths, which certify rejections. The interest changes from the sentimentalizing to the fate of the objects. Within limits, these dramatic episodes may occur as the closing of any sentimental stage, and an important difference among novels depends on this. Some novels, like *L'Éducation sentimentale,* keep the sentimental progress always in the foreground; others rather punctuate the stages of fixation with vivid dramatic episodes, in the manner of Balzac or Proust, the former usually tragically, but Proust often with colossal comedy.

The resolution is the part that follows the fixing of character and has the double object of giving the character in action and yet of retrospectively doing justice to the sentimental past. The ending of *L'Éducation sentimentale* employs the most classical devices for resolving a novel. First, "il voyagea": these are the actions that exhaust the sentimental energies among objects of no moment and bring calm. Then reminiscences: these revive the sentimental objects and interests, but as past and no longer disturbing. Further, philosophical explanations, like the thoughts of Deslauriers on logic and sentiment. Again, there is the curious formality absent from no nineteenth-century novel, whereby we learn, in one sentence for each person, what has happened to the others; this fixes them and certifies that the system of attitudes is abiding. Similarly, all mysteries are cleared up, like the mystery of the "tête de veau."

But of course the most striking incident of the ending of *L'Éducation* is the very last. Deslauriers and Frédéric, reminiscing, recall an amorous adventure that occurred before ever the story began, and "c'est là ce que nous avons eu de meilleur!"—"that was the best we ever had!" cries Frédéric. One is reminded of Alfred Adler's wry proposition that a person is immature when he imagines that there is some secret that he will learn when he grows up and that he is mature when he realizes that there is no such secret.

### THE PROPER PLEASURE OF NOVELS

In novels the dramatic scenes and reversals are fearful and grievous or variously laughable. But for the specifically novelistic feeling (if it is a feeling), namely, the motion of a sentimental sequence, we must look in the area of "sympathy."

Sympathy seems to be a recognition of the other and of the sameness of the other and one's self. The passions and mirth of drama are not sympathetic; there is not enough other; we identify with the directly presented and quickly moving plot, and feelings take us by storm. In novels we identify with the omniscient narrator; the sentimental persons are others. And in the sequences of sentimental occasions we find that the persons are understandable; they are, after all, like us or we like them. Following their careers and comparing them with our own: it is a verbal question whether or not to call this a "feeling"; it is reassurance, being understood, understanding, with the accompanying anxiety, tears, relief. So a critic has said that the chief use of novels is to learn that we are not alone or eccentric; others are as confused, hurt, and guilty. Contrariwise, we could say that a chief use of novels is to learn that other persons exist.

Besides, of course, since the persons are like us, their careers give us another world, an enlargement of our own. In adventure stories or romances this comes simply to having vicarious satisfactions. But specifically novelistic is the feeling of sinking into the world of a long novel, and we say "we know those persons better than we know our friends."

### THE NONSENTIMENTAL PART

So much for the story of Frédéric. But, as we said in the very beginning of this analysis, *L'Éducation sentimentale* is also a political history, and Frédéric's responses are mainly nonpolitical. Almost half the book is politics, not as a congeries of scattered occasions, but as a well-ordered history of opinions and events before and after the uprising of '48. Dambreuse, the capitalist, adapts himself to the era "like a barometer," from Guizot and the wondrous scheme of the social-minded trust, to his funk at the rebellion and his sudden socialism, and finally to longing for the dictatorship. His foil is Dussardier: his naïve republicanism, his enthusiasm at the fall of the monarchy, his bewildered opposition to the Communists, his disillusionment, his heroic death in the face of the *coup d'état*. Sénécal: the dogmatic radical who in the end comes to say the same thing as Dambreuse and kills Dussardier. The violence of M. Roque, the self-made man who was a peasant; and the fatuousness of M. de Cisy, the little aristocrat who ends up religious. The intellectual progress of the projected journal of Deslauriers and Hussonet, now progressive, now scientific, now anarchist, etc. And, occupying the central place, the great account of the uprising and Paris in arms.

In general, the combination of a sentimental plot with a background plot of history is common, ranging from *Ben Hur* to *War and Peace*. What are some varieties? The sentimental plot may be an example of the social conditions or an example of them and an effect of them; these are the sociological novels, opposite in effect to the epic plot, where the performing hero represents and causes the history. Or the persons in the sentimental plot may have important roles in the history as presented, which gives great and climactic occasions, as in *A Farewell to Arms*. Or many of the chief persons may have important historical as well as individual interests, so that their rise and fall coincide with the social changes, as in Proust. To the degree that the historical and "private" interests involve each other, the dual plot becomes single; and we get the great living sociology of Balzac or Proust, where the persons are motivated by "bourgeois sentimentality and ideals," "aristocratic sentimentality and ideals," and so forth. More trivially, again, the history may merely add picturesqueness and magnitude, as in most historical romances; and, where the separate parts are then brought together without an essential relationship, we have a melodrama of the historical romance, like *Ben Hur*.

Now in *L'Éducation sentimentale* we have already noticed one major relation between the two parts, namely, Frédéric as precisely nonpolitical: his friends talk politics, and he suffers from ennui because he is distracted by his love affairs; he misses the revolutionary rendezvous because of a rendezvous with Marie; his different opinions at the Dambreuses' depend on his amorous spite or satisfaction. But, besides this, the historical plot has an independent sequence, and how then is it one book? Let us consider a more indirect relationship.

If we ask at what point in the sentimental plot the Revolution occurs in the history, we find that it is just at the moment that Frédéric finally comes to possess a woman, a moment marked by the ending of Part II, and then Part III opens in an atmosphere of fulfilment and joy. But alas! the woman is not the Ideal Marie, who did not keep the appointment, but Rosanette, whom he brings to the room prepared for the other. Again, if we look at the moment of complete frustration of all his desires, the end of Part III, chapter v, we find that it is the moment when Dussardier, crying "Vive la République!" is shot dead. And between these two stages we are presented in both plots with progressive disillusionment and corruption, up to the pathetic tirade of honest Dussardier in Part III, chapter iv: "Vous rappelez-vous comme c'était beau?—nous voilà retombés pires que jamais!" This occurs in the midst of the sordid lawsuits, the death of the infant, etc. And so throughout the book. In the beginning both Frédéric's sentiments and the political remarks, though confused, are turbulent and hopeful; in the latter pages they are both disheartened, disillusioned, mendacious.

Now such a parallelism as we are suggesting might be handled by an author symbolically, giving a one-to-one correspondence between the elements of the two plots—as, Marie is the ideal Republic who misses the rendezvous, Rosanette is the temporary material satisfaction of—Louis Blanc(?!), Madame is Louis Napoleon, etc. But Flaubert by no means takes this line; he is a realist; he eschews the symbolical and mythological. But instead we are given a parallelism of character and feeling which in a wonderful way expresses the thought: "In those days *in fact* everything went from bad to worse." The book is a poem of reaction, concluding in the uneasy peace of 1867.

### THEME AND THOUGHT

We must distinguish the rhetorical, sentimental, and philosophical thought of the characters from the thought expressed by such a selection and combination of independent plots as we have been exploring; thought of this kind might be called the Narrator's Theme, and we might expect it to be closely related to the Narrator's Attitude or Style.

Narrator's thought appears also in direct observations on the action, persons, etc., as when Flaubert says, "La France, ne sentant plus de maître, se mit à crier d'effarement." Such direct observation, however, is less likely to be true, more likely to be rationalization, than what is expressed by the artistic handling itself, for that is the artist's power and act and constructs the truth. (Thus the narrator is not the man Gustave Flaubert but somebody likely wiser than he.) The choice of incidents and what is expatiated on, such things give the narrator's thought. The combination of foils (as Deslauriers-Frédéric) or the analysis of disposition by the play of different sequences (as Marie–Rosanette–Mme Dambreuse), these are the narrator's sociology and psychology.

Of the persons, we may distinguish: rhetorical thought, as Frédéric advocates easy divorce in order to shine at a dinner party; philosophical thought, as Deslauriers on logic and sentiment in the resolution (and we have previously seen that the thoughts in the resolution are akin to the narrator's thought); and sentimental thought of various kinds, as thoughts that are objects of sentimentalizing, are sentimental occasions, and thoughts that are the result of sentiment, like Frédéric's Dambreusian opinions. A usual thought occurring in novels is the result of sentiment and is used rhetorically by the hero to persuade himself to action in the same direction. Thus, Frédéric's timidity with Marie makes him think that "other occasions will present themselves, but a false step can never be recalled"; this thought is the result of sentiment, but the fact that he finds it persuasive, or thinks it and yet behaves otherwise, is also an occasion for sentiment. But then, besides, there is a certain philosophical truth of sentimental life here expressed by the sentimentalist, namely, that commitment is evil; that is, what the sentimentalist says about sentimentalizing is philosophical.

### THE NARRATIVE MANNER

Lastly, let us consider the Manner, in Aristotle's sense of "Narrative or Dramatic Manner." It is profitable to explore this distinction a little further than is customary. It seems to me that the following are all parts of the discussion of manner: presence or absence of narrator parts; immediate presentation or telling about important parts; unity of time and place; immediate expression of the time and place in the temporal flow and scene of the work, or indirect expression through something nontemporal and nonspatial.

1. The persons may be immediately presented, as in *Oedipus;* or spoken about by a narrator whose action, attitude, thought, and feeling may call attention to itself in various degrees. In one way we must say that every work is dramatic, because some part is always immediately presented, as Homer's part in the *Iliad*. The narrative may then become more dramatic in either of two ways: (*a*) by minimizing the narrator's dramatic role to a few lines and having the narrator assume the roles of the characters and speak for them, as Aristotle praises Homer for doing; or (*b*) by expanding the narrator's immediately dramatic role, as in the case of a lyrical narrative, for example, "The Solitary Reaper," where the emotions and thoughts of the narrator are a major part. On the other hand, almost no dramatic work is without narrative, for not only are there such set narrations as those in *Le Cid* or *Oedipus* but all thoughts, memories, and attitudes that are spoken of are narrative.

Pursuing this line, we may distinguish the manner of presentation of Frédéric from that of, say, Dambreuse. Frédéric is more immediately and dramatically presented in that the narrator chooses to view many of the events either through his eyes and feelings or in their relation to what he must feel if and when they come home to him; and Dambreuse is presented, for the most part, from this point of view of the narrator-and-hero. We might use this distinction as a means of defining a sentimental hero, namely, the person whose sentimental point of view is joined in by the narrator. At the same time the narrator—and we in our identification with the narrating—is detached; the narrator does not completely assume the hero's role; the hero is other. The narrator is omniscient of all the persons, though he sentimentalizes mostly with one; sometimes he even changes his sentimental point of view to another person, as to Deslauriers in his attempt on Marie, or to Marie when her child is ill (this then makes these persons more dramatic). And, again, long passages (e.g., the uprising) are told rather as pure narration, that is, as the narrator's dramatic action, disregarding the hero.

Clearly all this is relevant to achieving the specific novelistic feeling of "sympathy," recognizing the other and being like the other, and being understood. And we have seen how in this novel the shifting of the narrative point of view is a way of combining the sentimental and historical plots.

In an extreme case, like *The Waves,* the narrator enters freely into the point of view of each separate person, leaving no "narrator" at all; this would have to be called "sentimental-dramatic." Proust throughout achieves the marvelous effect that nearly all the persons are dramatically presented sentimentalizing: they are sympathetically X-rayed, and we see through their eyes; and yet at the same time the presence of the narrator Marcel is never lost—and his point of view, his drama (of remembering), is still more immediate than the others. In *The Counterfeiters,* again, a kind of hierarchy of dramatic manner is achieved, through the novelist-person writing a somewhat similar novel and a diary.

Let us consider also the contrasting set of cases, where in a prima facie dramatic work there is generated a narrative manner. The obvious example is where the speeches of certain characters are handled as the narrator's point of view, as in those plays with choral, reflective, or commentator characters who do not become characteristically involved in the plot; these of course make the other actors thereby less dramatic, for the others do not fill the whole presented world with their motives and acts. But even where the characters are all dramatic, the narrator may appear in the disposition of scenes, as when one scene follows another with an effect of irony, or when one scene is set as foil to another, and this sequence is not strictly probable. And, to go to the limit, we must say that any shift of scene at all introduces the narrator into the plot, since it distracts from the immediate presentation. This can be shown in many ways: a new scene involves a new partial beginning, and all such beginnings reveal the narrator's intent rather than the characters'; and to leave a scene before the ending of the play as a whole reveals the narrator's intent; etc. On these grounds we must say that Shakespeare is less dramatic than Sophocles; and a chronicle history, with its frequent shifts of scene, is less dramatic than a drama. Thus, for his special purposes, Brecht espouses an "epic" or narrative theater as against the more dramatic absent-fourth-wall of Ibsen.

2. This brings us to another principle of the definition of manner, the unities of time and place.

The dramatic is the absorption of the audience into the scene as though it were the actual world (potentially the entire world); this effect can be achieved by the permanence of place and the continuity of time; without such permanence and continuity, there is the introduction of the narrator's arrangements, and identification with the nonspatial narrating.

As the ancients understood—I am speaking of their practice, not of their theory—the measure for the unities of time and place is in the plot; it is not given by a "natural" clock or ruler applied from outside the play. When the characters are completely involved and defined in the action that is happening, the time must seem continuous, episode to episode, for what other stretch of time could lapse meanwhile? What would it measure? So the tragic or laughable action occurs in "less than a day"; and the more internal action of a tragedy occurs all in one environment, whereas a comic intrigue may need juxtaposed environments that can be comically joined or separated yet can be in the same quick action, say, "in one town." (Thus, unless the characters are acting the action, the mere mechanical fact that the scene does not change and the time of the play takes two hours is not unity of time and place, for the characters are not *there* anyway.)

Conversely, when the plot requires that we keep in mind some other action measured by time and having a place—for example, that Macbeth and Malcolm are both preparing—then we precisely break the unities of time and place. So changing the scene (if only by lowering and raising a curtain) itself implies a lapse of time, for example, aging, as in *The Winter's Tale*. The most violent break with continuity is making the time run backward, as to enact a past scene or a memory, and this implies that the character as first presented is not really all there.

As soon as such breaks and changes in the immediate presentation occur, there is to some degree implied an omniscient narrator, with whom we identify.

The retardation (the hindrance) in a sentimental sequence is a persistent withdrawal from direct dramatic involvement; the essential action, the fixing of character, is occurring in a different time from the presented time. This other time is given to us in our identification with the omniscient narrator.

The occasions are multiplied indefinitely, and still we are not lost.

The extreme case is the novel of "stream of consciousness," as frequently in *Ulysses* or, as we have said, in *The Waves*. The presented occasions become identical with the action of the narrator. To my taste, the effect is a lyrical one, neither novelistic nor dramatic.

3. This brings us, again, to another principle of defining dramatic and narrative manner: namely, immediate temporal sequences and those requiring the mediation of nontemporal parts—for example, the narrative case, where the narrator's attitude is nontemporal, contrasted with the dramatic case, where the change in the narrator's attitude is itself the presented plot. But this important distinction can be more conveniently discussed at length in the next chapter.

## [ *Preliminary Remarks on the Structure of "Hamlet"* ]

### DRAMATIC AND SENTIMENTAL AS FORMS OF APPERCEPTION

In the abstract, a dramatic character is a relatively fixed complex; the tragic combination threatens or destroys these whole unities; the comic suddenly expands them through some small detail. But a sentimental person is a relatively loose complex, and a sentiment is the rearranging of the loose structure by adding new elements; the disposition is the direction or tendency of such rearrangements. In the kind of novel we have been discussing the rearrangements are progressively more fixed; they are stages toward commitment, or rejection, a final rearrangement permanently including or excluding certain parts. Often the new fixed complex, of two committed persons, can serve again as a sentimental complex—consider the story of an amorous triangle in which there is an interloper in a marriage—and it may be dissolved through some persisting relative looseness in the commitment. But a different effect altogether is the progression from the more fixed to the more loose and sentimental: this antidramatic effect is noticeable in the ending of *L'Éducation sentimentale.* Supposing the original commitment is epic, then the loosening may be nostalgic, as so often in Tennyson's handling of epic figures. Or, if the original is tragic, the loosening may be poignant and assuaging, moral decay but lapsing back into nature, as in *Oedipus at Colonus.*

Now just as we here distinguish dramatic character and sentimental person, we shall in the next chapter find it useful to distinguish the character and the feeling of verses: where character is the identity along the regular modifications (e.g., the iambic rhythm), and feeling is any loosening or alteration of the regular, as the inclusion of a quickening anapest. If the alteration is then regularized, there is a character change in the verse, brought about either dramatically all at once or sentimentally by stages.

Any loosening of character or conviction that occurs in a tragedy in the tension of the conflict could be called "sentimental"; and this is not repugnant to common experience. We have already spoken of the waverings of doubt and of tragic recklessness as sentimental. And let us again distinguish passion and sentiment: passion is the straining of character toward absolute looseness and destruction; sentiment is the loose forming around some center or object. (Since sentiment involves an object, it is more like knowledge.) Tragic sentiment will always be passionate, for the tragic characters are originally fixed, and therefore, to be restructured, they must first be destroyed and "strain toward looseness."

### COMPARISON OF "OTHELLO" AND "HAMLET"

A good example of all these points is the tempting of Othello. Such an incident as the eavesdropping on Cassio and

Bianca is a sentimental occasion in so far as our chief interest is in the fixing of a new conviction in Othello. But it is still a tragic action in that his willingness to lend himself to such an occasion is, for him, the destruction of his virtue; and there is the imminence of a tragic reversal. The peculiar aesthetic effect of *Othello* that has been so often remarked (e.g., by Coleridge), namely, the almost intolerable suspense, can be explained, I think, by just this combination of the sentimental and the tragic; for sentimental occasions are in their nature retardative and slow-going, but, given an Othello we do not expect to wait for action and catastrophe, the tragic meanings are too imminently fatal for sentimental retardation. And we here approach again the oppressive effect of Kafka's "Burrow," an infinite number of incidents each one imminently fatal.

If we turn from Othello to Hamlet, however, we meet a protagonist who is not so much a tragic figure undergoing a change, and therefore very passionate and somewhat sentimental, as a sentimental person responding to a tragic situation in which he is unavoidably committed beforehand.

The "interpretation" of Hamlet and his action consists in the intrinsic relations, or lack of relations, between his sentimental and tragic roles; and there have been many such interpretations (the conflict of the barbaric and the effete civilized; of the mundane and the religious; the Oedipus complex; a patched-together text of a Spanish tragedy and a Shakespearean tragedy; etc.). In what follows, I do not wish to add to these interpretations but merely to point to some abstract relations involved in any such combination of the tragic and sentimental. And let us cover the ground under the following headings: "Fortinbras," "Hamlet's Disposition," "The King's Plot," "The Soliloquies," "Hamlet's Sentimental Development," and "The Magnitude of *Hamlet.*"

### FORTINBRAS

We saw how in *Henry IV* Hal avoided the tragic complexity of his father and of the nobles by living away from the court. Something similar occurs in *Hamlet.* To be in Denmark is to be involved in corruption; the time is out of joint, something is rotten in the state of Denmark, child actors reign, and people pay out a hundred ducats for the picture of Claudius. Indeed, "there is something in this more than natural, if philosophy could find it out."

Now there are three sons with fathers to avenge, Fortinbras, Laertes, and Hamlet, successively introduced in the beginning. Hamlet is in Denmark throughout; his attempt to avoid a tragic involvement is clear from his first speeches, "too much i' the sun" and such an aside as "the time is out of joint." Laertes leaves Denmark in the beginning, returns with a noble and justifiable intention, and is at once ensnared in the evil. But what a contrast in the handling of Fortinbras! For he is to escape scot-free and to be rewarded; he must therefore avoid involvement and yet must be importantly presented. How to present a character and not involve him? Shakespeare makes him important by introducing him in the beginning, the middle, and the ending (Acts I, III, and V); yet, so long as the complexity persists, he is merely passing through on his way to an epic exploit.

If Fortinbras appeared at the court, he would become involved in the tragedy; as it is, he appears when the corruption is dispelled and is the figure of resolution, for he inherits the good of Hamlet's sacrifice and is his eulogist. The bloody reversal of the last act, the stage piled with corpses, is repugnant and even a little absurd if the play is taken as a tragedy of characters, but it is an apt expression of the rottenness of the whole state: it is probable from the start that *only* the outsider can survive. This ending, then, is not the ending of a tragedy of characters but of what is expressed in the sweeping social, moral, and theological criticism throughout. The moral satires are not introduced just by the way; rather, the whole play expresses despair and disgust.

### HAMLET'S DISPOSITION

In the beginning Hamlet is presented as wishing to exclude himself from the main business of the court. So his relations to it are reflective and sentimental rather than dramatic. Now the disposition determining his sentimental responses can be considered in two aspects: he is a universal sentimentalist, and his disposition is particularly appropriate to the corruption of Denmark.

Universal sentimentality might mean the ability to sentimentalize on an infinite variety of occasions, like Tristram Shandy (this would be more likely to occur in a novel); or it might mean, as here, philosophical sentimentality, the thoughts of a person who has such general principles that he is adequate to (adequate to protect himself from) any occasion.

Obviously Hamlet is also a melancholy Dane. Now, taking these two aspects into consideration, Hamlet's responses make a fairly coherent complex: gloom, suicide, untimely wit, disgust for sexuality, manic enthusiasm, drawing maxims, elegance, subtility, curiosity, etc. But what is the unity and ordering among these parts? Is his sexual disgust melancholic, or is the melancholia the effect of sexual disgust? Is his love for Gertrude incestuous? What has made him a sentimental person in a dramatic situation? All these are the questions of concrete interpretations of *Hamlet* and come to the mad Hamlet, the idealist Hamlet, the Oedipus Hamlet, etc. Nevertheless, in any interpretation, we start with the following structure, a sentimental impasse: Hamlet's interests are balked, by whatever cause, and his response is the desire for self-destruction that we have discussed previously.[4] This is the situation that recurs throughout: "O that this too too sullied flesh" occurs in Act I; "To be or not to be" in Act III; and in Act V he is still engaged in graveyard speculations, though with a different confidence. Into this persistent impasse comes the tragic duty imposed by the Ghost. (The meaning of the Ghost, how far it is the creation of his "prophetic soul," etc., again will depend on one's concrete interpretation of the meaning of the play.) But again on any interpretation we have the following structure of the plot: (1) his tragic duty provides sentimental occasions, as he writes in his copy-book; (2) his disposition reaches a new stage because of a new cause of self-disgust, as "O what a rogue and peasant-slave am I"; (3) the revenge becomes a temporary object of interest and causes a certain development to a commitment; and (4) he then acts somewhat dramatically, as when he sets the Mouse-trap. Thus throughout Acts II, III, and IV he finds occasions in Polonius, in conversation with Rosencrantz and Guildenstern, in the players, in sololoquy, in Ophelia, in seeing the King at prayer, in the Queen, in seeing the soldiers of Fortinbras. The slaying of Polonius seems to be a dramatic action, but, accompanied by the pathetic query, "Is it the King?" it becomes the strongest possible sentimentality.

In sharp contrast to this sequence of responses, we are presented with Laertes, a dramatic character with a frailty of virtue and temper that makes him the King's prey and a subject of reversal. (Just so the stoical Horatio is a foil to the reflective Hamlet, for Horatio is an unsentimental philosopher.) But of course Hamlet is not merely a sentimentalist but a universal sentimentalist; and to the extent that we take his thought as true, and so we must, he is above his sentimental sequence, and the retarded action, instead of being exasperating, is every-

4. Cf. above, p. 148.

where resolving and thought-provoking. Thus the over-all effect, of dismay and world-weariness, does not come from Hamlet's sentimentalizing but from the proved argument in his sentimentalizing.

### THE KING'S PLOT

Claudius, the antagonist of the tragic plot, is not inactive, though he also is given a sentimental sequence, his remorse. From the beginning he is presented as provident and executive. For the most part, it is the episodes of the King's plot that furnish the occasions for Hamlet's sentiment. The King sets on Rosencrantz and Guildenstern; Ophelia; summons him to the Queen; sets Polonius to watch; sends him to England; finally sets on Laertes. We then have the following structure: there is a tragic action, not of Hamlet against Claudius, but of Claudius against Hamlet; Hamlet is laid open to it because of his own tragic motive (the Ghost); but to the deeds of the King he responds sentimentally; yet, in each stage of fixation, Hamlet is present again as an antagonist, perhaps more dangerous. (Thus it can be argued that Hamlet is "not mad" but is cleverly parrying the enemy's thrust.) If the King did not drive the plot forward, Hamlet would never be avenged. And in the finale it requires the elaborate triple threat—the unbated rapier, the poisoned point, and the pearl in the cup—to finish the play; as if to say, the King will not stop at anything.

For Claudius too has a sentimental plot, his remorse; but, unlike the sentimental hindrances of Hamlet, Claudius' remorse drives him on, like Macbeth, to greater enormities. Yet such a progress in violence, as in *Macbeth,* is itself something sentimental; it leads not so much to discovery and reversal as to commitment at any cost.

### THE SOLILOQUIES

The most sentimental of Hamlet's responses are his soliloquies, for these are either not rhetorical at all, like ordinary dramatic speeches, or are that sentimental rhetoric whereby the hero generates reasons to persuade himself of his own disposition. The structure of many of the soliloquies is as follows: (1) an occasion is presented in the dramatic action; (2) Hamlet takes no part in the dramatic action but broods inwardly; (3) when he is alone, he bursts forth with his sentiment; (4) this sentiment fixes him even further from his tragic role; and (5), but *therefore,* since his role is unavoidable, it returns him to his duty. The first soliloquy, "O that this too too sullied flesh would melt . . . ," cannot reach the fifth point, because his duty is not yet announced; and this makes it end in the uneasy impasse, "Break my heart, for I must hold my tongue." This is a strong gratuitous probability for the entrance of Horatio and the sentinels. The next important place is after the Ghost has sunk down, "O all you host of heaven"; and here we have just the opposite movement: his duty is pressing and immediate, it threatens to destroy his disposition, "all trivial fond records, etc."—but therefore he absorbs the event sentimentally into his disposition, writes an observation in his copy-book that is quite off the issue, and then writes down the words of the Ghost. The couplet, "The time is out of joint, O cursed spite," presents in miniature the dramatic-sentimental structure.

Note in all these cases the commencement of the response with an exclamation, as "O." Such exclamations express the energy dammed up by the inhibited dramatic interest and, conversely, by the disproportion of the dramatic role that he allows himself to the far greater energy of his sentimentality, so that, when he can launch on his own responses, he can cry out. Further, the great speech

> Now I am alone.
> O what a rogue and peasant-slave am I!

first sets the condition for sentiment, solitude, and then breaks forth in the exclamation. Similarly the marvelous soliloquy,

"How all occasions do inform against me," commences with "I'll be with you straight. Go a little before." These two speeches are alike throughout; they are occasioned by incidents not directly in the tragedy—Hecuba and the expedition of Fortinbras. They absorb these into the disposition with its tragic bent; and they end with a fuller tragic resolve, "The play's the thing" and "From this time forth my thoughts be bloody."

Now, except for some such analysis in terms of the sentimental and the dramatic, I do not see how these impressive episodes can be made part of the play—yet every audience has always considered them the essence of the play. But, if we are dealing with a sentimental person and a character-fixation, just such nonessential introduction of the occasions is pat.

"To be or not to be," the next soliloquy after "Now I am alone," is spoken as if the Ghost had never appeared, as if we were back in the impasse of "O that this . . . flesh would melt"; but, no, for the thoughts cast up by this stage in his disposition curiously turn to resolution and the pale cast of thought and enterprise losing the name of action. He is turning against his own sentimentalizing; the very next moment he will do the deed—but he sees Ophelia. Thus there has been a sentimental advance. But then, on the contrary, the next soliloquies, after the play and when he comes on Claudius praying, move again in the opposite direction, away from action, for here the tragic act is again too imminent (as just after the Ghost has vanished); and this is expressed by the double and triple "now": " 'Tis now the very witching time . . . now could I drink hot blood," and

> Now might I do it pat, now he is praying;
> And now I'll do it—

so that, of course, the sentimental hindrance at once generates a contrary feeling and a contrary argument. The next important soliloquy is "How all occasions do inform against me!"

### HAMLET'S SENTIMENTAL DEVELOPMENT

What is the progression of Hamlet's sentimental sequence? It has become the vogue to argue that prior to the trip to England Hamlet is vacillating but that, after his return, he is determined to act, for the King has attacked his very life; now he has documentary evidence against him; etc. But it seems to me that Hamlet's compliance to the bout of foils tells fatally against any such view: the "determined avenger" who is willing to engage in such play is no different from the one who says, "From this time forth my thoughts be bloody," and nevertheless boards the ship. Hamlet, I should say, does not commit himself to his tragic role; it is the King who generates the catastrophe; and, if this were not the case, all probability would be thrown to the winds. But it does not follow that Hamlet does not commit himself at all; on the contrary, the conversations with Horatio in Act V show a *fixed* Hamlet, but one not fixed *on* action, but fixed in not standing in the way of action. "There's a divinity that shapes our ends," he says, and "Even in that was heaven ordinant"; one may therefore rely in "indiscretion . . . when our deep plots do pall," on some rapid chance for "a man's life's no more than to say 'One' "; and, lastly, to sum up: "We defy augury. There's a special providence in the fall of a sparrow. If it be now, 'tis not to come; if it be not to come, it will be now; if it be not now, yet it will come: *the readiness is all.*" This prose is the rhythm of a fixed opinion. Why it is this particular opinion and its attendant attitude would have to be explained in terms of one's central interpretation. (In my opinion, what Hamlet suffers from is conceit, the need to think away the world in terms of himself; and once he admits the existence of anything else, even chance, he is ready for action.) But, in any case, if we find the direction of the sentimental plot toward such a fixation of character rather than toward a determination to act, then the catastrophe is altogether probable: Hamlet is ready and the King is culminating his mad career. Then we can dispense with Goethe's theory of the "ironical accident"—a theory not unattractive in itself (it is, e.g., the ending of *Coriolanus*) but too weak an ending for so large a structure.

### THE MAGNITUDE OF "HAMLET"

We are not, to repeat it, here analyzing the play itself but merely looking abstractly at its structures without inquiring what any of it means (but probability, like any demonstration, is grounded in concrete meanings). We have, rather, been seeking in the extrinsic structure for a number of places in which the concrete forces of the plot can be evaluated: as, in the soliloquies, what particular thoughts or feelings lead to the temporarily allaying fixations, what interruptions prevent these, and so forth?

The advantage of the sentimental-dramatic structure is simply this: that the vast magnitude of parts of action and thought, which to the taste of so many has expressed one meaning as a whole, is unifiable in this structure. I have not mentioned the comedy in *Hamlet,* but the kind of comedy is one possible relation between an independent sentimental point of view and a tragic role; for in a moment of self-reliance the detached person will see the tragic *sub specie alterius,* a kind of comedy, as when Hamlet cries "Hide fox, and all after!" or when he taunts Polonius. And, being a universal sentimentalist, Hamlet can see things *sub specie aeternitatis,* another kind of comedy. Hamlet's comic sarcasm is thus the converse of his despairing inability to act: the sarcasm depends on the perception that he is he and that is that; the despair, on the perception that he is not that.

So, the sentimental, the tragic, the comic: love, art, and power, and instinctual disgust and disgust in the world, and death—these constitute the magnitude of *Hamlet.* But if the attempt is made to hold them together in too simple a structure, that does not give room for the scope of the hero, then the unity is inexplicable, and the critics have recourse to explaining the failure by historical causes, revenge plots, and Renaissance psychologies.

## [ *Plot Structure of "The Castle"* ]

### INTRODUCTION

Finally, let us turn to another novel, a very curious one subject to many interpretations. But I should like to show how, in this difficult case, a close reading of the structure obviates the need for other interpretations. Allegorical meanings of the Castle and Village, in Kafka's *Castle,* are not far to seek. They are present in the text, and critics have sought them out; but the book can be better unified in terms of the literal fate and heightening passion of speech of the protagonist. Likewise the latent, unconscious meanings are always important, but there is less need to explore them because the character reads itself off in its surface behavior. We turn, therefore, directly to the plot structure: separating the several plot strands and relating them—a unique structure of epic, mysterious, tragicomic, and lyrical parts. (The following analysis is reprinted with slight changes from *Kafka's Prayer*.)[5]

### K.'S EPIC VIRTUE AND HIS HIGH CASTLE-DESTINY

1. First there is the plot strand of "K.'s purpose." Whatever this purpose is—it is expressed in such terms as "ambition," "enemy," "freedom of action," "underestimating his strength," "to attain and go beyond," "best to be unobtrusive"—the line of this purpose does not change in the course of the book. K.'s stubbornness, his courage, his force and fraud, and what

5. Paul Goodman, *Kafka's Prayer* (New York: Vanguard Press, 1947), pp. 204–19.

might best be called his squirming, are always bent to one end.

It is this inflexible line that gives to the book its epic, rather than tragic or novelistic, expression. An epic virtue is a fixed habit, whereas a tragic character is itself at stake in the action, and novelistic sentiments are molded by the occasions. K.'s epic virtue is his watchfulness.

Yet this epic has a tragic coloring, for K. is shaken, not in his purpose or in his method, but in his confidence in these: under the impact of the events, he becomes more clinging and desperate, and he comes to ask what he is about and whether he is about anything at all.

The work is not planned as an epic, for it is not the case that K.'s virtue will be effective, active, whether successfully or unsuccessfully; that is, he will not see that which he is watching for—and nevertheless he does not, cannot, give up his epic watchfulness. It is this cross in the construction that gives to the work its metaphysical or "absolute" expression: no event will ever occur not subject to K.'s watchfulness and interpretative wit, and never will he see what he is watching for.

2. But answering to K.'s inflexibility, and making it something more than stubbornness, is an unchanging line in the events: namely, the explicit decisions of the higher authorities, especially Klamm. For we must distinguish sharply between these official pronouncements, for example, Klamm's messages and the messages in the so-called "ending" (reported by Brod), and the divagations of the subordinate officials, K.'s dealings with whom bear a closer relationship to his own career in the Village. There is no evidence that K.'s relation with the high authority in the Castle, his purpose toward it and its purpose toward him, are in the least influenced by his career in the Village or his brushes with the subordinates. (This is brilliantly exhibited by Klamm's "outdated" message, completely irrelevant to foreground events; like the pronouncements of the

court of Pekin, these messages are archaic and eternal, they are not in the same time sequence as the Village.) It is the sense of this separation that expresses the antinomianism so peculiar to Kafka, the incommensurability, as Brod says, of the human and divine values. But which sign, positive or negative, is to be assigned to the antinomian justice of the Castle, whether it is divine or diabolic, depends on one's Castle-interpretation, which, I am arguing, is not important. (My impression is that the "sleepy" Castle gentlemen can be equated with the "good" father whom Kafka describes in the Letter to His Father as *so* good—when he is asleep.)

The separation, the absolute separation, constitutes the serenity, the humor, the miraculous-in-the-offing; for comedy is the sense that destruction takes place without harm, and miracle is the intervention of probabilities outside the foreground plot line. Nevertheless, the story is not one of happy anticipation but of sorrow, anxiety, and passion, for at every moment K. extrapolates from the Village to the Castle. He considers his Village-predicament as hopeful or fearful for his purpose; and he must do so because his watchfulness and constructive will cannot rest. He is miserable because he does not cease striving.

### K.'S VILLAGE CAREER AND HIS LOVES

The lines of K.'s career in the Village show a steady decline: for example, from the room at the inn, to the schoolhouse, to living with Pepi and the chambermaids; or, again, from land surveyor to janitor, etc.—and ultimately to the deathbed of the reported ending. His relations with the subordinate officials, likewise, show an increasing complexity and perplexity, more and more humiliating and desperate. These two lines of decline make each other probable; taken together, they mean, prima facie, that K.'s unfortunate relations with the under-officials destroy his credit in the world and that his relations with the villagers prejudice his case with the underofficials. Looking more closely, however, we see that it is his too desirous striving to get on with both that destroys both sets of relations. This is shown precisely and explicitly in the history of the Barnabas family. After the insult to the Castle messenger, their situation has gone from bad to worse, *not* because of any doing of the Castle—for there is no crime, no charge, no penalty—but simply because of their own efforts, their sense of guilt, and their striving to atone. So, in the decline of K. in the Village, it is his constructive will that condemns him to sorrow and apparent failure. His constructive will is in the service of his hopelessness; it is a means of exacerbating his hopelessness.

An extremely important movement of the plot is from the Frieda-connection to the Barnabas-connection. Now Frieda and Amalia, the younger sister of Barnabas, have had opposite fates: Frieda, the mistress of an official and therefore attractive to the usurping K.; Amalia, the unique rejector of an official, haughty, solitary, and peculiarly displeasing to K. Yet we must expect that it is Amalia that K. will eventually come to; she is his deeper disposition.

If this is so, what a light it casts on the previous episodes! That K. is unsuccessful, is rejected, because he is the rejector; he sees to it that he is not welcomed. If this is where the story were to lead, it is not hard to understand why Kafka could not carry through the scheme, for the events would be too sexless, too temporarily deadening to the animal spirits. It is impossible for a man who has suffered too much frustration (especially when it is self-imposed) to put his faith in the simple axiom that through renunciation one comes to fulfilment. K. cries out, therefore, "*Something* is there!"

It is clear that after the first few days with her, K. no longer loves Frieda. Yet he clings to her and tries to reclaim her when she finally leaves him for the assistant whom he has dismissed. What shall we say of K.'s possessiveness? He must keep everything, with methodical anality. It is not sufficient to say that he pursues his purposes with the aid of women; even when his purposes are no longer furthered, he clings to every connection, meantime reaching out again for other connections. He is setting up a counter-Castle.

A counter-Castle of every love but the love! This growing glut of nonsatisfactions and complexities is the fixing of character toward which K.'s sentimental sequences are tending. His hindrances prove to be his entire disposition. Nevertheless, of course, there is his epic mission to which all this is completely irrelevant and which makes it a serene comedy. And there is the persistent tragedy that he cannot help but feel, while he keeps on striving, that his Village career *is* relevant to his mission.

### LYRICAL PASSAGES IN ABNORMAL SITUATIONS

Lastly, there is a series of remarkable passages of a lyrical kind that do not form a continuous line of plot, and yet they have a unity of function and structure which makes them be taken together. These are K.'s manic responses in abnormal states of consciousness. Considering that his character is watchfulness and awareness, the unity of these spontaneous responses is, of course, of capital importance. Taken as a whole, they form, to the turmoil of the plot lines, a counter-statement of fulfilment and satisfaction.

Since the expressiveness of these places is so largely in their tone, I shall quote at length the four most striking.

First, where K. walks through the snowy night with Barnabas; he is exhausted, melting with love for the silk-clad youth, and confident that they are bound for the Castle:

They went on. . . . The effort which it cost him merely to keep going made him lose control of his thoughts. Instead of remaining fixed on their goal, they strayed. Memories of his home kept recurring. . . . There, too, a church stood in the market-place, partly surrounded by an old graveyard which was again surrounded by a high wall. Very few boys had managed to climb that wall, and for some time K., too, had failed. . . . The graveyard had been no mystery to them, they had entered it often through a small wicket-gate, it was only the smooth, high wall that they had wanted to conquer. But one morning—the empty, quiet market-place had been flooded with sunshine, when had K. ever seen it like that, either before or since?—he had succeeded in climbing it with astonishing ease; at a place where he had already slipped down many a time he had clambered with a small flag between his teeth right to the top at the first attempt. Stones were still rattling down under his feet, but he was at the top. He stuck the flag in, it flew in the wind, he looked down and round about him, over his shoulder, too, at the crosses mouldering on the ground, nobody was greater than he at that place and moment. By chance the teacher had come past and with a stern face had made K. descend. In jumping down he had hurt his knee. . . . At that moment, Barnabas stopped [to K.'s woeful disappointment].

How sweetly it is told, in a flowing series of commas without relatives or connectives though the sentences are complex, yet no heavier punctuation is needed!

What is the structure of it? (1) The loss of conscious control and single purpose, the giving-in, made possible by physical exhaustion and emotional trust. (2) This makes possible full potency and satisfaction. (3) The exploit is performed with ease, without striving, in a sunny clime different from the endless snow and night of the Castle Village. (4) There is no danger to watch for, yet he anxiously looks about to make sure. (5) All is cut short by a sudden authoritative voice, and his trust is disappointed. (6) He is castrated (hurt knee).

Next, with Frieda under the bar, K. is mastered by sexual desire, and, being with Klamm's mistress, he is again confident that he is attaining the Castle:

They embraced each other, her little body burned in K.'s hands; in a state of unconsciousness which K. tried again and again, but in vain, to master they rolled a little way, landing with a thud on Klamm's door, where they lay among the small puddles of beer. . . . There, hours went past, hours in which they breathed as one, in which their hearts beat as one, hours in which K. was haunted by the feeling that he was losing himself or wandering into a strange country, further than any man had wandered before, a country so strange that not even the air had anything in common with his native air, where one might die of strangeness, and yet whose enchantment was such that one could only go on and lose oneself further. So it came to him not as a shock but as a faint glimmer of comfort when from Klamm's room a deep authoritative impersonal voice called for Frieda. [It is Klamm, and next moment K. cries to himself:] "What had happened? where were his hopes?"

(1) Here again is unconsciousness with, as a forepleasure, the confidence that he is advancing his purpose. (2) The new element is the "strangeness"—and it seems to me that a passage like this is fatal to the theory that K. is a stranger who wants to establish himself as a native. On the contrary, what he consciously desires is to establish himself on his own terms, and what he evidently unconsciously wishes is to be a stranger, getting away from himself and his own terms. (3) It is easy; there is no hindrance. (4) The sense of self-loss, of orgasm, rouses in him the greatest anxiety: "one might die of it." (5) Again all is cut short by an authoritative voice. (6) The castration is projected onto his notion of himself, his hopes rather than his body.

Third, waiting to accost Klamm, K. stands in the snow by his sledge:

He slipped inside. The warmth within the sledge was extraordinary. . . . One could not tell whether it was a seat one was sitting on, so completely was one surrounded by blankets, cushions, and furs; one could turn and stretch on every side and always one sank into softness and warmth. His arms spread out, his head supported on pillows which always seemed to be there, K. gazed out of the sledge into the dark house. . . . As if stupefied by the warmth after his long wait in the snow, K. began to wish that Klamm would come soon. The thought that he would much rather not be seen by Klamm in his present position touched him only vaguely as a faint disturbance of his comfort. . . . Slowly, without altering his position, he reached out his hand to the side pocket. . . . He pulled out a flask, unscrewed the stopper, and smelled; involuntarily he smiled, the perfume was so sweet, so caressing, like praise and good words from some one one likes very much, yet one does not know clearly what they are for, and has no desire to know, and is simply happy in the knowledge that it is one's friend who is saying them. "Can this be brandy?" K. asked himself doubtfully and took a taste out of curiosity. . . . Then—as K. was just in the middle of a long swig—everything became bright, the electric lights blazed. . . . [The coach is driven back to the barn, and as K. stands forlorn in the snow] it seemed as if at last those people had broken off all relations with him.

(1) There is a blessed state of surrender (we must remember that Kafka himself was an insomniac and an abstainer from alcohol). (2) The praise is not in fulfilment of his Castle-purpose but in forgetting it, for one does not know what the praise is for, and one does not wish to know. (3) It is cut short. (4) What is cut off from the self is its social world, "as if," in the extraordinary words with which the chapter ends,

as if nobody could dare to touch him, or drive him away, or even speak to him . . . as if at the same time there was nothing more senseless, nothing more hopeless, than this freedom, this waiting, this inviolability.

The last manic passage I want to quote is from chapter xviii, not printed in the American edition. By a mistake, K. stumbles on an official who by a freak might grant his every Castle wish and is wooing him only to ask for something, but K. is too sleepy:

K. slept; although it was not a real sleep, he heard Buergel's words possibly even better than before, when he had been awake but dead-tired; word after word sounded in his ear but that annoying consciousness was gone, he felt free, Buergel no longer held him, it was rather K. who sometimes groped for Buergel; he was not in the depth of sleep yet, but he had dipped into it. No one could rob him of it now. He had won a great victory. And already there was a social gathering to celebrate it and he, or was it some one else, raised a glass of champagne in honor of his victory. And in order that all might know what it was about, the struggle and the victory were gone through again, or perhaps not gone through again but were just taking place, and had been celebrated before, and there was no end to celebrating it, because happily the outcome was already certain. An official, naked, very much like the statue of a Greek god, was being engaged in battle by K. It was very comical, and K. smiled gently in his sleep, because the official's proud pose was repeatedly upset by K.'s sallies which forced the official to use his lifted arm or his doubled fist quickly in order to cover himself, yet he was never quick enough. . . . Was it really a struggle? There was no serious opposition, nothing but a squeak from the official every now and then. This Greek god squeaked like a girl who is being tickled. At last he was gone. K. was alone in a large room; pugnaciously he turned around looking for his adversary, but there was no one . . . only the champagne glass lay shattered on the floor. K. crushed it completely under his heel. But the splinters cut him, he awoke with a start, nauseated like an infant when it is awakened. Yet at the sight of Buergel's bare chest, the dream-thought passed through his head: "Here is your Greek god! Why don't you drag him out of his bed!"

(1) Again, as in the previous passages, there is a consciousness in unconsciousness; it is only the annoying self-control, the inhibition of surrendering, that is relaxed. (2) Primarily, and perhaps even most deeply, the victory, the power, is just to sleep; but at once a secondary meaning is given that explains the inhibition to giving in: the love for the hypnotic "good"

father is revealed as hostility. The official squeaks like a girl; it is an easy triumph. I cannot help but feel that the clause "in order that all might know what it is about," coming in this late chapter of the narrative, is a formal invitation to the critic, much as Buergel is at this very moment wooing K.; and really I cannot see here, in this father-raper and father-punisher, a seeker of grace. (3) He awakes with a start, "nauseated like an infant." How interesting that Kafka seems to think this is a normal simile, but I think that the infant is nauseated when the suckling has been soured by the fear and guilt of the usurper, and this certainly is the sense of the dream-thought: the official has no breasts; drive him out of bed. (4) The castration is again a cut foot, but it must be understood not only to the general Western custom of breaking the glass after consuming the bottle but also to the Jewish custom of the bridegroom's crushing the glass with his heel at the wedding. The social gathering is a wedding where K. ousts his father and wins his mother. The Castle then is not the goal but the ordeal.

### THE PLOT STRUCTURE OF "THE CASTLE"

What is the meaning of these beautiful passages that are a pleasure to copy out? What is their relation to the continuous strands of the plot?

In a bald diagram the structure of *The Castle* is as follows. There is a turmoil of conflicting plots in two sets: K.'s purpose and the high authorities; and the village, Frieda, and the women of Barnabas—and this turmoil is so managed and so kept in motion by the protagonist's character and fixing disposition that it can never come to an end. Meantime there is a series of lyrical passages that point to a resolution. The catastrophe is the final exhaustion of the protagonist, in death, putting to a stop the motion of the turmoil without an issue either way. But the dénouement, never written, should be the full expression of the lyrical resolution passages. The pattern of the book then is to exhaust the watchful, wilful, and stubborn protagonist and carry him away with the satisfaction that comes with finally giving in.

We must envisage a resolution passage in the ending not unlike the four just quoted, but with one important difference: it is not manic; it does not belong to an abnormal state of sleepiness, drunkenness, or sexual fantasy; it is an open-eyed view of the actual scene and *therefore* spontaneous and unwilled.

So, if we look at *The Castle* structurally, the meaning of the book is not obscure. The particular allegories (I have been suggesting an Oedipal one) are important not in content but in form, just as a man substitutes one ideology for another and still is unchanged in character and destiny.

[CHAPTER V]

# Lyrical Poems: Speech, Feeling, Motion of Thought

LET US NOW TURN MORE MINUTELY TO THE IMMEDIATELY PRE-sented texture of poems. In this chapter I want to discuss the relations among the rhythms, sounds, and lexicon of speech; feeling; the motions of thinking (e.g., reflection); and the attitude in the style. I shall choose for analysis a few lyrical poems, for in most lyrical poems the words, the feeling, the reflection, the image, and the attitude are the chief parts.

But of course they are equally parts in tragedies, comedies, and novels; and usually in such longer works the most moving passages are speeches and paragraphs that have a lyrical excitement, when out of the background of the over-all plot there is an immediate flowing unity of speech, feeling, thinking—a lyrical poem. But in the longer works, we have seen, it is the plot of action, character, and nontemporal thought (e.g., a thesis) that provides the structure in which the lyrical speeches make sense and are telling. Such a plot is not the immediately presented surface; it requires abstracting and recalling. A short poem, however, is what is heard, felt, and thought from beginning to end in an immediate experience. This is what Poe meant when he said that only a short poem is a poem.

Reverting for a moment to our discussion of the distinction

between dramatic and narrative manners,[1] we might say that the dramatic is what is immediately presented and that the narrative is what is mediately presented; then a short lyrical poem is an extreme case of the dramatic. This is the distinction implied in the common advice to young writers, "Tell it; do not tell about it." But it seems to me that, in a long work, there is a right time to tell about it and a right time to tell it, falling and rising with the subject; for it must be remembered that, in the places where a certain narrative distance is being maintained, we are identifying with the artist's synoptic point of view, necessary for the large experience.

I have chosen a little poem of Catullus as an example of direct feeling without complexity or stanzas; also because any poem of Catullus in his favorite meter shows very simply the relation between attitude and style. The sonnet of Milton is an example of both complexity and stanzas in feeling, and it gives a convenient opportunity to discuss what I mean by "motion of thinking." Tennyson's "Morte d'Arthur" (1842) shows how, by a system of images, an apparent action is transformed into a reflective symbol.

Since these poems are short, I can treat them in rather minute detail and also have space for more widely ranging generic discussion than up to now.

### [ *Analysis of "Iam ver egelidos refert tepores"* ]

Iam ver egelidos refert tepores,
iam caeli furor aequinoctialis
iucundis Zephyri silescit auris.
Linquantur Phrygii, Catulle, campi
Nicaeaeque ager uber aestuosae:
ad claras Asiae volemus urbes.
Iam mens praetrepidans avet vagari,

1. Cf. above, chap. iv, p. 158.

iam laeti studio pedes vigescunt.
O dulces comitum valete coetus,
longe quos simul a domo profectos
diversae varie viae reportant.

[*Carmen* xlvi (text of Merrill, but reading *varie* for *variae*)]

(Now spring brings back ice-free warm weather, / now the rage of the equinoctial sky / is quiet in the pleasant breezes of the west wind. / You must leave, Catullus, the fields of Phrygia / and the rich land of steaming Nicaea: / let's fly to the famous cities of Asia. / Now my fore-trembling mind wants to wander, / now my joyful feet grow strong and eager. / O farewell sweet intercourse of comrades, / who set out at the same time from home far-off, / whom different roads variously carry back.)

### FEELING AS A MODIFICATION OF RHYTHM

This is a set of Phalaecean verses, on the scheme

|| –– / –∪ / ∪– | –∪∪ | –∪ | –∪ | –∪ ||.

Catullus handles this meter as a lively conversational speech. There is a continuous sequence of modifications that are a mounting excitement, allayed at the close. The "meanings" of the words, what he is "excited about," also are in a mounting sequence of personal involvement, broadening out at the close into a bit of sentimental reflection. Finally, this lively conversation roused to this excitement and its termination is itself an example of the style of Catullus pervading the whole, simple, direct, and intimate, idiosyncratic and elegant.

1. The eleven syllables are an easy speaking breath (between our pentameter and the classical dramatic iambic trimeter). The verses are end-stopped or, moderately end-stopped, broaden out to couples. The flow is easy: both in that the words are not hard to say together (generally easy consonant com-

binations) and in that there are plenty of polysyllables, speeding things up. The words pass freely over the metrical feet, so that the meter cannot establish itself too strongly and prevent a conversational tone; likewise the accents on the words freely hit or miss the metrical beats—except that, since in Latin a long penult is accented, in the last foot of each verse the accent and the beat coincide, and this keeps the verses firm through the conversational flow. Also, for the most part, the words seem free of the meter, but the phrases and clauses fall rather strictly in meter.

Any trochaic rhythm is rapid, for the foot is short, and there is a touch of energy at the beginning. But the variety in the first foot of each Phalaecean keeps the trochee-rhythm from too strongly establishing itself. (Continual trochees, unless they are expressing a chase, soon become doggerel: rhythm established against meaning and feeling.) The second foot, the dactyl, is of course the characteristic mark of this meter; it is lilting. This lilt would in itself become painfully obtrusive, but Catullus uses this meter always for quite short poems.

To sum up, the metrical base is easy, lively, conversational, lilting, and yet formal and not loose.

2. The emphatic "Iam . . . iam . . ." is an exclamatory beginning, the first verse giving a complete summary conception, the second at once broadening out to the third, slowing down the conception while at the same time speeding the utterance, in polysyllables. Verses 4 and 5 are again a couple, as if this were to be the norm. But then verse 6 is again monostych, with shorter words, introduced without connective, and brought to a full stop. At this stop, and therefore with the greater energy required to begin anew, comes again "Iam . . . iam. . . ." The lines are crowded with light consonants, explosive without heaviness, and ease into the vocalic *u*'s, with alliteration ("a*v*et," "*v*agari," "*v*igescunt"). Taken

together, verses 7 and 8 form a couplet, the same in the beginning, alliterated in the end, yet both are monostych: the couplet is then a strong pause. But the first "Iam . . . iam . . ." ran six verses to its pause, the second only two verses; there is an increasing impetuosity. Into this impetuous stop breaks climactically an exclamation proper, *O*. The exclamatory line, verse 9, is again full of light consonants, but these are no longer in random variety; but there are three *c*'s, three *t*'s, and "comitum" is balanced by "coetus": the explosive excitement is delicately formalized, calmed, and conception is slowed by the lapidary pattern. There then begins, in verses 10 and 11, a periodic syntax unlike anything else in the poem: the syntax of reflection rather than of simple excitement. The last line is a very smooth sonant alliteration; and the trisyllables "profectos" and "reportant" make a couplet in sound and meaning; and "reportant" ends the syntactical period. There is thus an effect of stopping finally and smoothly, so we do not expect another beginning.

Verse 1 is a summary statement of the external situation; the couplet of verses 2–3 specifies it. In verses 4–5 the situation comes home personally to the narrator addressed in the second person. In verse 6 the narrator is in the first person, and the sentence has a certain boastful panache. By verses 7 and 8 he is feeling his feelings and body. Meantime the time has shifted from a pervasive present to an immediate future, the most exciting tense. This leads to the most intimate person of speech, interpersonal direct address (vs. 9). The farewell is the climax of inwardness, and the concluding couplet shifts from the dramatic manner altogether; it is narrative and retrospective, a sentimental reflection, rather peculiar and idiosyncratic, almost as if witty in embarrassment. (Consider the alternatives that the poet eschews: either to proceed more deeply into feelings for his friends, or—in the manner of

Horace and other poets—to sentimentalize more generally about spring and departure, as, e.g., "Solvitur acris hiems" leads to "pallida Mors aequo pulsat pede." But Catullus finds a courteous middle, a thought about his friends.)

We thus see that from the background of easy and lively verses a simple over-all mounting and fading movement appears in the handling of the words, the syntax, the tones, tenses, and persons of speech. This movement is given in an immediate experience; for example, the second "Iam . . . iam . . ." comes when the first is fading but still present, and excitement is heightened by its reinforcement at just this point, after the rich brash "let's fly to the famous cities of Asia."

In this sense an over-all immediate motion of speech, tone, syntax, etc., is not presented in *Oedipus;* rather the over-all sequences are given in recognized individuals and remembered thoughts. In the beginning the King is sensuously introduced, in tone, rhythm, and spectacle; but it is as a named individual that we carry him along as the agent of later incidents. In the short lyric the separate words are part of the plot; that is why they must be attended to so carefully.

Feeling exists in such short sequences of immediate experience, and we can say that lyrical poems imitate feelings. The longer works imitate dispositions to feeling, characters, habits; they are feelingful at the climactic turns of the plot, and then, as we have said, the texture of speech often becomes lyrical.

### OBJECTS OF FEELING AND VEHICLES FOR FEELING

In these verses of Catullus there is nothing problematical in the relation of what he is telling about—spring, departure, prospect, farewell—and the feelingful modifications of the rhythm and the sequence of the narrator's involvement in the situation. There is *something* to be excited about, and he speaks *excitedly,* and *he* is excited; this is direct feelingful speech. But in many lyrical poems this is by no means the case; often there is no (direct) relation between what is told about and the mounting excitement conveyed, so it is profitable to make a distinction between the direct and what I shall call the "vehicular" expression of feeling.

An exclamation directly expresses feeling; but any word may be said in an exclamatory tone (e.g., a name called in a tone of anguish). If the poem turns not on the particular words but on their intonation, the words are vehicles. So further certain properties of grammar and syllogism are feelingful: there is agitated speech, confused speech, leaps of thought; all such require sentences to be feelingfully modified, and these sentences may directly imply the feeling or may be vehicles by which the feeling is conveyed. For instance, in a novel, conversation about the weather may express amorous embarrassment because conversation of another kind is expected. Contrariwise, when in *Philoctetes* the embarrassed Neoptolemus falls silent, the silence is directly feelingful, since his dilemma leaves him nothing to say; but, if he showed his embarrassment by turning to a tangential subject, the subject talked about would be a "vehicle," but the tangent would be the direct expression. Very different aesthetic effects result from the more or less use of vehicles and their distribution among more or less striking parts. Ring Lardner and T. S. Eliot, to instance two modern writers, achieve a kind of contemplative satire by the feelingful modification of trivialities; and Henry James relies heavily on feelingful tangential avoidances. (These are mixed-ethical vehicular effects.) "Understatement," again, with its peculiar effect, is just the other side of the medal; what is told about evokes feeling, but the rhythm and involvement are neutral.

The speech of Catullus is unusually direct. (Sappho, Li Po,

and Tu Fu come to mind as the only obvious comparisons; perhaps Wordsworth when he is writing about his childhood.) More typical lyrical poetry seems to me to have the following structure: The narrator is telling about something that is conventionally, symbolically, or otherwise indirectly moving; this subject matter forms a pattern with the verse, the imagery, the rhetoric, and this pattern may be very beautiful, but it has no motion of feeling or involvement of the narrator; nevertheless, feeling, involvement, and motion of thinking occur, using the pattern of the subject matter as a vehicle; and perhaps, toward the close, a more direct subject matter emerges that may or may not be akin to the apparent subject matter of the poem. Readers who happen to share the same character defenses against direct speech as the poet do not perceive that the subject matter is a vehicle, and they think they are moved by what the poem is "about." Critics, on the other hand, tend often to say that the poetic quality, the lyrical feeling, has nothing to do with the subject matter.

### PERVASIVE ATTITUDE, STYLE

Let us return to Catullus' poem and see if we can find what gives this poet his pecular power. It is his attitude or, what is nearly the same, his style. The style pervades the verses from beginning to end—it is always immediately experienced—but it is habitual; it does not have the motion of the particular incident and feeling; and, indeed, it is the same as in dozens of other poems, with different feelings. We do not much look, in Catullus' book, for great single poems, but we hear everywhere a single voice. Yet the power and charm of this voice are just that, again and again, it allows for the direct expression of different feelings; it is not a "style" apart from the feelingful occasions, yet they gain importance because they are given in the style of Catullus.

The attitude is at the same time both completely direct and intimate and yet elegant and curious (Alexandrian); elegant but rarely sought out, for it is always easy. We have already noticed this attitude in the conversational yet quite formal handling of the lilting meter. Notice, too, the narrator's assumption that all the biography necessary for the action and feeling is known or obvious; there is a naïveté and self-centeredness, yet the "I" appears from the environment and merges into a thought of his friends with modesty and courtesy. The sentences are short and easy to conceive, yet the accurate meteorology and geography of the first five lines are completely Alexandrian. "Praetrepidans" is a little odd, just as the rich "ad claras Asiae volemus urbes" is a little campy, and the alliterations call a little attention to themselves, and "profectos-reportant" is a little neat; yet the over-all motion is so direct, and the subject is so matter-of-fact, that everything seems unaffected.

It is an educated and high-born style that yet (or with luck, therefore) remains free-born and happy, with plenty of youth, friends, sex, and self-esteem.

## [*Milton's "On His Blindness": Stanzas, Motion of Thought*]

### TOPICS OF DICTION

In poems long and short the first presented parts are (spectacle and) the sounds and meanings of the words and the attitude and style of the speaker, whether actor or narrator. We have seen how in a short lyric the structure of these parts goes from the beginning to the end. Let us list some of the topics in discussing such a structure: sound, utterance, type of words, weight, tone, meter and rhythm, lexicon, metaphor, syntax. It will be seen that any of these and their combinations generate larger wholes.

By *sound* I mean the vowels, sonants, consonants, and accents; the distinction of light and heavy consonants, high and low vowels, long and short syllables; rhymes, assonances, alliterations; and thence we get meters, etc. By *utterance* I mean the combinations easy or hard to say, or quick or slow, in the given context of meaning and rhythm. The utterance depends also on the *type of words;* in polysyllables many sounds are given in an habitual unit (thus children who have not learned the unit speak them slowly and with difficulty, but adults speak them more rapidly than the same number of sounds in monosyllables); also auxiliaries and content words, as, in "to the house," "to the" is auxiliary and conjunctive; it is glossed over rapidly, but "house" has content and is slower. The content words have more *weight,* the auxiliaries less weight. It is meaning rather than sound that most arrests attention or drives the speech on (if, e.g., the meanings are making up a larger meaning being rapidly grasped); so content words, and phrases composed of auxiliaries and content words, determine the rhythm of a verse at least as importantly as the number and sound of syllables, or often they determine the rhythm that is heard in counterpoint to the meter. For example, in English pentameters we usually hear three (or two or four) beats to the blank verse, and the nearness or distance of the fall of the rhythm and the counted meter gives disposition and feeling. It is profitable to speak also of the weight in sound and utterance of images and propositions; for example, important true thoughts are heavy in a passage, and, if because of the feeling the passage must be read rapidly, the effect is hammer-like, terrible, or explosive. *Tone* is the immediate expression of feeling and attitude in the sound and utterance, as an exclamatory tone, by being either loud or surprisingly hushed; the tone may be crisply terse, or frankly given out, or slurred over, swallowed, talked away; or aside or parenthetical (in a different voice). All such things are dramatically expressive of the interpersonal relations and count very strongly in the structure. *Meter* is more the counting of the pulses and alternations of the body: the rate and flow of breathing, and the various gaits of locomotion, as walking, marching, skipping, etc. A verse is, in general, one breath. *Rhythm* is, as we have seen, more the modification of the pervasive meter by feeling, growing strong or faltering, tending toward a goal; we have spoken of it mainly as a sequence in short stretches, in short poems, but there are of course also the long waves of rhythm, toward the climax of the plot or conclusion of thinking. (Consider, to sum up so far, how all these might interrelate in the expression of a sudden discovery: accent, monosyllable, aposiopesis, defective meter, accelerating rhythm, exclamation, inference, quick utterance, and long pause.)

*Lexicon* is the choice of vocabulary, such as standard, learned, colloquial, neologist, including the appropriate (or clashing) grammar; very important for the connotative overtones in poetry is the nearness or distance from the etymology (like Dryden's beautiful "deviate into sense"). In the English language we notice especially, in a subdued but ultimately powerful way, whether the words are Saxon, Norman, or Latin. The choice of words gives character and disposition, social status, the role assumed for the speech; and the change of lexicon expresses always a powerful feeling (it is the giving-up or the taking-on of what the Jungians call a "new *persona*"); for example, a broken man reverting to the vocabulary of his early years.

The *syntax* of sentences is extraordinarily telling; it may express how the speaker is "in" the world, his logic, and his fundamental belief about the nature of things. To discuss syntax, we should have to explore a new range of topics:

co-ordination and subordination of clauses, inflected and un-inflected (analytic) combinations, mood, tense, the persons of speech, active, middle, and passive verbs, etc. Contrast, for example, a run-on style connected by co-ordinate conjunctions, like Hemingway's, with the periods of antithetic subordinate clauses of Gibbon: the former expresses a passive sensibility to which things "happen"; the latter, a deliberate ego exploring but also appropriating the world. Proust's syntax, again, is full of subordination, yet run-on, as if growing into experience but unable to come to decisive periods. Often the syntax of a paragraph gives the entire plot and theme *in parvo*. An analytic and generalizing language like Basic English is in the world in a different way from a highly inflected and specific primitive speech; thus Cocteau imagines "une traduction de Proust en sauvage où un seul mot désignerait la jalousie qui consiste à ... ou celle qui consiste à. ... On verrait des pages réduites à une ligne." A textured poem is like a complex primitive word. Tenses and change of tense often express degrees of involvement, as, for example, an account in the past alienates the subject and then warms into an historical present and becomes excited in an imminent future. We have seen how Catullus in a few lines passes from the third to the first to the second person, expressing the intimate and generous; and the peculiar rather timid sociality of Horace is strongly expressed by his continual recourse to the second person to begin ("Vides ut alta stet nive candidum"; "Iam te premet nox"; "Tu ne quaesieris"; etc.), leading often to a first plural, as if having found a safe identity. The expressiveness of the mood and voice of verbs is obvious.

Thus we see the tendency to poetic combination in the least elements, the parts of diction. I have chosen strong, but not far-fetched, examples in order to show that the close analysis of texture is not picayune. For the most part an element is expressive by calling attention to itself, deviating from normal expectancy, as "an unusual number of heavy consonants in the line"; but attention is a matter of degree—a very slight expressiveness may become powerful when it is pervasively repeated. Also, the so-called norm itself may be expressive of character, attitude, Weltanschauung. Certainly most individual speakers are unaware of the expressiveness of their habitual speech; and so with social groups: the speech of an individual seems neutral because it is standard, but the standard itself is powerfully expressive. In this way, finally, whole languages are said to have their peculiar "genius."

On the other hand, of course, the actual expressiveness of any element, rather than its "tendency to combine," is selected and altered by the whole ongoing structure, the poem itself. Words like "then" or "so," which in most poems are auxiliary, might be heavy in an intellectual poem of Donne, where there is syllogism and enthymeme; or, again, where in many poems adjectives are less weighty than nouns, in a given imagist poem the pattern of adjectives of color and sound might be the chief structure.

### VERSE FORMS AND STANZAS

When a meter is well established in a poem, there gets to be in the counting alone a certain probability. And in a conventional verse form (e.g., a rondeau) there is in the counting of the lines and rhymes a probability of the ending. The simplest relation of a verse form to the other, nonconventional, parts is that the verse form is a framework by which we go from the beginning to the end, as in certain enumerative ballades or in twelve lines of Shakespeare's sixty-sixth sonnet. The other extreme is that the conventional form is "naturalized," that is, that every metric division of the form expresses the motion of the other parts; and this extreme is approached in several sonnets of Milton, to which we will shortly turn.

Stanzas are metric units of more than one verse or breath. When a poem has stanzas, the relation between the stanzas and the other parts offers the following interesting possibilities.

1. There may be a free movement, across the stanzas, of the syntax, thought, feeling, etc. The meter then becomes a kind of musical background, and the dissociation might be expressive of freedom of fancy, continuous description of the object or situation as if not poetizing, etc. (This is an effect much cultivated by Marianne Moore.)

2. Having established the dissociation of (1), by then changing to a stricter correspondence of the other parts with the stanza an effect may be attained of summary, drawing conclusions, earnest involvement of the poet's voice. Thus, in *φαινεταί μοι κῆνος ἴσος θέοισιν*, Sappho freely describes the beloved and then more earnestly subdivides her own responses. In "O Fons Bandusiae" Horace describes his own action freely, but he praises the spring formally.

3. Along the same lines, the syntax, thought, and image may seem to be moving freely across the stanzas, and yet the periods happen, as it were, to fall near the endings or the beginnings of the stanzas. This gives a certain witty or unexpected elegance. I mention it especially in contrast to (5) below.

4. Or there may be a strict adherence of the syntax, thought, etc., to the stanzas. In a mounting feeling this gives the effect of definite stages, a kind of learned passion, as in the sonnets of Dante. In a poem of action such an adherence to the stanzas creates an arbitrary discontinuity; and in a simple ballad, where it is common, the effect is a naïve charm, for the action seems to be made suited to the convenience of a rude singer. In a motion of thought, adherence to the stanzas emphasizes the logical relations.

5. Last is the case important for the analysis of Milton's sonnets. Here it seems that the motion of thought and the mount-

ing feeling will adhere to the stanzas; but for an internal reason the bounds are broken. In "Avenge, O Lord" the passion of the description breaks down the orderliness and overflows. So overfulness of thought might overflow the boundary. Or in "On His Blindness" the stanza ending is anticipated—there is a sudden contradiction. It is clear that this passionate effect is not to be confused with the delicate or witty effect of (3) above; for there we have free fancy generating wit, but here passion degenerating order. Very expressive also is the passage from (4) to (5), strict order breaking down; or from (5) to (4), as when passion calms to resolution.

There is an important, but rather elusive, set of relations that occurs in somewhat longer poems that have repetitive verses and especialy repetitive stanzas. As the same pattern is repeated again and again, its succession to itself becomes more and more probable. Now this probability may, on the one hand, attract too much attention to itself and quite destroy everything else; this is a peculiar chanting monotony, the doggerel of larger units. (So often in Longfellow.) On the other hand, the probability may seem, in a strange way, to be transmitted to the progressing action or the ongoing thought, with a powerful increase of feeling, conviction, necessity; the utterance that is causing the effect is not noticed, the inevitability seems to belong to the incidents or the reasoning; the effect is hypnotic. Perhaps the condition for this kind of success is that with the long series of stanzas there is also a strong progression in the other parts and a great fulness and variety, so that the monotony cannot be heard; then, when these conditions exist and when the rhythm is modified, in speed, excitement, or solemnity, suddenly the monotonous regularity of the stanzas begins powerfuly to reinforce the climax, and we have such sublime organ points as "Or go to Rome" in *Adonais.* Something similar occurs from time to time in long sonnet sequences. The fact that a strong and rich poet can thus gain power also by being monotonous, whereas a weak poet becomes all the more boring, is an illustration of the text, "To those that have shall be given, and from those that have not shall be taken away even that which they have."

### MOTION OF THOUGHT AND ASYMMETRICAL THOUGHT

Sonnets are divided asymmetrically into two parts, the octave and the sestet (or the three quatrains and the couplet). This asymmetry has been used to convey a certain asymmetrical motion of thought; indeed, the sonnets with such a motion of thought and its feeling outnumber all the others together. Let us first discuss "motion of thought" and then "asymmetry of motion."

Thoughts in a poem may be immediately presented or mediately operative as background conceptual sources of probability. For instance, the particular indefinite judgment, "The Oracle demands a murderer," is immediately present, thought and said by the characters, in one episode; but it is mediately operative throughout *Oedipus* as one explanation of what is going on, if such an explanation should be called for. As a judgment, it is at rest; but, when the explanation is called for and we get the enthymeme, "The Oracle demands a murderer and therefore demands Creon," the judgment becomes part of a motion of thinking.

How is the motionless thought given in the motion of speech? We saw that a motionless habit (e.g., character) is given by a certain similarity in a series. Thought is the taking together, as one whole, of meanings given successively; for instance, a subject is given and then a predicate, and, when they are taken together, it is a thought. The successive giving of the meanings may occur with a mounting feeling, in which case the thought is an object of the feeling. Or the dialogue and argument may circle round or come to a thought, in which we take together what has been said. Or an image or images may reflect, as in a mirror, a thought.

But a motion of thought may itself directly organize the flow of words. For instance, in the sentence, "Oedipus murdered his father and committed incest," the "and" is a kind of taking together—namely, co-ordinate conjunction—that directly organizes the sequence of words. And, more elaborately, in any kind of dialectic some thoughts generate other thoughts, and there is a sequence.

(The sense in which terms have meaning or propositions have compounded meaning or inferences have validity: this does not seem to me to be a topic of poetics. The meaning of terms or the validity of inferences is neither at rest nor in motion and cannot be analyzed in a concrete poem; but the thinking or saying or giving of the meaning can be part of a poem. I do not at all mean by this that such meaning is unimportant to the poetry; but it is the "life" in the "imitating of life," and I must therefore repeat what I said in the first chapter: "It is just *because* important parts of the combination have been taken from life and concernful parts of life"—indeed, from where else could they be taken?—"it is just because the works *are* imitations, that the poet and critic can prima facie neglect the extrinsic reference and concentrate on making a self-contained whole." That is, since terms have meaning, their poetic combination is bound to have meaning or be nonsense, both major poetic effects.)

Now inference is an asymmetrical motion of thought in that the end somewhat contains the beginning and cannot be taken as co-ordinate with it, equivalent to it, or disjunct from it. Consider kinds of inference: judgment, or the passage from a rule to a particular; induction, the passage from a particular (or collection) to a rule; syllogism and enthymeme, the passage from premises to conclusion; or cause to effect; or effect to cause; question and answer, a passage from possible alternatives to no alternative; etc. In all these, especially if presented as immediate acts, we have a motion of thinking and likewise a probable ending of the motion. They are then capital for directly organizing poetic sequences.

It is such motions of thought that in very many cases are part of the over-all plot of sonnets, another part being the asymmetrical structure of the stanzas, and another the rising and ending of a feeling. Let me give an intricate example, "The World Is Too Much with Us": Here the octave describes an undesirable state of things; there are unexpressed premises rejecting the state and embracing a contrary condition; it seems as though the undesirable state of affairs will continue, for the octave overruns into the ninth line, "It moves us not"; but then the sestet breaks through with an exclamation, obviously moved, expressing the suppressed premises and the dammed-up opposite (a device we observed in the soliloquies of Hamlet); and, without explicitly stating the contradictory rule, the sestet describes an example of the contrary state. Throughout, the inferential thought is in violent motion, the violence being beautifully conveyed by the inability to come to the explicit statement of the premises, since that would be too slow:

> For this, for *everything,* we are out of tune,
> It moves us *not.*

This summary is already too close to the conclusive judgment of the deadness he feels; he will not tolerate it and certainly not say it, but instead the contrary wish breaks through, and the dreamy fantasy of the pagan, Proteus, and Triton is exquisitely probable. (Compare and contrast all this with "Milton! Thou Shouldst Be Living at This Hour": Here the life-problem is similar, but the motion is less violent. He comes to a more explicit judgment, "We are selfish men"; but his exclamatory denial, "O raise us up," is an exhortation rather than an angry dismissal, for he believes that the return of Milton is in some way possible; and then the ending is, again with exquisite probability, close to the everyday: "Thy heart the lowliest duties on herself did lay." Alas! the Triton sonnet has to do with spontaneous feelings that we cannot revive by willing to; "Milton" deals with deliberate ethical behavior that is somewhat in our control. In the first case, nothing will serve but disgust, despair, and anger, and they do not "really" serve; in the second case, calling attention and exhortation are of some use. My point is that all this is adequately conveyed by the motion of the thought, the handling of the stanzas, and the tone of the images.)

A simpler case: in the sonnets of Shakespeare usually the couplet is a conclusion of inference; but, to judge these poems rightly, we must bear in mind that, although often the couplet is not sufficiently prepared, and does not have enough weight, to contain the premises, yet, if the sonnets are read as part of a sonnet sequence, the probability is sufficient. Thus, in "Tired with All These, for Restful Death I Cry" the twelve lines are an elaborate collection; the first line of the couplet states the rule, the second, with no weight of feeling or evidence, refutes the rule; but the probability of the refutation is given in the sequence of sonnets.

### MOTION OF THOUGHT AND STANZA STRUCTURE

Let us now explore some possible relations between the inferential thought and the stanzas of sonnets.

1. Suppose that there is only a two-part division, eight and six or twelve and two. The conclusion may begin with some inferential words, "But since . . . ," "But if . . . ," "Then . . . ," "Yet him . . . ," "Unless . . . ," "Therefore . . . ," etc.

2. The octave may be divided into two quatrains. These may be the premises from which the sestet concludes; or they may contain a subordinate movement of thought, as cause and effect, rule and example, or vice versa, that the sestet contradicts, or further generalizes, or applies to one's self, etc. (So the three quatrains of English sonnets might be three examples, two examples and a rule, etc.)

3. The octave may be divided for the thought, as just described, and yet be a single mounting feeling. This is common, the sestet then either climaxing the feeling or reversing it and climaxing it. But consider the opposite possibility: that the thought is single throughout the octave but the feeling is divided; this might, for instance, express a wry or sardonic or paradoxical or flippant mood (what I have been calling a mixed-ethical effect). I have no example in mind, but no doubt that exists.

4. Again, the sestet may be divided into tercets, or quatrain and couplet, or couplet and quatrain. Now a very important arrangement, that I shall call a "complex sonnet," is that where the first tercet or the quatrain reverses the octave in such a way that a catharsis is required, and this is then given in the remaining tercet or couplet. "The World Is Too Much with Us" is such a case, and we shall find others among the sonnets of Milton.

5. In any case, a final couplet has a peculiarly summary or antithetic quality and arrests the thought. Its motion is briefer than the norm of quatrains, and therefore the tonal effect will often be witty, contemptuous, sharply angry, or dismissing. Many examples could be cited from Donne.

6. A division of the sestet that I myself often have employed is couplet then quatrain. Then either the couplet sharply reverses the octave, and the quatrain is a more leisurely view of the new situation; or the couplet emphatically summarizes the

octave, bringing the poem to a premature close, and the concluding quatrain looks elsewhere, gives a *deus ex machina,* etc.

Then, further, let us return to the discussion of verse forms and stanzas[2] and ask about the handling of the stanza boundaries. The motion of thought is most in the foreground when the quatrains and tercets (and couplet) are most strictly adhered to. The characteristic overrunning or falling-short in Milton and Wordsworth expresses impetuosity, passionate fulness of thought; and it is the probability for a more striking reversal. The boundaries may have transitional words, as "But Patience, to prevent" in "On His Blindness," or there may be a leap of thought with no transition, as in "The World Is Too Much with Us"; the first is a more sober, the second a more excited, consideration.

### THE REFLECTIVE THOUGHT

Milton's "On His Blindness" is a motion of thinking, reflection on a problem, introduced by the formula "When I consider." But the reflection is peculiar and can be understood only if we consider the feeling accompanying it. The relations of the thought and the feeling are given in the rhythm, syntax, and handling of the sonnet form. And we shall see that this particular combination of thought and feeling is probable in the pervasive style. Let us take up these propositions in turn.

The reflection is an argument on justification by works. In the octave (vss. 1–7⅗) there is a justification of the self before God; this is given in the profusion of first-person pronouns, "I," "my," "my," "me," "my," "my," "my," "I (fondly)." In the sestet a virtue declares God's position in the argument: "God," "His," "His," "Him," "His," "His"; and further the first person is negated in the words "man's," "Who," "they," "thousands," "They," "who." The transition is given in the alienat-

2. Cf. above, p. 197.

ing epithet "*That* murmur" rather than "this" or "my" murmur. The octave is divided to give a subordinate motion of thought: "these being the circumstances, I therefore say"; the sestet breaks in on this reasoning, indeed before the eighth line is complete, and contradicts it.

But look more closely at the sestet; it too is divided (at vs. $11\frac{4}{5}$) into two tercets; what is the motion of thought expressed by this division, introducing an entirely new idea? For the first tercet presents the correct argument with regard to man's justification: "Who best / Bear His mild yoke, they serve Him best." This is the end of the normal argument; what more remains to say? But, no; now *God* is glorified (vss. 12–13). This further reflection, though logically probable from " 'God doth not need . . .' (because He has)," is nevertheless extraneous, and perhaps even impious, in the apparent unity of an argument on justification.

### FEELING: COMPLEX SONNET

But if we consider the feeling rising through the poem, however, we see at once that the passion in the octave is not merely the appropriate anxiety at not being justified, not being able to play one's role, but even more it is despair at the deprivation and inaction, mounting to almost anger and insolence, in verse 7. The "one talent" of verse 3 is, of course, first the talent of Matt. 25:15–30, that belongs to poverty, incompetence, and timidity to put out; and that talent is "one" in the sense that it is not two or five. But the talent is here also the poetic gift, that is one because it is unique and great, and that is "death to hide" because such a talent feeds on action and fame and otherwise "I" dies.

We are thus not at all in the feeling of an humble reflection on justification. Then, can the feeling be resolved by the correct injunction of Patience, "Bear His mild yoke"? Not at all;

for the "I" must be not only justified but *satisfied*. It is this satisfaction that is given by the joyous anthem, "*His* state / Is kingly." *God* is justified, and by identification "I" is satisfied. We may then come to a satisfactory Patience, the confidence of "wait." The feeling of the octave is not resolved until this ending.

This is everywhere the Miltonic theme. In the early sonnet "On His Having Arrived at the Age of Twenty-three," "my late spring no bud or blossom shew'th"; but just wait! for "that same lot however mean or high / Toward which Time leads me"—and he means high. And in "Cyriack, This Three Years' Day" his blindness is "justified" by "my noble task / Of which all Europe talks from side to side." Or again, "But not the Praise! / Phoebus replied, and touched my trembling ears." Fame is the "last infirmity of noble minds." And, of course, the justification of God to be even more satisfying than Satan's pride is the theme of his epic.

(This is, I say, his conscious theme; and of course it is only a great soul that can identify so explicitly with such a dark and wicked theme. Psychoanalyzing the same theme, we should perhaps begin to ask—taking *Samson* as his most intimate poem—why is it that to have strength means the same thing as to abuse it?)

By analogy with tragic plays, we might call this and similar sonnets "complex," for the thinking suffers a reversal prepared from the beginning, and then there is a catharsis. Further, by analogy with miracles, we could say that the conclusion of the argument on justification is an impasse, for the thought does not do poetic justice to the gratuitous suffering, nor is it a sufficient reward for the talent; but that God is kingly is a reconciliation *ex machina*.

### MODIFICATIONS BY RHYTHM, SYNTAX, AND HANDLING OF THE FORM

The following considerations bear on the expression of feeling in the over-all rhythm: the quantity, weight, and obviousness or difficulty of the ideas; the co-ordination and involution of the syntax and its plainness or difficulty; the relation of ideas and syntax to the meter and sonnet form; and the rhythmic modifications in the metric verses and the stanzas themselves. Let us use the last, the rhythm of each of the fourteen lines, as the framework for discussion.

Throughout, a good iambic pentameter can be heard. The style (the man) does not neglect the standard; and yet he is always sounding the quite different rhythm of his thought and feeling.

*When I consider | how my light | is spent |*

This, three accented phrases to the pentameter, is the norm of iambic pentameters expressing meaning rather than sounds (for the principle of rhythmic accent is meaning, not syllabic feet). I prefer to read "I" as without accent, to give a quiet beginning to the self-justifying. "Light" and "spent" are a little sharper after so many previous slight syllables in the verse.

*Ere half my days, | in this dark world | and wide, | |*

This is a heavier consideration, expressed in the longer vowels, in the alliteration on a heavy consonant ("*d*ays," "*d*ark," "*w*orld," "*w*ide"), and the assonances on sonants ("*w*orld," "*w*ide," "d*ar*k," "wo*r*ld"). Spondees weight down the end of the line. The increase to four beats despite the harder utterance is a kind of heavy excitement. The full ending, with a periodic couple and a broad vowel ("world" and "wide"), closes the meaning and makes of the first two lines a unit; it is the first premise of thought. (I accent "dark" by contrast to "light.")

*And that one talent | which is death to hide*

This is a much quicker excitement: there are again four beats but only one caesura (if indeed the whole line must not be read without caesura) and no end stop; the utterance is much lighter but made agitated by the antimetric accent on "one." "Death" is perhaps heavier as the heir of the *d* alliteration. But, most important, the syntax has now begun to involute; for we expect an independent clause to complete the "when"-clause, but rather we embark on an "and"-clause within it. And this beginning of involution is matched by impeding the flow of thought with the difficult image of the talents, especially since there is a pun. Yet the line goes on rapidly into

*Lodged with me useless, | though my soul more bent*

(A remarkably expressive verse.) Here are only two phrases as previously, and we must read quickly; and yet because of the heavy spondees this is very hard; and yet the whole is despondent because of little accented beat. The beat is taken out of the line by the ametric trochee of "useless" and the ametric emphasis on "more." I read "useless" emphatically, as a kind of groan. And now the syntax that had begun to involute has begun to tangle, for we start a "though"-clause with the "when" and the "and" still incomplete. Likewise, as the image generates more points of resemblance, the strain of attention increases: we must bear in mind that the thought, the syntax, the learned image, the pun, all become complicated. The idea "soul . . . bent" is itself constricted. Finally, though we have come to the end of the quatrain and expect a breather, we are driven onward.

*To serve therewith my Maker, | and present*
*My true account, | lest He returning | chide: | |*

Again in the first of these lines there is only one caesura, and it comes so late in the line that the pentameters are thrown into agitation; I read a heavy emphasis on "serve" in contrast with "useless" and then on "account" and "chide," making of these heavy beats a quite ametric rhythm across both the meter and the beats of rhythmic speech; this is an effect of heavy breathing, groaning, or gasping. The despondency is succeeded by a more rapid and agitated excitement; the fifth line is as fast as the first, but rougher; the sixth line is even rapid, with short vowels in the unaccented places, a quick light alliteration ("presen*t*," "*t*rue," "accoun*t*," "les*t*," "re*t*urning"). Speed, yet the syntax and the image have become only more tangled: "therewith" refers backward; the "though"-clause within the "when" generates an infinitive and still another conjunction; and with "lest" the involution becomes extreme—"returning" is hard even to say, it is so out of the flow—and "chide" is isolated and harsh by position, sound, and sense. (I read "He" without accent both for rapidity and to keep the big "He's" for the sestet.) This is headstrong agitation, rapidity in difficulty. The isolation and length of the rhyme word "chide" creates a pause. It is, finally, the end of the "when"-clause, but this is not clear for another line and a half.

*"Doth God exact day-labour, | light denied?" |*

It seems as if the syntax has collapsed, for there is no independent verb until "ask" in the next line; the inverted order throws the difficult syntax into the boldest relief. And how well this confusion serves as the background for the surprise in meaning: we expect that the poem's quotation marks will tell the chiding of "He," but instead they tell the complaint of "I." There are six beats; but, where five make a rapid verse, six make a nervous one. This nervous speed is, too, among heavy consonants, a *d* alliteration ("*d*oth," "Go*d*," "*d*ay," "*d*enie*d*") and a *g* alliteration ("*G*od," "e*g*zact"); this is a heavy nervousness (anger). Yet there are four good iambics, and the verse, though broken, is unflagging to its loud ending; and the good beginning (two definite iambics) and the end-stop make a conclusive verse after all the previous indefinite meters and overflows. But, most important, instead of the expected chiding, there is a touch of insolence: this is given in the witty contrast of "day" and "light," enforced, as it is, by the *d-l* chiasmus ("day-labour, light denied"). In the nervous anger there is room for a rhetorical figure and an insolent wit. But of course it is just the modicum of insolence permissible in this place to this author—he is wise and humble, but indeed he has a bitter complaint.

∪ / ∪ /
*I fondly ask.* ||

The syntax is finally untangled, and there are two good iambics. We are returning to the norm, the nervous anger is already lost in judgment; and the judging word "fo*ndly*" may perhaps be heard as the heir of the *n-d-l* of "light denied."

It is the end of the octave, though we have not filled the eighth line. There has been an agitation mounting to a nervous anger with a touch of insolence, all involved in a confused syntax; but all is calmed in the judging word "fondly," and the syntax reaches its period. The first quatrain of the octave is more despondent, the second angrier. The boundary of the quatrains is "my soul more bent / to serve."

∪ /̲ — ∪ ∪ /
*But Patience,* | *to prevent*

∪ — ∪ — ∪ /̲
*That murmur, soon replies,* |

Breaking into the octave at verse $7\frac{2}{3}$, yet not suddenly, for the agitation is already spent in the regular "I fondly ask." The passage is transitional to a contrary freer moving rhythm; from now on, for several lines, the sense and stronger rhythm move quite in disregard of the verse endings—we must pause at "replies," "gifts," "best," "kingly." In the octave the lack of correspondence of sense and verse was handled tensely ("more bent / To serve"); but here openly, freely. But the transition to calm freedom is especially given in the sound: the sharper sounds of "But Patience, to prevent" allaying to the lovely smooth long syllables on the beat, "That murmur, soon replies"; and allaying is the succession of *p*'s ("*P*atience," "*p*revent," "re*p*lies"—the last a little delayed)—for where a quick alliteration, like the *t* alliteration in verse 6, is accelerating, a retarding alliteration recalls attention to the sameness and is calming. (Cf. in "Captain or Colonel or Knight-in-Arms" the same *p* alliteration with the same effect: "s*p*are the house of *P*indarus when *t*emple and *t*ower wen*t* *t*o the ground, and the re*p*eated air of sad Electra's *p*oet had the *p*ower." Or the same effect in slow assonances, e.g., Poe's "To Helen": "thy hyacinth h*ai*r, thy classic f*a*ce, thy Naiad *ai*rs.") Further, the relaxed free motion of the sestet is given in temporarily establishing a choriambic (swinging) base: "Patience-prevent," "murmur-replies," "God-doth-not-need." "Murmur" is the sound inside the head; "replies" is the clear word spoken out.

/ ∪ ∪ ⁄
*"God doth not need*

∪ ∪ ⁄ — ∪ ∪ ⁄ —
*Either man's work* | *or His own gifts.* |

From the start the syntax of Patience is direct, one simple clause following another. "God doth" reverses "doth God," a new meaning, a new atmosphere. The free-swinging choriambs continue in "man's work . . . His own." Contrast, for example, the ametric beat on "man's" to that on "soul móre bent"; in the free swing the effect of the ametric strain is earnestness rather than agitation.

*Who best*
*Bear His mild yoke,* | *they serve Him best.* ||

The stronger meaning-rhythm is going freely past the verses, but the speech-rhythm has nicely returned to a normal three phrases to the pentameter. In this clause the earnest consideration is given more strongly: the choriambs lose their lilt to spondees, and one could almost read "théy sérve Hím bést." The soothing *p* alliteration deepens to a *b* ("*b*est, "*b*ear," "*b*est"). Each word seems isolated. And, most important, this is a conclusive clause; it is a periodic formula; "serve" answers the question of "bent to serve"; and the repeated "best" at the period requires a strong beat and a pause. It is the end of the first tercet. Yet, of course, it is not the end, for a foot is missing to the line.

*His state*
*Is kingly.* |

The last tercet again breaks in prematurely. I read "His" fortissimo, to top "best" and recommence after the pause; and as the climax of "God . . . His own . . . His . . . Him." (It would be attractive, alternatively, to lay the strong beat on "state," and I guess this would be the more seventeenth-century reading. But I prefer the loud choriamb and the emphasis on the personal.) In any case, the sentence is exclamatory by its brevity. We have begun to generate, in one burst, a new excitement after the earnest consideration.

*Thousands at His bidding speed*

This change to trochees is immortal. These are the heirs of the choriambs, as if, through a transition, iambics had turned into running-rhythm. The diphthong in "Thousands" is as loud as can be, it tops "kingly" and launches on the trochees with hardly a breath. No pause at the end of the verse.

*And post o'er land and ocean without rest.* | | |

After the trochees, a complete line of rapid iambs without caesura: it is a climax of excited pleasure and fulfilment. We are hurried into it by the s*p*-*p*s of "speed-post," for, where such an effect within a verse would be retarding, here it is a bridge of easy utterance. And, indeed, the verse of trochees and the verse of rapid iambs form a wondrous choriamb, so to speak, of verse against verse. But the rhythm breaks with the spondee at the end and prevents running on into the last line. Since the last line is isolated, the pause may be dramatically exaggerated.

Thus far in the sestet, then, we have a freer motion marked by an easy disregard of the verse endings and continual choriambic effects; increasing in earnestness; and climaxing suddenly in joyous excitement, marked by the return to pentameters, first trochees, then good and rapid iambs.

*They also serve who only stand* | *and wait."*

This famous line is syntactically isolated by the lack of a conjunction and by the previous pause. In feeling and thought it resolves the poem entire. The feeling is not merely that proper to God's court, joy, but also the special feeling of patient confidence: this is given by the firm march. There are five iambs, all good, yet not quick, for there is an important sonant in every foot ("a*l*so," "se*r*ve," "o*nl*y," "sta*n*d") that slows utterance without creating difficulty; the vowels are exceptionally long, yet low-pitched and not loud. But especially there are the medium-slow balances in the first four feet: "they-who," "also-only," "serve-stand": balance in syntax, word length, vowels, consonants. Yet all this in the most unobtrusive way, so that seriousness is not distracted by figures of rhetoric. Lastly, these balances isolate "and wait," which is further isolated by the somewhat difficult utterance "stand and w . . . ." Thus, the balances give the line stability, but the isolation of "and wait" opens a new prospect. I should then read "wait" in a higher pitch—by no means as a period, and ever so faintly stronger. The line as a whole is an epigrammatic thought, therefore is an ending, for nothing can be said after an epigram.

These remarks have been somewhat minute (though by no means exhaustive); and, in becoming thus minute, I have introduced many idiosyncracies of my own. I doubt that any other reader would scan this poem exactly as I have. But, in any case, there are certain main motions that are beyond dispute: the difficulty and agitation of the octave, in thought, sound, and syntax; the easy thought and syntax of the sestet as a whole and the freedom of the choriambs and overflows of the first tercet; the climax at "His state is Kingly"; the speed and excitement of the twelfth and thirteenth lines; and the slower, resolving, conclusive epigram.

### ATTITUDE AND STYLE

But the minute description I have been giving is, by critical magnification, a caricature. I speak of the syntax collapsing or of a climax of nervous anger, but no such shocking events come to the fore or make us for a moment forget the controlled intellect, aware always of the more inclusive whole, whose syntax knows no collapse and who is not excited by a poem. The turns of thought and the modifications by feeling are never destructive of logic or meter; they are never far from a "serious" norm. The epigram is not a stinging one, the "excitement" comes down to mild alterations of rhythm, and the "fortissimo" is a voice somewhat stronger, certainly no shout. Nevertheless, the anger and excitement are there. It is the expressiveness in so restrained an expression that makes this style.

The attitude is serious in the following sense: the feeling bears only on the thought, and the thought is determined by the feeling. The "I" must face this problem; the diction is a means by which he faces it, but it is a servant to the problem: it does not call attention to itself. (The hint of an exception, "day-labour, light denied," confirms the rule.)

The choice of words is the graver class of the ordinary, the ethical and philosophical speech of all men when personally involved in a serious matter. There is no question but that the blind man considering is real, not imaginary; "half my days, in this dark world" means something about the narrator's true age. And all this, again, makes the choice of the metaphor from the Bible neither out of place nor technical (dogmatic) but appropriate and personal. The style is serious and personal enough to be able to include the scriptural in the ordinary flow of the verse.

Mostly in the sonnets of Milton there is no style; it is the speech of earnestness personally involved and calls all attention to the thought and feeling. Given a similar theme treated by Donne, for instance, much would have to be said about the style; or, in speaking of *Paradise Lost* or *Lycidas,* we should say independent things about the style, as we did in discussing the verses of Catullus. We can speak of "no style" in three senses: the sense of Milton's sonnets, where a powerful diction is artistically neutralized in the interest of the thought and feeling, and this neutralizing itself is then expressive of attitude; the sense of a nonliterary writing, where the writer has never gotten into contact with his speech—this is "no style" absolutely; and the sense of poor poetry, where "no style" is a confusion of styles.

## [ *Remarks on "Morte d'Arthur"* ]

### TOPICS OF DICTION GROUNDED IN THE RELATION "STANDING-FOR"

The poetic use of words in imitating Action, Character, Feeling, Thinking is such that, in the poem, the words directly *are* the Action, Character, etc. Specific combinations of words are these different parts of poems, as, for example, I have been trying to show how rhythm is often character and modification of rhythm is feeling. But Metaphors, Images, Symbols require us also to think of the words as *designations,* as "standing-for" something. For, as Aristotle says, "metaphor is giving the thing a name that belongs to something else," and so our attention is called to the fact that it is a "name," a designation.

Let us put this another way. All words are, of course, designations; as the semanticists say, "The word is not the thing." But the genius of poetry is that the words, and the combinations of words, *are* the thing; they present us with a constructed reality. Thus, in the end, the function of poetry is not to "communicate meanings" but to have a direct effect like any other important experience, to make us have gone through something. The words start as designations and become the designates. In the case of metaphors and images, however, the "standing-for," the self-conscious use of language, is played with. Thus metaphor has always been considered peculiarly appropriate in poetry, since it is playing with the language function itself; and critics who speak of "pure poetry" generally mean pure metaphor (embellished by sound).

Or let us take still another tack (but all these come to the same). Metaphors, images, and symbols call attention to the likeness and keep the likeness as part of the whole structure, whereas in the method of presenting character (e.g., as "similarity in a series"), the character is presented just when the likeness merges into the background. Or, to take another example, a rapid modification of a basic rhythm is "like" a mounting excitement; it is a natural sign of it, but it does not "indicate" or stand for emotional speech—it *is* emotional speech. But a trotting rhythm is "like" a horse, is appropriate to describing a horse race.

The various distinctions of metaphor, simile, etc., turn on this fact of calling attention to the likeness and therefore the difference. Since the similars are not identical, the off-naming might be mentioned explicitly with the word "like"—these are the similes—or more or less implicitly, as in the metaphors, metonymies, onomatopoeias, etc., where the boldness consists in affirming an identity of the nonidentical. Often in the similes of Homer, the likeness is drawn from one aspect to start with, but then, as the simile develops, a likeness appears in some other aspect, and he returns us to the original with a "so"; this is a compounding of simile. Or in my "Your Face, Your Profile," the simile develops into an independent episode, and this is reversed back to the original.

There can be more or less unlikeness of the sign and the designate, more or less emphasis on the standing-for, a vaguer or sharper or developing standing-for, and so forth. For instance, we might start with a word taken in a conventional sense and calling no attention to itself as a sign, but then suddenly make use of its etymology and so generate a metaphor or simile.

In poems of action the relationship of foil characters and parallel plots may profitably be explored as an image. In Spanish plots the servants are comic images of the masters, or Fortinbras is an image of Hamlet. But where the foil is taken as equally *actual,* that is, as occupying the same kind of time and place, we do not generally then consider it as imagery *until* the analogy is explicitly called attention to, as in drawing a moral, as when Hamlet says, "How all occasions do inform against me!"

### IMAGES AS PARTS OF THE PLOT

As with other parts of diction, kinds of metaphor—Images, Descriptions, Symbols—may continuously organize the whole and be parts of the plot. (This is commoner in short poems but applies also, obviously, in long allegories.) In "On First Looking into Chapman's Homer" the image of traveling organizes the whole, and the change in the type of travel is the chief expression of the thought; but "came down like a wolf on the fold" is a metaphor by the way.

In analyzing *Richard II,* Act III, scene 2, however, we saw how a series of such ordinary metaphors can combine into an image system, developed by reinforcements of weak analogies, until it organizes the whole scene.

In short poems, where every part of the diction is kept in mind, the poet must take care to prevent anomalous, non-reinforcing, relations among the metaphors; for, if he writes metaphorically at all, he is bound to generate an image.

Images differ in manner too. Often the standing-for is given directly by the narrator with a formal comparison, as "The Lover Compareth His State to a Ship." This works well in short poems, where the way the language function is played with can directly convey feeling; but in long allegories the effect is, to my taste, almost invariably frigid. In other cases, the comparison develops immediately from the description, as when the lapping waves generate a melancholy sentiment. Sometimes there is a change of manner, for example, from a description to an appraisal of its meaning to the narrator, as in "This Lime Tree Bower My Prison," or in all descriptive poems with morals ("To a Waterfowl"). Or, contrariwise, the image is introduced by an explicit analogy but then is freely developed as an independent episode—so Horace in *Odes* ii. 13 exclaims, on a narrow escape, how nearly he came to see the realms of Proserpine, which are then described for the rest of the poem. A very dramatic kind is where what seemed to have only an analogous relation is suddenly made an action, as when the narrator of "Les Fleurs du mal" punishes "sur une fleur l'insolence de la Nature."

Crudely we might say that an image is analogous throughout but an analogous description at the beginning or end; but poets have explored every intermixture. For instance, in "Dover Beach" the scene is at first analogous to the feeling but relatively independent of the thought; then, in verses 15 ff., the feeling generates an appropriate thought, and, responding to this, the description suddenly appears as a full-blown image, the Sea of Faith.

We may sense that an image is analogous throughout and yet be quite unable to grasp the precise analogue. This is true of many Imagist poems, where it is clear enough that they are not descriptions, but we cannot quite hit what is being analogized; in some cases it is the order of perception, therefore the action of the soul; or the structure of associated memories. The grand master is Mallarmé the "symbolist," whose obscurities turn out to be (after a certain amount of detective work) exquisitely precise descriptions of simple matters of fact—the reflection in a wine glass, the foam after something has occurred to disturb the sea—and the effect is an immense awareness.

An image may be a framework to convey the analogue rather than an important analogy of it. In the first two stanzas of Poe's "To Helen" the figure of traveling is an analogy of the feeling (I am a wanderer), but it is a mere framework for the thought of the cultures of Greece and Rome; but the cease of travel, in the third stanza, is analogous to the thought and feeling both, "as a man stands and gazes, so I know the Ideal and so I feel."

To images and descriptions we may add analogous actions. These must first be distinguished from such mutual implications of thought and action as in *Oedipus,* where the relation is probability rather than analogy. But it is interesting when we find both relations at once, as in many poems of Wordsworth; in "Daffodils" the dance of the daffodils is like the feelings of the observer, but on the Wordsworthian theory of perception (which, by the way, is psychologically correct) it is also causal of them. It is this that makes his images of nature so actual, whereas even a fine poem like "To a Skylark" is a mere descriptive image with a moral. Because of the causality, we feel that only daffodils are like Wordsworth's feelings, whereas Shelley might have found some other bird or beast or the wind. So in a complicated instance an action may play at once all the following roles: framework for the thoughts, probable occasion for the thoughts, image of the thoughts, occasion for the feelings, vehicle for the feelings of which the thought and the action are the objects. And, if the action is long, it may have an independent probability of its own, with agents and their intentions, and the independent incidents may be more or less analogous in detail.

Genetically considered, a way of arriving at the complicated case just described is to submit to general reflection a story that then reveals a system of symbolic meanings, as when a sophisticated poet retells an old legend. Such is Tennyson's "Morte d'Arthur," to which let us now address ourselves.

### THE REFLECTION AND FIXING OF BEDIVERE

In "Morte d'Arthur" (edition of 1842) the chief action might appear to be an epical one, the casting-away of Excalibur and the departure of the King. Yet our interest is certainly not in this exploit or in heroic virtue; and, indeed, the diction, background, and subsidiary incidents belong rather to "romance" than epic. The feeling is not admiration for the exploit but nostalgia for the bygone, pleasure in the colorful, escape into the marvelous, and so forth: "looking wistfully with wide blue eyes as in a picture," or "clothed in white samite, mystic, wonderful," or the Three Queens. But, if we consider still more closely, we see that the motion of the whole is not the action, whether of epic or romance, but is the thinking and coming to a conviction of Bedivere. The events work on him until his climactic thought action of lines 181 ff., "his own thought drove him like a goad," and his climactic speech of lines 226 ff., "Now I see the true old times are dead." This is a psychological action, and the famous rhythms of the poem mainly express just such thought action: doubt, decision, agitation; or, first, he is dazzled by the ornamental sword as a present thing, then he already sees it as a relic, and then, having cast it away, he looks at Arthur "remorsefully" as at one dead.

What is this thinking about? It is more than the events themselves; it is a system of meanings interpreting the events. The adumbration, clarification, and affirmation of these meanings proceed *pari passu* with the process of reflection. From the first (ll. 12 ff.), Arthur interprets what has occurred: "The sequel of today unsolders all the goodliest fellowship of famous knights. . . . I perish by this people which I made,—though Merlin sware that I should come again." But, by the time Bedivere is willing to grasp this idea, the meaning has immeasurably expanded, for in line 234, "The whole Round Table is dissolved which was an image of the mighty world." And in this wider context Arthur can show that the events are quite rational; he can justify them, for "The old order changeth, etc."

To reach such a universal meaning, it is obviously useful, though not indispensable, to start from a great or epic incident; and the particular meaning here, what it means to pass away, is made somewhat probable by the nostalgic and archaizing handling, whereas an objective actual epic style would be less effective.

### TIME AND SCENE

What is the Time and the Scene of the action? It is midwinter night; the moon is full, the ice shines; and there are rocks that the sparks fly from with a jangling noise. Further, there is a chapel, "a broken chancel with a broken cross, that stood on a dark strait of barren land." It is Lyonnesse, that will sink beneath the waves. But Arthur is to cross the water to Avilion (if indeed he is! for in true Tennysonian spirit optimism is a faith but hardly a conviction), "where falls not hail or rain, etc." That is, not only is the Table Round an image of the Mighty World, but its destruction and Arthur's resurrection (and perhaps return) are an image of winter and the revival of the year.

Let us pursue this tack a moment. What, let us ask, is the season of the *Iliad?* There are no doubt geographical reasons why there is none; but what would weather add to the *Iliad?* Neither action nor sentiment depends on it. Even the scene of the *Iliad* requires but a shore, a plain, a river, and a town. The environment becomes more important in the following cases: in a novel, where it gives occasions for sentiment; in a sociological story, where the character is made of the environing causes; as an image (e.g., in *Macbeth*), where the environment reflects the inner struggle of the character; or symbolically, as here. In "Morte d'Arthur" we might indeed consider the winter, the broken chapel, etc., as images of the death of the King; but this death itself is so handled that it rather becomes an image of the winter or of every other cosmic and cultural change: death of the year, death of religion.

By the time Bedivere comes to say, "Among new men, strange faces, other minds," we are feeling the Victorian plight, and we understand Bedivere as the representative of the narrator. (It is his point of view that the narrator adopts and lavishes on him the psychological rhythms.) The thinking, finally, is not about the passing of Arthur, but it is a general dialectic struggling somehow to reconcile obvious value and the admitted loss of it. So the role of Bedivere surviving is to be the narrator of the *Idylls.* And the same generalizing extension holds for the incidents of Arthur's reign—it means something else—the sword is brandished thrice and sinks, Bedivere goes thrice and throws it, Three Queens come and take the King away; but he will return (Tennyson is not so sure of this), for the dawn is about to break.

### SYMBOLIC STRUCTURE

Thus, along with the action and the reflecting, we must add as a major part the structure of symbols. We might distinguish this from a system of images as follows: images point to that whose images they are, as the seasons in *Richard II* point to the historical theory and the feelings of the King; the designate of the images is given in the other parts. But the parts of a symbolic structure express only one another through persistent analogies; what is directly conveyed is simply "meaningfulness," that may or may not then be given content by historical, sociological, psychological, or religious considerations.

The role of the marvelous in a poem like "Morte d'Arthur" is not obscure. It is improbable for the action that the agents should come to a "broken chancel with a broken cross"; but this detail is analogous to the broken King. The dreamy world of Romance makes easier the fabrication of such a structure of symbols. And, at the same time, the greatness of the action allows an easy combination with cosmos and history.

The structure of the poem, therefore, could be given in the following formula: the discovery of a symbolic structure developed on a framework of action, the framework itself being an analogue in the symbolic structure, by a progressive reflection whose progress is part of the action.

[CHAPTER VI]

# Special Problems of Unity

THROUGHOUT WE HAVE BEEN LOOKING FOR THE STRUCTURAL relations among the parts of a poem that make it one thing, a "whole animal," for experience. I pointed out at the beginning that it would be profitable, to cast light on both the poem and its importance to us, to explore also its extrinsic relations, for example, the change in Sophocles' style between *Oedipus Rex* and *Oedipus at Colonus* or the Victorian plight in "Morte d'Arthur." But this book is restricted to "formal analyses," the consideration of self-contained relations. I should now like to turn, however, to a few special problems where, in the nature of the case, the application of the methods of formal analysis takes us beyond what could be called a single work. Consider a poem that is a translation of another poem; prima facie one would proceed by comparing the two separate works, but I would like to show that in the formal analysis of the translation itself we can often find the two separate works in an uneasy relation. The analysis of a bad work or a confused style also will show, on analysis, an internal conflict among the parts. Again, there are works that, formally, are even excellently unified and yet, because of the handling, make us muse and feel something beyond what is conveyed in what is "presented"; such works have a mysterious or sublime or symbolical effect.

The decision to call a work "bad" or an "unsuccessful adaptation" depends a good deal on the intention or amiability of the critic; there is a question of finding the proper critical distance and allowing the proper latitude. To an unsympathetic half-an-ear *Phèdre* sounds like pompous verbiage. Reading many of the poems of Shelley separately, we might think they are thin, brittle, and silly; but, if we take them en masse, they win our respect. In every case the lover of literature tries to take the work in terms of its strongest expression and at the distance where it shows to advantage.

I have chosen Dillon's translation of "La Géante" of Baudelaire, since Dillon is himself a poet and since "La Géante" is in a vein and has a subject quite peculiar to Baudelaire's genius and different from Dillon's. I chose *Un Chapeau de paille d'Italie* to say something, in this book, about a movie. Longfellow is an obvious choice for a poet with strong powers likely to write many bad poems. I chose "The Minister's Black Veil"—as a simple example of mysterious effect—because Hawthorne is my favorite writer among the Americans. Lastly, I include some remarks on Corneille's *Horace* that combine formal and genetic modes of criticism, in order to come full circle back to the introductory chapter of this book.

## [ *Dillon's Translation of "La Géante"* ]

### STRUCTURE OF A TRANSLATION

We call a poem a translation when there is a prior poem that has important parts in common with it, including parts of the diction, but not the tongue. Now, since every part in a poem is expressive—and especially in a short poem, as we have said, the elements of diction are parts of the over-all plot—where there is a difference in tongue, there will be other differences. For example, to be idiomatic in the new tongue, it is always necessary to change the word order, and this must result in new emphases in the sentences and verses; on the other hand, if the word order of the original is retained, the feeling (perhaps of naturalness) is altered. Again, one language is inflected, whereas another uses auxiliary words like "have" and "shall"; then the relation of the thought to the metric feet will be different, for the auxiliaries will, for the most part, be the unstressed syllables. In excellent translations entire systems of relations are altered or neutralized in order to save certain parts that the translator believes to be crucial; the imagery is altered in order to save the rhymes and stanzas, or the rhymes are sacrificed in order to save the imagery; the incidents and references may be completely renovated in order to keep the attitude of topical satire; and so on as far as Cowley's Pindar. Good translation is grounded in practical formal criticism, for the translator must estimate just what parts are strongly functioning in giving the effect.

Certain passages are said to be "untranslatable." But it is not especially those poems in which diction plays a major part that are untranslatable; on the contrary, often in such cases the expressiveness is so strong in the diction in the original tongue—unusual figures, archaism, neologism, etc.—that the translation is even easy, by finding equally strong and peculiar equivalents. Rather, the difficulty is where the relations between a part that has to be altered and those that are to be conveyed are so intimate that they cannot be dissociated. Consider an obvious illustration: Catullus has a little hymn to Diana (*Carmen* xxxiv); how to translate the first line, "Dianae sumus in Fide," or even "Dianae"? The feeling in the reference to the institution and the goddess is related in the closest way to the simple but hieratic elegance of the whole poem; the difficulty is not that we do not know what this feeling is (indeed, certain scholars know it perhaps better than Catullus!) but that our feeling is not related to anything like those words.

Suppose now that we look at the translation itself as a poem. From the above considerations we can predict something about the structure of such a poem. First, in so far as there were "untranslatable" passages, the translation-poem will contain lapses in structural unity; there is likely to be a discrepancy between the feeling proper to the thought and the new vocabulary and rhythmic modification. But, second, if the translation is by a poet with a strong habit of feelingful speech, there will appear a new organization of his own, and it is likely that the lapses in formal unity will attach to the new organization. Instead of a "translation" we begin to get a commentary on the original, and indeed the poem that the poet would write inspired by the original but unencumbered by translating. In a typical case the translation-poem will contain two independent systems of design—the first comprising thought, action, character, and descriptive image; the second comprising attitude, feeling, lexicon, rhythm—and these two interpenetrating and modifying each other, sometimes with a unique expressiveness.

### CHARACTER AND ACTION

## LA GÉANTE

*By* Charles Baudelaire

Du temps que la Nature en sa verve puissante
concevait chaque jour des enfants monstrueux,
j'eusse aimé vivre auprès d'une jeune géante
comme aux pieds d'une reine un chat voluptueux.

J'eusse aimé voir son corps fleurir avec son âme
et grandir librement dans ses terribles jeux,
deviner si son cœur couve une sombre flamme
aux humides brouillards qui nagent dans ses yeux;

parcourir à loisir ses magnifiques formes,
ramper sur le versant de ses genoux énormes,
et parfois en été, quand les soleils malsains,

lasse, la font s'étendre à travers la campagne,
dormir nonchalamment à l'ombre de ses seins
comme un hameau paisible au pied d'une montagne.

THE GIANTESS

*By* George Dillon

In times of old when Nature in her glad excess
brought forth such living marvels as no more are seen,
I should have loved to dwell with a young giantess
like a voluptuous cat about the feet of a queen;

to run and laugh beside her in her terrible games,
and see her grow each day to a more fearful size,
and see the flowering of her soul, and the first flames
of passionate longing in the misty depths of her eyes;

to scale the slopes of her huge knees, explore at will
the hollows and the heights of her—and when, oppressed
by the long afternoons of summer, cloudless and still,

she would stretch out across the countryside to rest,
I should have loved to sleep in the shadow of her breast,
quietly as a village nestling under a hill.

Let us consider the differences between these two poems. In the English poem, "In times of old"—on the formula "in days of old"—imports at once a regret of the bygone; reinforced by "glad" and "living marvels as no more are seen," it is the thought and feeling of a golden age of fable. "Glad excess": Nature in that time was not niggardly; "living marvels" are peculiar and delightful things. These give the character of the "young giantess."

In the French, the time is stated without nostalgia, an alien past. Nature has creative power; her children are monsters.

The emphatic words (the rhymes) are "puissante," "monstrueux," "géante." Such is the character of the "jeune géante."

From the outset "I" is nearer to the "giantess" than "je" to the "géante." He dwells "with" rather than "auprès de" (near by); he curls "about" her feet rather than lies "at" them. As we shall see, the "giantess" and "I" are not absolutely different, not different in species; and so "voluptuous," probable to curling about, is a word of the 1890's, perverse sentiment. But "voluptueux" is a physical word (lustful); it is given in contrast to the other rhymes, "puissante," "monstrueux," "géante"; "je" and "géante" are different in species, and the coming-together is terrible, objective, and comic. The Baudelairean image of cat and queen may be taken as an objective picture; Dillon's belongs to "a cat can look at a queen" (because he is like).

Already "I" is running and laughing beside her; "je" can as yet but watch. Her games are terrible, and this makes "I" afraid (her size is "fearful"); that is, he is playing with fire; he *sees* the "flames of passionate longing": the thought of "longing" is, I think, foreign to the French poem. The French is again objective and more restrained: the games are terrible, but they do not frighten the observer; the "sombre flamme" is guessed at as an act of independent curiosity. She grows "librement," distinct from "je"; but her size is "fearful" because "I" puts himself in the way.

In the sestet, "I" continues his movements; he has gotten closer to her in "to scale"; and "explore at will the hollows and the heights" must be taken in two senses—let us wink at the phrase "of her" that has a real Hibernian intimacy. In one sense it is sexual; in the other, she is a landscape and not a giantess at all. These two senses, of sexual intimacy and of mere descriptive landscape, are kept in a rather uneasy combination until the end. The scene is developed picturesquely in "long afternoons of summer, cloudless and still"—"I" is not asleep, "nestling" in the shade of her breast—nestling is the heir of "curled about her feet."

The French is very different. In the sestet, "je," who has been standing off, observing, now first begins to move, and this is closely related to the stanza structure, as we shall see. The emphatic positions are "parcourir," "ramper," against "magnifiques formes" and "énormes." And the feelings attributed to "je" are just those following from his distinctness and independence: "à loisir," "nonchalamment" (i.e., "without heat," whereas "at will" is the language of sexual mastery). The description is not picturesque: "soleils malsains" is functional; it is the explanation of why she stretches out tired, so he, also tired, can lie in the shade. Then the last line comes not as the end of a landscape description but as a stroke of wit and, as such, creates a sudden comic impression of absolute hugeness and of protection rather than of intimacy; or, to explain the wit and the image, as carefully repressed incest rather than a sensual fantasy. "Paisible," finally, comes as almost the only sentiment in the poem, rather than one more possible mood: all feeling has been repressed, until we suddenly have perfect satisfaction.

From these considerations it is clear why the "giantess" is a "hill" but the "géante" is a "montagne."

Baudelaire believes in the "géante" as an objective character and tries to make her credible; Dillon does not believe in the "giantess" but in the possibility of feeling and fancying about such an object.

### RHYTHM, SYNTAX, ORDER OF THOUGHTS

Metrically, the English is an eccentric iambic hexameter with complete irregularity of caesura and, as the poem proceeds, increasingly free overflows. The feeling is rapid and nervous but nicely calmed down in the more regular concluding lines. The syntax and thought are similarly ad libitum; "run and laugh," "see," "scale," "sleep" develop on no definite principle either in concept or in emphasis by position; and similarly, again, the traits and actions of the giantess are developed ad libitum. The stanza structure, then, is not—and should not be—closely tied to the thought; there is a free play of thought and fancy.

The contrast of the French is striking. These are normal alexandrines with perfectly regular caesura and (for 1850) no enjambement—except after "malsains," where, we shall see, we have a special effect very closely related to the stanza structure. The syntax is ordered to the verse and stanzas; the principal verbs occupy the emphatic places; "je" reflects in the octave, moves in the sestet. The first quatrain gives the situation; verse 5 mentions "corps" and "âme," and the second quatrain takes these in turn; verse 9 mentions the over-all "magnifiques formes," and the rest of the sestet particularizes. Most important is the emphatic position given to the one notion of hugeness; eight lines end so: "puissante," "monstrueux," "géante," "terribles jeux," "magnifiques formes," "énormes," "à travers la campagne," "montagne." And against these, emphatically, the progress of "je": "vivre," "voir-deviner," "parcourir-ramper." There are thus independent careers for "je" and "géante," so that their final coming-together is a dramatic and witty reversal. This is a dramatic rather than a sentimental action. Consider the stanza structure: it is two quatrains bound by a common rhyme, a couplet, a concluding quatrain. (The typography is of course two tercets merely by convention.) The first quatrain presents "géante" and "je." The second develops the thoughts and motions of "géante," while "je" observes and reflects. The couplet turns sharply to "je"—the asyndeton "parcourir . . . ramper" is sharp and summary. The last quatrain broadens out into a four-line period, the only long clause in the poem, including the enjambement after "malsains"—and this is the "paisible" togetherness, namely, "dormir." "Au pied" directly inherits from "aux pieds" at the end of the beginning.

In the English, the "puissante" endings are reduced to five weaker ones: "excess," "giantess," "terrible games," "fearful size," "hill." The systematic development of the verbs is destroyed by "run and laugh beside"; etc. But the point I am making is not that these omissions are defects in Dillon's poem; on the contrary they are efforts toward the expression of his own poem: a free fancying on a particular sensual theme.

### GENRE AND THEME

The two poems are different in genre. In the first place, "La Géante" is comic. A sharp distinction is maintained between the two characters, and, because of their incongruity, their relation is necessarily an extrinsic one. (But of course just because the nonsensuality of the relation is so strong, what is expressed, and wonderfully expressed, is hot incest, and the witty—repression-breaking—flash of the ending.) There is a comic reversal at verse 9, when attention is suddenly called to "je" as against the monster who has grown before our eyes. "Corps fleurir avec son âme" sounds to me a little mocking.

In Dillon's poem there is an attempt to bring the characters sentimentally together; we feel, or at least he hopes, that the "first flames of passionate longing" are for "I"; perhaps he is tall and looking into her eyes, or even looking *down* into their "depths"! They take part in games together; and all is diffused by a cheerfulness going back to the "glad" of the beginning. Having played together in the sun, they lie down in a common lassitude to sleep.

Second, Baudelaire's poem is epical. The action and characters are objective. Feeling belongs to the whole arc of the action; it is given not in any important words or modification of rhythm but only in the one over-all movement.

The English, on the other hand, is a lyric of sentiment; there is a pervasive feeling directly told about and an emotional rhythm. The action becomes rather a descriptive vehicle for the feeling than the chief part of the poem. There is an emotionally modified landscape description.

(Obviously, I do not mean that Baudelaire's poem conveys less feeling than Dillon's—the French is a powerful lyric, the English a weak one—but that Baudelaire achieves this impact by restraint and comedy and epic.)

Psychosexually, the French poem is an early dream, absolutely different from adult waking; the English poem is a regression to late boyhood and adolescence, the love of an older sister.

Now, if we consider "The Giantess" as an independent poem, we must first say that it is obviously embarrassed by being a translation. It is clearly not precisely *this* object that is the "objective correlative" of the feeling of the narrator; his feeling is not about mythical marvels. It is implausible that he would run and laugh beside such terrible games; and is that laugher the same one who is compared to a voluptuous cat and to a nestling village? How does the peace of a quiet village follow from the previous sentiment? It is too deep a peace—Keats's "pillowed on her breast" would be more appropriate.

But more striking than these lapses of unity is the prevailing unity of attitude and feeling in "The Giantess." And this is not achieved by random failures in conveying the original but by a systematic overhauling of the original: the omissions, the substitutions, the shadings, all tend, in one direction, toward

Dillon's own poem. "Glad" is in the translation, not in the original; "nonchalamment" is in the original, not in the translation; "nestling" substitutes for "au pied." The rhythm and stanzas are profoundly modified in the same direction, to convey glad, run and laugh—free fancy. The lexicon, "in times of old," "hollows and heights of her," goes in the same direction. Everything is being plastically molded by the habit of the poet.

## [*"Un Chapeau de paille d'Italie": Adaptation in Another Medium* ]

### ADAPTATION

Like a translation, an adaptation takes important parts from another work, the differences being in respects other than the language. Thus, the "modernizing" of a play in costume, social institutions, or so forth could be called an adaptation; and almost all such adaptations reveal internal incoherencies, like translations. It is a question of convenience at what point we choose to say a work has been "suggested by" or is "after" another work rather than "adapted" from it. We say "suggested by," etc., when what is inventive in the new work occupies the foreground and is powerful in the effect. Thus a parody or travesty of a work would not be called an adaptation, because the effect is very different.

The most usual meaning of adaptation is a work varying primarily in manner, as a change from the narrative to the dramatic manner in adapting a play from a novel. Variation in medium, on the other hand, is rarely considered adaptation; we say a tone poem or a painting is "suggested" or "inspired" by the poem, for the sensory surface strikes us right off.

The exception, in common usage, is the case I now want to discuss: the cinematic rehandling of a literary work, especially a play; here there is a variation in medium (and of course in manner), yet the new work would be called an "adaptation." But this, it seems to me, is because there is a common ignorance of what constitutes cinema; and practically this ignorance has had a disastrous effect. Many a play has, indeed, been "adapted" to films, as if the medium were not always crucially in the foreground; to my taste such are invariably thin art works, for they lose the reality given by the materiality of the original and do not invent enough materiality of their own.

In Clair's *Un Chapeau de paille d'Italie,* no such thing. The synopsis of the play is recognizably conveyed, but we have in every important way a different art work. And the superficial sameness in the "story" enables us to see with great clarity the crucial importance of the change in medium. Put crudely, in cinema the structural relations of painting and music are far more important than those of literature; and of course cinema has its own specific properties as well. Naturally in a book on literary structures there is no place to discuss the structures of another medium altogether. But it is profitable in this last chapter to compare Labiche's play and Clair's film in order to show the limits of the literary analysis.

### CHANGES IN PLOT AND THEME

Labiche's play is a comedy of humors inflated, reversed, and deflated in a few situations; the fun is in intentions coming to naught and verbal embarrassments. In the film very many of the strands of the comic inflation are omitted; a few of a specific kind are added; the humors are transformed into faces and hands; and much (if not, indeed, most) of the comedy is in reversals of spectacle rather than thought and character. These changes, of course, depend directly on the change in medium and manner, and we shall explore them as our main subject.

Besides these, however, the film has a different theme: the

presentation of bygone mores *qua* bygone. This explains why an "adaptation" was made rather than starting from the outset with cinema, as if to say, "See how *their* story looks in *our* medium." So the first title is "1895." (Labiche's play, by the way, appeared in 1851! but obviously Clair wants to draw on something nearer to his childish memories.) From this subtitle on there is a meticulous detailing of costume, furniture, makeup, behavior, and ceremony that everywhere fills the screen in close-ups and poses. Labiche's contemporary play takes all these things for granted; it is bourgeois comedy for the bourgeoisie; the rather gentle comic malice is turned against our ideas and prejudices, embarrassing them and releasing other wicked ideas. But the film aims rather at the peculiarity of objects—makes the world strange again as to a puzzled child—and the release is in smashing the furniture.

(Another way of handling the bygone is to make it actual, as in the serious retelling of classic stories, like *Phèdre*. The aim in such cases is to portray what is generally, unhistorically, human; and in principle plays like *Phèdre* may be given in either Cretan dress, or the dress of Versailles, or modern dress, or an "abstract dress"—so long as the scene is kept harmonious and calls no attention to itself.)

### DIFFERENCE IN DEPLOYING THE INCIDENTS

Labiche tells his story in the following scenes: Fadinard, in quest of the hat, is at home (Act I); he goes to the milliner's (Act II); to the Baronne's (Act III); to the Beauperthuises' (Act IV); and to the street (Act V). In all these places the wedding guests soon follow and crowd the scene, with consequent embarrassments and comic reversals. Meantime the wedding ceremonies have occurred, as we learn, as if by the way, in the narrative soliloquy of Act III, scene 6. This "by the way" is, of course, the point of the comedy: the distraction from the normally important business.

Clair's film takes just the opposite tack. We follow the wedding from the beginning to the end—a continuous accelerated chase—at the bride's home, at the groom's, the presents, the carriages, the city hall, the oratory, the carriages, the banquet, the dance, the carriages, the nuptial bed. This gives the frame for the systematic presentation of the objects, types, and mores of "that period" in an important ritual; and it allows for the montage of an over-all flowing motion, the chief part of cinema. From this straightforward motion, however, the groom is continually distracted, to the milliner's, to the Beauperthuises', and we are constantly cut-back to his home, to the officer, to Mme Beauperthuis'; and these distractions are again the comedy of humors, but not as the main plot, but as its persistent railing accompaniment.

First, here, there is the prima facie difference in manner. The stage of Labiche (and the stage in general) is restricted to a few locales; in cinema, as in the novel, there is apparently no limitation of locale. (But, of course, as we argued above,[1] the narrative locale is even more fixed, to the one screen and the one telling, so that film and novel rise often to the most intimate drama, the lyric.) What is humorously narrated in the play, as the marriage or the encounter with the lieutenant (I, 3), is shown in the film; even the "narrations" in the film are shown, as the narrative to Beauperthuis, where the director distinguishes the actual action from the mental action by differences of tone: what is thought and told has artificial light, stiff limbs, dummy horse, wishful events.

Yet—and this is the significant point—despite the possibility in the new medium of showing "everything," the film has in fact many fewer incidents than the play. Virginie, the Beauper-

1. Cf. above, chap. iv, p. 185.

thuises' maid who knows Fadinard's valet, is missing (Acts I and IV); Tardiveau is absent (II, V); the former relation of the milliner and Fadinard is missing, and the mistaking of the milliner's for the city hall (Act II); the entire situation of the Baronne, the Marquis and his Brise du Soir, Signor Nisnardi, the father-in-law as accompanist, the mistaking of the house for the cabaret—this is all absent (Act III); the pervasive complication of Bobin the jealous cousin is absent. *In place of these* are the incidents of the wedding and the officer at home and especially all the pointing-up and play with the hands, objects, and faces.

The incidents that Clair omits are just the main substance of Labiche's play, for they constitute the farce of situation. Each situation is prepared by an introductory scene with new humors; into this setup plunges Fadinard; and into *this* setup the wedding pursues him; that is the comedy. To motivate the situations, Labiche assigns a few traits to every humor, as characteristic desires, background, thought, habits of speech. Thus Nonancourt is a "pépiniériste" (which explains the myrtle, which in Clair is pure period); he is always saying, "Mon gendre, tout est rompu"; Bobin loves the girl; etc.

Clair's people too are strongly and tersely differentiated, but for the most part—I should except the officer and the deaf uncle—differentiated as faces and characteristic movements, not as desires or habits of thought. They do not motivate the same kind of humor-thought-and-action farce. The difference is simply given in the two casts of characters: the persons of Labiche have personal names and social traits, as "Fadinard, *rentier*"—his income is one of the main motives of the wedding. Clair's persons are of two kinds: those with roles in the comic distraction but who are not, as such, persons—the "Bride," the "Officer," the "Married Woman"—and those with characteristic faces and movements—the "Man with the Tie," the "Man with the Glove."

### MAIN PLOT OF THE FILM

Fundamentally, the film is a unified complex motion of the spectacle of hands, objects, faces. These are given in the opening shots; they are combined in different rhythms and at different speeds—the comic reversals occurring in abrupt changes of direction or pace—and the harmonious resolution of movements (and rests) is the ending.

Now several of the objects appear prominently in the play: the hat is the goal of the entire action; the tight shoes and the pot of myrtle are continual occasions for the reversal of Nonancourt. But in the film the number of objects is enormously increased: the wreath, the gloves, the tie, the clock, the shoes, the myrtle, the hat, the ear trumpet, the bust of Justice, the chairs, the cushions, the cigarettes, etc. Obviously all these do or could appear in the play, for they are obvious stage properties; but in the film they become strands of the plot: they are first close-ups, then the camera returns to them, then we see them from another angle, and so forth. Typical is the handling of the kissing-on-both-cheeks, which is important in both the play and the film. In the play it is a tic of the bride's family and a comic reversal for the groom. In the film it is introduced again and again in the first shots, lightly but without any especial comedy; as they are about to leave the bride's house, the kisses come thicker and faster; and then suddenly, with immense comic effect, we have a marvelous view from above of the screenful of heads meeting like jigging molecules. The process of "adaptation" is to find in pictorial terms the meaning of verbal incidents, to find symbolic gestures and objects; but we get cinema when there is invented a new combination of the moving pictures.

Let us pursue the same point concerning the language. For instance, talking with hands. Most simply, hands point to the persons or objects talked about; excited argument is rapid motions, determination is strong abrupt ones, the mellifluous rhetoric of the mayor is flowing prones and supines. The hands are also nervousness by twitching and drumming, embarrassment and distraction by fiddling, and character, as in the case of the formidable *pianiste*. Further, hands engage in actions proper to hands, as in putting on gloves. Now we get cinema when all such movements are heightened from a symbolic, sign, or auxiliary-active role to an independent sequence with its own internal probability. Thus, in *Un chapeau de paille* (film) there is a beautiful sequence where the groom's nervousness during the oration makes him drum on his hat, a sign; the deaf uncle, not understanding the sign, imitates the motion; these two kinds of hands are cut against each other and against the posing hands of the orator. Suddenly the groom's hands begin to clap, although the speech is not over, and everybody shakes hands all around, and all rush out!

In sum, the verbal ideas and the emotions can be adapted to gestures; but gesture is a motion in a system of motions. Pantomime starts as narrative, but it becomes dramatic action. In cinema we are handling a single sensory system, sight, rather than a double one of subvocal sound (thought) and sight, mediated by meanings. (But what I tried to show throughout the last chapter is that in poems, too, we are dealing with a single system; not internal thought and overt speech, but the motion of meanings, given in the syntax, etc. *This* is what constitutes literature, and it is this aspect of literature that cannot be adapted to cinema or anything else.)

The directors of talking films neglect these considerations, with disastrous effect; their films must bore because they do not directly, sensorily, move us. The opposite of the simple moving art is the use of talk or subtitles that arrest the motion and require the shift to a different sensory taking-in. (But subtitles themselves, of course, can be cut in with great power, e.g., at natural pauses, as so beautifully in *Le Sang d'un poète,* or to slow down, as Eisenstein used to do; and speech is also a motion.)

What has been said of hands applies equally to faces. The motions in which faces are the major elements are, perhaps, generally slower than hands—unless I am too much beguiled by Dreyer's *Joan of Arc.* If so, this is because faces claim attention so strongly and do not so readily initiate other motions by their own motion; we concentrate on the face before we allow its gaze or speaking lips to initiate a pan or cut. The motionless parts of faces, hair and features, give character. The motions express feeling. The possibility of great subtilty in this expressiveness is given not only by the ability to close-in and focus attention but also by the peculiarity of cinema-miming that the picture can be originally turned under any conditions and as many times as required and only the successful bit be spliced into the art work itself. In *Un Chapeau de paille* the faces are humors but not important motivators of cinematic action; the facial comedy consists mainly in panning or cutting from one humorous face to another, as they respond differently to the different circumstances, as drunk, asleep, or so forth. Sometimes, of course, they more directly give the action, as when the groom and the officer stand "frowning brow to brow" or when suspicion develops in the husband's eyes, forehead, chin.

### THE MAIN KINDS OF CINEMATIC MOTION: MONTAGE

Hands, faces, objects, bits of gesture, and gross actions (e.g., running and dancing) are worked into patterns of visual motion. That is, we have an adaptation of the story from a complex of moving words, thoughts, jokes, humors, and their intentions; from a farce of situation to a comic movement of images. The comedy of the images is, for example, the reversal of a man to a normally trivial part such as a glove.

There are three main kinds of cinematic movement: motion

of objects across the screen, panoramic motion of the camera past the objects, and cutting from scene to scene. The motion of objects within a scene, with relation to one another, and their parts, and also across the scene—this is much exploited in the play, as when the *noce* follows after Mayor Tardiveau in Act II. Further, in the play, there are the entrances and exits. As in many farces, these motions are exploited to the uttermost. But, in the film, we add to such movements across the screen, first the peculiar motion given by the panoramic motion of the camera, as when we move from face to face, or when we follow an object and the background flows past. Such panning may be done at any speed up to the absolute limit of leaping from face to face by cutting the film and pasting together the strips ("montage").

Cutting, or the motion from filmic scene to scene, is the most important motion in the medium of Clair. (Cutting also may occur at any speed, e.g., by dissolves or with brief interludes of blackness, or at once.) In any play only the persons disappear, the scene remains until the curtain; thus each act is developed as a whole motion immediately presented; Act II recommences with the incidents of Act I as its mediately given conditions. In film, however, the objects, persons, and scenes are continually vanishing and reappearing, and the persistent flow among them is comparable to the flow of music. (Just as the design within a scene draws on the relations of painting.) In cinema the motion of cutting is more important than any other because the act by which the mind loses an entire scene and must recognize the next is stronger than that by which a persisting object is followed from place to place. The cutting may occur at any speed; it may be rhythmic, a steady march or a waltz (there is cutting in waltz time in, if I remember, *Old and New*). The cuts grow out of, are made probable by, previous motions and rests within the scenes;

for example, a head turns to gaze, and we cut to the object looked at; or, again, a still object may be decomposed and cinematically reintegrated in a series of shots: a distant view, a close-up, an angle.

Finally, there is the speed of turning itself, in slow or quick or reverse motion. Such effects of speed must not be underestimated in literary plays either; many scenes of Labiche's play are certainly to be acted at a speed quicker than normal speech. But the film of Clair is as a whole run off in quicker motion; and he also employs the accelerations and decelerations for special effects, with as much freedom as in music. For example, against the rapid motion of the dance—which is made crazy and confused by shooting too close to get a clear view, and shooting slightly out of focus—the groom's stationary head begins to think (cut) of the chairs slowly sailing out of the window (cut); the dance accelerates (rapid cut); the chairs come quicker and many men in black evening dress (cut very fast) carry out the bed (cut as quickly as possible); the house falls with a bang! (cut as fast as possible) to a still.

Such considerations make us see that the change in manner and medium makes a change in the points of interest carried over, so that the episodes of maximum laughter and glory in the play and film are no longer the same. The comic motion of the film would have to be explored in terms of the cinematic elements and the cinematic kinds of motion. After a previous excitement, for example, we have the delicious slowness of the banquet, where all gestures are slow and alcoholized and the light is a golden haze—cut against the stillness and small nervous movements of the officer back home and his pile of cigarette butts and the anxiety of the groom—and then the accelerating chaos of the dance. Or, again, in the beginning we have first a still, then normal shots and ordinary cuts of putting on shoes, a pair of gloves, rapidly accelerating in motion and agitation, up to the shot of the moving molecules that we have mentioned. But in the end we have a motion of resolution, with rather long, but not unlively, shots of nearly still objects, the hat, the shoes, the missing glove found at last, the quietly joggling carriage, the bed, the intent gaze of the officer, and, at last, reverting to the very beginning, the bridal wreath, but now put away forever under its glass bell.

We saw that Labiche's play was presented in five separate situations, whereas Clair's film is the continuous movement of the wedding party from place to place, always getting in and out of the carriages. Labiche's handling gives the pyramiding of the farce of situation; Clair's, an adaptation to the cinematic flow. Clair is using the classic principle of cinema: to arrange the story in such a way that it consists in the main in a continuous local motion, directly given by a montage of movements across the screen, dissolving and cutting from scene to scene. (The movie is told like a Japanese picture story on a continuous strip.) Such are the pursuits on horseback of western stories, the great chases of the American comedies. Perhaps the perfection of this form is in Clair's later film *Le Millon,* which is nothing but the pursuit of the missing lottery ticket from beginning to end. As the chase progresses, other groups join in, with comic crowding and increase of pace; and the changes of direction become more abrupt as the ticket falls from one group to another. Such abrupt changes of direction are pure comedy of motion, almost apart from the humors involved.

## [ *Longfellow's "The Builders"* ]

### "BAD" POETRY

There is no point in subjecting to criticism poems that are weak, whose parts do not add up, and whose style, borrowed from the ordinary ragbag, has no relation to a particular experience. To set going a powerful intellectual function like criticism there must be a need, a problem. When a critic calls a work "bad," it is because he has gotten involved and has been frustrated by internal incoherency; he has to explain the unpleasant experience away. Such an explanation usually finally takes the form of showing extrinsic reasons, from the poet's biography or society, why the poem *cannot* express something; the poet will not allow it to.

To put this another way, in a bad poem there are not only strong warring parts but there is also, built in, a principle of frustration: the poet *means* to bore and disappoint you, to put you off, to see to it that you too are kept from a live experience. Thus we speak of a "crashing bore," a "thunderous bore," a "colossal bore"! Obviously such terms indicate a positive aesthetic effect, not a mere negation.

We might distinguish between a weak poem, without plastic power; an inept poem (like Dillon's "The Giantess"), in which an expression is emerging but cannot dominate the difficulties; and a bad poem, which is an abuse of poetic powers.

### EVERYMAN'S DICTION

It would be possible to analyze such poems as Longfellow's "The Builders" rhetorically, as didactic exhortations. Rhetorical analysis is in terms of the effect on a particular audience, and it is plausible that the maximum persuasion of a particular audience may require an abuse of poetry in order not to offend or make anxious. In the case of "The Builders," however, it is probable that the frustration of combination is internal to the poet and shared by the audience.

Let us say something about the hortatory attitude, the ethical thought, the rhythm, the image, and the vocabulary. Up to a certain point all these combine strongly, for even in works like this Longfellow is not a weak poet (but rather lacking in originality and distinction; he is a great academic). There is a charmingly unsought relation of thought, image, earnest tone, and appropriate rhythm and diction.

1. The vocabulary is ordinary (middle-class) cultured sobriety, somewhat on the following formula: no unusual or long words, yet no insistence on naïve monosyllables—allowing "materials," "minute," "entire," "incomplete," "ascending"; at the same time a preponderance of monosyllables of serious import, "Fate," "work," "time," "deeds," "great," "rhyme," "man," "care," "Gods," "lives," "days," "strong," etc.; a selection of dignified colloquialisms, as "idle show," "yawning gaps," "feet stumble," "strong and sure"—extending these even to phrases of complete thought, "Each thing in its place is best," "the Gods see everywhere," "let us do our work." To this strong everyman's diction is added a coloring of technical words from the image of building, "massive," "ornaments," "blocks," "stairways," "base," etc.; but the image itself is so chosen from the fundamental yet noble things that these words do not seem colorful but merely reinforce the sobriety (in general, food, clothing, and shelter are fundamental, and shelter is almost always noble, being arduous, large, unpassionate).

2. The same character is expressed in the syntax: direct, short unperiodic clauses and arguments, without however the naïveté of simple co-ordination; and a certain intellectual ethical tone given by such connectives as "for," "else," "then," "thus." Inversions are few, but they are boldly taken—"useless is, or low," "with materials filled." They are justified by the strong rhythm; they avoid commonplaceness without obtruding.

3. The rhythm is simple hymn time, though not very songlike in its kind. (E.g., "A Psalm of Life," with its alternating feminine rhymes, is more lilting.) Catalectic trochees of this

kind, across a solid diction, are very vigorous. And working in this hymn rhythm is a rhythm of gnomic utterance, brief couplets expressing complete thoughts, as "Our todays, etc." The trochees are slow, earnest rather than tripping, and the vigor is heightened by the regularity. There is a continual co-ordination of verse and syntax. We have thus, to sum up, the rhythm of resolute and somewhat pious thought.

4. The image carries the same feeling. Building is dignified and effortful. And, again, as an image it is functional and everyman's. The motion of building is the motion of living a life; the progress of building is a framework for gnomic thoughts, making them seem to form an argument with direction—toward height and completion. The hortatory attitude climaxes with the completion of the thought, the tone becoming more resolute still, "Build today then, etc." and freely broadening out, "where the eye sees, etc." The historical reference to the Middle Ages(?) is pat for the thought of humble, social effort—the passing of time—and that we stand on what our fathers wrought for us.

All this is quite domestic; it is nonetheless effective. It is not so easy, for instance, to write trochees of such regularity and vigor without becoming sparse and harsh, as Longfellow is not.

### HINDRANCES TO THE EXPRESSION OF FEELING

Once we attend more closely to the poem and get past its surface texture, we find that everything falls apart. There are powerful hindrances.

1. First, in the rhythm. The motion across the stanzas is hopelessly static and hinders the progress of the argument and image and, most important, completely prevents the development of feeling; the poet does not believe in what he is saying, for he does not warm to it; rather, he believes that this is the kind of thing that should be said.

There are gnomic stops at the end of each stanza and more fatally in the middle of each stanza—in seven of nine stanzas the second line has a semicolon or its equivalent. Such a pattern at once becomes probable and prevents feeling. Contrast, for example, FitzGerald's *Rubáiyát:* here each stanza marks the end of an image and a thought—we are not meant to progress—but within each stanza we are kept in motion both by the rhyme scheme and by the free overflows. In "The Builders" the *a b a b* rhyme in closed couplets makes us wait for 3 and 4 to conclude from 1 and 2, and, when they do not fail to do so, our expectation is too perfectly fulfilled; but, when they fail to do so, we are disappointed, and the stanza has no structure. And, when by exception the second line overflows, as in "In the elder days, etc.," then the reader is caught in a neat trap. The free overflow in the last stanza does express the broadening vista, the end of effort; but by then it is too late for such expressiveness, and we have nothing but a poetical flourish, as is indeed clear from the vocabulary and image, which are what might be called the "trivial sublime."

Turning to the verses, we find that the strong regularity soon becomes so strong in the absence of any developing rhythm of feeling that we can no longer hear the sense for the beat. Further, the handling of the catalectic trochees is such that after each explosive rhyme we must recollect our forces to hit the opening of the new line: this lays great emphasis on the first word in each line, but in half the cases this word proves to be a mere grammatical auxiliary, "each," "and," "for," "our," "are"; thus nothing makes sense. Soon we have doggerel, the destruction by the beat of the relation of sound and sense; and the doggerel is woefully reinforced by the static stanzas into boredom. Contrast with this over-all rhythm the even elegant simplicity of the first stanza, before the beat has gathered force through repetition.

We have thus found ourselves making an apparently contradictory criticism: the very elements, such as regularity and gnomic brevity, which we called expressive are now called inexpressive. No; for the rhythm is right in character but wrong in feeling. What is such character without feeling? New England, 1840, to a sensitive, learned, and cosmopolitan poet who can catch the tone of his beloved society, but he cannot passionately affirm it (he knows better), and he cannot break from it (he is afraid).

### HINDRANCES IN THOUGHT

2. Turn now to the image. When an image is used in a poem in passing, only the point of comparison need be clear. But, when the image is part of the plot and many points of comparison are drawn, there is a difficulty; for the things compared are not identical, and therefore pains must be had to prevent awkward discrepancies or else to work them into the design.

"Massive" and "ornaments" in the first stanza are neat; but in the second stanza "low" is catastrophic, for "low" can apply to building, and it is the foundation, which is not a trivial thing, but ethically it is what is contemptible. Again, how to square "walls of Time" with "Time is with materials filled"?—are we to displace the old blocks for the new structure, as the Italians destroyed the Forum to build hovels and churches? Syntactically, "truly shape and fashion these" must refer to "todays and yesterdays"—but how to reshape the past? Again, "ornaments of rhyme" are architecturally "idle show," but how, architecturally, do they "strengthen and support the rest"?—unless he means them to be Gothic gargoyles, which were rainspouts (this would not be a bad idea in a comic way). Again, the unfinished "unseen parts" are going to become stumbling places and "broken stairways"; this is very strange.

Again, the temporal use of days in "elder days of Art" is not square with the structural use of "Our todays and yesterdays are the blocks."

What is the over-all movement of the image? The ending belongs to a movement upward; the clause, "make the house, etc.," belongs to a movement toward completion. The order of description seems to move from the materials to the manner to the purpose. These separate sequences fail to reinforce one another.

3. The case is that the thought itself is confused, and it is this confusion that infects the rest. The opening two stanzas are ambiguous: it seems that they are philosophical and not hortatory (and this would be Longfellow's better elegiac vein); but by the fourth stanza it is clear that they were the premises for an exhortation. As such, the universal indicative "Nothing useless *is*" must be taken to mean, "Everything *can* be put to some use." "Idle show" is useful only when "strengthening and supporting the rest"—however that's done—that is, poetry can support morality. But, finally, we come to suspect that it is only the days "with a firm and ample base" that are truly justified—and this would probably exclude those that are merely "ornamental." The elegiac beginning does not prepare us for any such development as this.

The ending is even more confusing. What is the purpose of the building? Three or four different answers seem to be given. First, the purpose of the building is just to make it well; but then we find that this is because the "Gods" will punish and shame us if we don't; and then that the building is being made for the gods to dwell in. (By the way, who are these plural gods in the "elder days of Art," surely the Middle Ages, for ancient builders did not fret much about finishing off the unseen parts?) Suddenly, then, still another purpose is announced: we build well for posterity, for clearly it cannot be the gods whose feet will stumble because of our mistakes; and the chief purpose in the end seems to be that "we" (our children) may attain the turrets, etc. There has been a great change of purpose from the beginning—for there it seemed that the good was in the effortful building, but in the end it seems that the purpose, the chief good, is in viewing the infinite scene, something not at all effortful to do; and it's quite sure that the ornaments of the building itself cannot be of any use at all. Such are the struggles of the poet with his pragmatic religion: good work is its own reward; but the gods reward; the gods are the judges of value whatever man may think; but it is as an aid to progress that anything is of any value. It is this confusion that leads him into the fantastic architecture where what "no man sees" becomes "broken stairways." Nor can we expect that any feeling will develop in the rhythm, for what is there to believe?

Who are the inhabitants, who the builders, what the materials? The soul is the builder, the days the materials; but the lives stand in the wall; and, if the gods are the inhabitants, the souls are, perhaps, the materials. Etc.

To my taste Longfellow has strong poetic powers: full and sweet language, sensibility, a warm and fertile imagination, a concern for all kinds of scenes and persons, very considerable learning. Yet he wrote little that is simply beautiful or profoundly true or extraordinary (I think much of *Hiawatha* is extraordinary). Obviously this cannot be by his merely falling short, for the exercise of the powers he had should have been more productive. We must say that he had in him positive principles of frustration (that would not be far to discover). His warmth comes only to nostalgia; his learning to pictures without much life; his presentness to acceptable sentiments. So the poet of "good character" proves in the end to have been lacking not so much in feeling and thought as, precisely, in character.

## [*"The Minister's Black Veil": Mystery and Sublimity*]

### FORMAL STRUCTURE OF THE SUBLIME

So far in this chapter we have been considering internal *discrepancies:* poems where no system of relations sufficiently unifies the whole. The contrary would be: poems in which several alternative systems of interpretation adequately account for everything presented. We have already discussed such a case in "Morte d'Arthur," a "symbol"; for we saw that the passing of Arthur or the death of the year or the decline of Christian civilization in England, etc., could by systems of analogy account for the "meaning"—though we should probably choose one particular symbolic distance as giving the most adequate view. The decline of his culture seems to me to be what Tennyson had in the foreground of his feeling.

We may distinguish such a symbolic poem from a proper allegory like *Pilgrim's Progress.* In the symbol the unifying relations operate at even no symbolic distance; thus, we could say that the poem imitates the passing of Arthur and that the wintertime is emotionally appropriate. But, in the allegory, it is only when we come to the precise distance of Bunyan's morals and theology that the work makes sense—for example, to explain the nature of Christian's obstacles.

But quite different again is the case where, without symbolism or symbolic distance, nevertheless alternative interpretations seem to be suggested by what is presented. Consider a Delphic oracle, where the same words have a double set of meanings. In such ambiguity we are directed outside the work for clarification—for instance, we think of the well-known cunning of the Tripod. But it is just by dwelling on the unity of what is presented, with its embarrassment of riches, that we are forced to feel and think beyond what is presented.

The property of being brought, through a presentation, to a knowledge (clear or vague) beyond what is given in the presentation—this makes us think, at once, of Kant's notion of the sublime. Kant, of course, was thinking of the absolute overstraining of the faculties in trying to synthesize an experience, and hence he denied that there was any such thing as sublime art (for no unified work made by a man is absolutely ungraspable by our senses—though, it sometimes seems to me, Beethoven makes us hear sounds that we cannot hear, and an endlessness that we cannot measure). But certainly in less arduous experiences there is often a temporary breakdown of the faculties, and it is historically convenient to call everything with such a structure "sublime," keeping the grand distinction between the "beautiful" and the "sublime." Sublime effects, in this structural sense, can occur in both art and nature and often quite trivially; *trompe-l'œil* is trivially sublime, the uncanny or chilling is sublime, etc. In this sense symbolic works are all sublime, and most allegories do not fail, before we apply the key, to give a presentiment of higher meaning. A striking kind of artistic sublimity is that where, despite or even because of the self-containedness of the unity, we feel the power of the artist as something beyond and sublime. Tragic irony and the tragic plot are relatively sublime, for the one hero has many meanings; but the progress of the work brings us back to a cathartic beauty. The miraculous resolution of an impasse is more unreservedly sublime.

The extreme case would be where the presentation is unifiable on an indefinite number of interpretations but the higher meaning of this plurality is not to be grasped by any act of imagination, feeling, or thought. Such are the theological mysteries. Poetically, Kafka, for example, explores such mysteries by the odd devices of an even excessive realism, somehow meaningful as a whole and yet not quite graspable.

### SYMBOL AND MYSTERY

In the works of Hawthorne there are numerous examples where his ubiquitous symbolism passes over into mystery. In *The Marble Faun,* "The Minister's Black Veil," and "Ethan Brand" the mystery seems to express the following thought: that diabolic crime, lust, sin, etc., is not to be named or described, for any namable crime, such as murder or rape, could be condoned, explained, shown to be relative. In "The Prophetic Pictures," "The Ambitious Guest," etc., the thought seems to be that there are certain inexplicable powers in art, Providence, the commonwealth.

Let us look more closely at the combination of symbol and mystery in "The Minister's Black Veil."

First, Hawthorne generates an expectancy of symbolic meanings for the whole by the employment of explicit metaphors: for example, the Minister rushes from the bright wedding into the night, "for the Earth, too, had on her Black Veil." Such metaphor makes us look for still other metaphor, and the Veil becomes a universal notion and the presented action itself a symbol of it, as in "Morte d'Arthur." In the end this symbolic expectancy is explicity fulfilled: "I look around me, and lo! on *every* visage a black veil!" This universal application is the end of a sequence that began in the first paragraph when we were presented with the old people, the children, the bachelors and the maidens, at that moment all in sunshine; and whose middle was the Veil at the funeral, at the wedding, in love, in death, in all the special and common chances of life.

But the symbol is itself mysterious; for we must also obviously take the Black Veil realistically, that is, without symbolic distance. The Veil exerts power on nonsymbolic characters; it makes the parson an efficient clergyman whose election sermon tinges the legislative acts with gloom. In most such cases of its effect, a plausible "realistic" explanation is stated or apparent, as that the "gloom enabled him to sympathize with all dark affections." As these explanations multiply, they form what in chapter iv we called a "sentimental point of view"—a device excessively common in Hawthorne (e.g., in "David Swan" or "Sights from a Steeple"). But here, in place of using the device for sentimental exploration, he leads us to wonder just what is the source of these various effects of the Veil.

Contrariwise, other incidents are stated matter-of-factly when no easy explanation is apparent, as that the oldest of the parishioners is slow to take cognizance of the Veil. Indeed, the immediate wonder of the congregation at so simple a thing is somewhat mysterious. Still further, there are out-and-out preternatural occurrences, as the shudder of the dead girl when she sees the Minister's face, but these far-fetched incidents are few and delicately placed and carefully moderated by such phrases as "it was said" and "there is a legend."

The over-all structure is a continuum of the ordinary, the plausible, the odd, the wonderful, and the preternatural, with the dual effect of making the meaning of the Veil actual, that is, continuous with the actual persons and scene, and yet inexplicable. (To my mind the superlative master of this technique is the theologian Karl Barth, who so X-rays the obvious that it passes beyond the bounds of belief.) Another way of attaining the same effect is by contradictions: each of two given explanations is plausible and actual, but they are contradictory, and we are led to think beyond either.

The climax of mystery and sublimity in this story occurs in the very passage which is handled as if it were to be the explanation, "Why do you tremble at me alone? etc." The stage is set for a resolving explanation: Parson Hooper is on his deathbed, his beloved is near, and he is accused of shielding a crime. But his explanation is—that the Veil is a symbolic mystery: the mystery of friend to friend, of lover to beloved, of creature to Creator. The explanation of the mystery is a compounding of the mystery, for we ask, what is it that a man hides? *He* doesn't know, for he hides it also from himself! And this remarkable scene gains enormously in magnitude from the fact that the universality of the symbol, whose career could be traced from the beginning, becomes the nonsymbolic mystery that only compounds the mystery; there *is* a fact, but it is mysterious. This uncanny paragraph cannot be read without dread and awe. After this climax of mystery, the resolution is that, though dead and buried, the face has "mouldered beneath the Black Veil."

Let us notice the character assigned to Parson Hooper. First, it is made clear that it is by no natural motive that he has put on the Veil, for he is often horrified at himself; his natural happiness, made impossible by the Veil, is still desirable to him, etc. To resist his natural will, he is a person of the utmost earnestness and resolve. Yet he is by nature not a strong character—indeed, he belongs to the line of Dimmesdales and Coverdales, Hawthorne's sentimentalists. The paradox is important, for in Hawthorne's psychology the strong character devoted to an apparently antinatural mission is really a *fanatic*—like Hollingworth or Chillingworth—and fanaticism, far from being a way to mystery, is the great passion of the demonic ego. The character must be weak just so that his power may be seen to come, not from him, but from the Veil; but strong, so he may be loyal to his Veil. Lastly, Parson Hooper is possessed of a curious and persistent smile, the sign of secret resources; on occasion it is a gentle or sad smile, but pre-eminently it is a quizzical smile.

## [*Critique of Corneille's "Horace": Combination of Critical Methods*]

### BACKGROUND OF THE PLAY

Let me round out and conclude this book of formal analyses with a study that combines formal analysis with some other modes of criticism, moral and genetic. It will be seen that there is criticism of the object of imitation, in its historical setting, and of the act of imitating, as a problem of the author, as well as of the work as an imitation. At the same time the work, the old play, is taken as a present experience of ours; the question that is being asked is: "Is it true? How is it true and how is it false?"

In the following analysis of *Horace* I try to show how a structural defect in a play leads us to important considerations outside the play, in our social existence. But this is true, of course, of many "bad" poems. *Horace* is not, however, merely a "bad" poem but a work of extraordinary power that carries us away. Then we are confronted with the question how such a work by such an author can contain such a lapse. And in answering this we find a discrepancy in our social existence. Corneille fails because we fail. Our society, as at present, will not bear a better play than this on this theme.

To a psychologist, war—whatever else it is—is a means that people have of destroying their self-conquering egos and of most strongly affirming the imperial will of those egos. It is a mass (guiltless) suicide and, like any masochism, is a desperate effort to release repressed feeling.[2] And the institutions of authority, the authoritarian family and eminently the state, are the expressions of this self-conquering will, and they therefore tend to nothing but the war that they themselves make necessary. With this orientation we may turn with sharper eyes to tragic poems of war, cries of the outraged spirit. And not only to the works of the Greeks—the *Iliad,* the *Trojan Women*—for the Greeks understood the carnage too clearly for what it was and therefore did not explore under the surface; but to the modern tragedies that concern precisely the moment in the

2. For the psychology see Perls, Hefferline, and Goodman, *Gestalt-Therapy,* Part II, chap. viii, esp. pp. 345 ff.

soul where nature resists and the imperial will asserts itself the stronger. And then especially to Pierre Corneille, who lived in the period of the consolidation of the personal-impersonal warring state, when the psychological problem was clearer than now, for the state still seemed, somehow, to be the will of a man; at just this period he saw tragedy in the conflict of "love" and "duty." And Corneille returns again and again to the idea of Rome, the *patria* in the supreme sense, the will that strips the soul of every resource but the collective affirmation of will, proved by the oracles of the gods assigning empire as a destiny. And among the tragedies and the Roman tragedies of Corneille, we must look precisely at *Horace,* the tragedy of the Roman family, whose pivotal character is the paterfamilias subordinating himself in all things to the state and impressing his character on the youth. Here, in the scene of early Rome, we have the psychological elements in their purity and in their connection: affection and natural ties, the honor of the ego, fatherly authority, and the state—the elements that are divided in *Le Cid* and *Cinna.* The strength of this masterpiece is the severe analysis of the psychology of war, when the gods, the state, and the father impose a single pattern of authority. Its weakness, especially in the conclusion, is the inability of the honest artist to energize the consequences of his plot (and of history); or, conversely, it is the unwillingness of the man, writing, to show the situation truly and to draw the more terrible consequences.

Let us look first at the story in Livy (i. 22–26): It establishes that the war between Rome and Alba was "most like a civil war, almost between parents and children." Therefore, against the inclinations of the Roman king, the Alban dictator suggests that a means be found to decide the issue without general slaughter, for, "if the true rather than the specious reason be told, it is the desire for Empire that spurs the two neighboring and cognate peoples to war." (But how on earth *would* such a desire begin to realize itself except by the murder of the cognate and neighboring?) So two pairs of three brothers, the Roman Horatii and the Alban Curiatii (unless, as Livy says, the names happened to be the other way!), are set to fight as champions of the two armies; and, after his two brothers are slain, the third Horatius by a ruse, feigning flight, slays the separated pursuers. Then,

Horatius went home, bearing before him the triple spoils; and when his sister, who had been betrothed to one of the Curiatii, came to meet him, recognizing on her brother's shoulders the mantle of her beloved that she herself had made, she loosed her hair and tearfully called on the name of the dead. The sister's grief, in the midst of his victory and the public joy, enraged the fierce youth. With drawn sword he pierced her through, spitting out the words, "Away to your betrothed with your immature love, forgetful of your brothers dead and live, forgetful of your fatherland. So always away with the Roman woman that shall mourn an enemy!" Arrested for this atrocious crime, Horatius was nevertheless not executed, for his father claimed that the girl was justly slain, and the people were moved more by admiration of his valor than the justice of the case.

### HANDLING OF THE STORY BY CORNEILLE

To this ancient legend, whose sacrificial meaning is psychoanalytically obvious, Corneille makes numerous additions. The slain sister is his Camille, but to her he adds Sabine, in a parallel situation, the sister of the Curiatii and the wedded wife of Horace. He brings the betrothed Curiace on the stage, and there is a scene between the lovers. Further, he adds Valerius, the rejected suitor for Camille, who prosecutes Horace for her murder; and Julie, a Roman matron, as confidante of Camille and Sabine. Lastly, he makes enter the King, to pardon the murderer. Thus far, these additions seem to be nothing but the seventeenth-century propensity to sentimentalize and subplot a simple stark episode; but, in fact, they are used by Corneille to bring his analysis to a deep inwardness—though not to the extreme of inwardness.

*Horace* is ordered as a plot of suspense, threats, and temporary reliefs. At first the women grieve because of the civil war and are relieved by the truce; then Horace is chosen and even congratulated by Curiace; then Curiace is chosen, and the horror of the women is made specific, but it is relieved by the mutiny of the people against the unnatural combat and the pause to consult the gods. Then follows the catastrophe.

Curiace is a foil to Horace. Following the hint of Livy that the Albans are less fanatical and more human than the Romans, Corneille divides the will of the youth several ways: he doubts the piety of the conflict; he admires Horace and is proud of him and somewhat desires him not to lose; when he himself is chosen as the Alban champion, he curses his fate; and, when he must meet the imploring of Camille, it seems to be more his desire not to lose personal honor than his patriotic duty that steels him; and he is about to succumb to her tears. (All this, of course, makes probable his defeat.) But to Horace, self-esteem, personal glory, family training, and patriotic zeal are one single drive. "Alba has named you," says Horace, "I know you no longer." "I know you still—" says Curiace, with that marvelous Cornelian flourish. Nevertheless, the character of Curiace, unlike that of Horace, is rather shallow. Something is missing; it is that he does not fear death, not for one moment. For Horace, this fearlessness is inevitable; he suffers an infatuation that includes also his need to die as well as to kill. But it is by a false convention of noble behavior that Corneille takes away from the more human champion this depth of humanity, the fear that Achilles and Hector are not exempt from. But Corneille cannot round out the portrayal of a flexible human character, as Homer could, because then the war would reveal itself as an intolerable waste.

A similar strength and weakness are disclosed in the portrayal of the pair of Camille and Sabine. Camille is handled simply: her motives are love and family love; at no point does she take seriously the authoritative ideals of *patria* and honor; and she is skeptical of the gods—not of their power (that would be idiocy) but of their affection. At the same time her grief for the betrothed is not the natural spontaneous outburst indicated in Livy but a set design to provoke her brother and hasten her own death: "Offend his victory, irritate his wrath, and take pleasure in displeasing him"; "you blame my grief, you call it cowardly; I love it the more the more it angers you." This is not a natural impulse but a will formed precisely on the rebelliousness of nature. Perhaps this raising of the conflict always to the level of the reasoned will—a necessity of the Cornelian theater—seems artificial; yet in this case it seems to me to be probable and beautiful, and it almost carries the bombast of the famous tirade that ends, "May I see the last Roman heave his last sigh, myself alone the cause of it, and die of pleasure!" (How grand!) This is an insight: the rebellion of simple unself-regarding nature against lunatic authority to end in—egomania.

But Sabine is more difficult, and Corneille eventually fails. The wife of Horace and the sister of the Curiaces, she speaks the first words of the play with a heavy heart for the civil war, yet she will not weep: "If I do less than a man, I do more than a woman." On the one hand, except in this one war, she shares the ambition of the Roman conquest; on the other, her natural relation to her brothers is more than a feeling—it is a moral principle. That is, her conflict is already more intense and irreconcilable than Camille's; and from this beginning her first great action follows admirably: when it becomes known that

Horace and Curiace are the champions, she rushes between them with the strange conceit that they must kill *her* and so remove the natural bond between them, in order that they may then kill each other without impiety. This is quite mad; it is her maleness—proper to the sister of the more feminine Curiace—and it is a soul busy forming illusions. And when we next see her, when the men are actually engaged in the fight, we have the promise of the creation of one of the greatest figures in literature. She proposes to herself to dismiss the conflict from her mind and to take joy in any outcome whatever, for if Horace wins, it is her husband's glory; if Curiace, her brother's, etc. "Fortune! whatever evils you sternly send, I've found the means to get from them joy; I can see the fight without fear, the dead without despair, the conquerors without horror." At this moment, in brief, we are presented with a madwoman. The conflict that men have invented is in fact irreconcilable; and the will that will not succumb to it and die (as she threatens) can still take leave of reality. Alas! for Corneille this depth of nature is impossible; there are no madmen in this theater (and therefore there is no extreme of truth, as Shakespeare tells the extreme truth); the reasoned will is itself imperial. Sabine descends into rationality and says, "A flattering illusion, etc." From this moment on she is unimpressive; it is agreed by all critics that her last scene, pleading for Horace before the King, is perfectly frigid and almost silly.

Julie is a "Roman matron." She sympathizes with the two other women; having seen two Romans slain in the fight, she comes away, unable to bear the rest. So far good. Suddenly one is forced to ask: But why does Corneille not dare to bring a mother on the scene (not only in this play!)? Euripides had no such fears. Suppose that the mother of Horace were presented? What then would this Roman tragedy look like? This Roman tragedy would be simply this Roman butchery, for the poet would not falsify the issue by copying off a mother of Coriolanus. But this deep reach of social nature, the bond between mother and child, prior to the formation of the ego, will, and imperial suicidal need, is rigorously excluded from the Cornelian theater and from almost *all* the modern theater of battle and duty—but not from the *Persians* or the *Trojan Women.* (Partly these mothers are excluded because many of the mothers that we see in so-called real life, who could take part in these warlike intrigues, are so unreal, so lacking in *vraisemblance,* beyond belief to a conscientious poet.)

Lastly, the denouement is the entrance of the King as the dispenser of justice. (In the history, we saw, it was the feeling of the "people" that exonerated the murderer.) To me this scene seems tiresome from the very beginning; but one must suppose that to Corneille and his audience of divine-right theorists the royal presence itself had a certain theatrical force: "I love to render justice to all, at every time in every place; it is by justice that a king makes himself a demigod." So. And what is the justice that the demigod renders at this time and in this place? Valerius, the only person with a natural tie to Camille—the tie of a rejected suitor! (for her father has disowned her)—pleads against the murderer: "In this place Rome has seen the first parricide; the sequel is fearful, the hatred of heaven. Save us from its hand, respect the gods." We can recall the similar moment in the *Oresteia,* when Athene herself decides. But the King says—this is his justice and wisdom—

> This crime, though great, enormous, inexcusable, comes from the same hand that today has made me master of two states. Without him, I should obey where I give the law; I should be subject where twice I am a king. . . . The art and the power of making strong the crown are gifts that heaven grants to few; such servants are the strength of kings; and such also are above the law. Let the laws then be quiet.

All this is true enough; it is even subtile. But it is not the resolution of a tragic play; it is not the resolution of what has gone before in the tears and the rebellious tirade of Camille, in the portrayal of the fanaticism of the younger and elder Horace, in the death wish of Sabine, in the dubiety of Curiace, in the return of Horace hot from carnage and ready to slay again. But it is precisely the resolution of the weaknesses of the play that consist especially in the *omissions* of the poet (what he does not dare): this weak resolution follows from the fact that he has omitted to show a warrior willing to fight but fearful of death; that he cannot allow Sabine to pass over into madness; that he dares not bring the mother of Horace on the scene. If such things were not omitted, what would the resolution look like except just what it is, no resolution at all but a continuation of the infatuation, a cause of the same tragedy again and again?

There is a remarkable episode in *Horace* that does not appear in Livy. Let me quote it. The fight between the trios is about to begin when suddenly (Julie narrates it),

> no sooner did they appear, ready to measure one another, than a murmur arose in the two camps: to see such friends, persons so close, come to mortal combat for their fatherlands. One is moved to pity, another is seized with horror, another wonders at the madness of such zeal; this one lauds to heaven their unequalled virtue, that one ventures to call it sacrilegious and brutal. But the differing opinions all come to one thing: all accuse the chiefs, all condemn their choices; and unable to tolerate so barbarous a fight, they cry out, they advance, at last they separate them.

Nevertheless, the infatuated boys wish to continue, for their honor, and they turn their swords against the people; but

> the two camps mutiny; they cry for a general battle or other champions. The presence of the chiefs is hardly respected; their power is doubtful, their voices scarcely heard. The King himself is as-

tonished, and as a last effort he says, "Since all are so hot in discord, let us consult the sacred majesty of the great gods and see if they agree to a change. What impious man would dare rebel against their will when they let us see it in a sacrifice." These words of his cast a spell. . . .

(The scene is lifelike and oh! familiar.) To continue:

*Sabine:* Sister, I have good news for you.
*Camille:* I know it, if that is what you call it. But I see nothing in it to allay my trouble. This delay in our evils will make the blows fall all the harder. The only consolation to hope for is that we can wail later what we must wail for.
*Sabine:* The gods did not inspire this tumult in vain.
*Camille:* Say rather, sister, that to consult them is vain. These very gods inspired the King in his choice, and the voice of the people is not always their voice. They do not so easily come down to the lower grades as to the souls of kings, their living images, whose independent and sacred authority is a secret ray of their divinity. . . . Heaven acts without us in these events; it does not rule according to our feelings.

Camille proves to be right; the sacrifice turns out adversely. The same gods that have given to Rome the destiny to conquer empire decree that the brother must slay the brothers-in-law and then also his sister. This is simply the nature of things. But how did Pierre Corneille dare to declare that the people might mutiny, if only so far, and even the King be astonished?

# Glossary

[This glossary was prepared instead of an index of topics in order to present in a striking and concise form the specific nature of structural analysis as an intellectual approach. May I ask the reader to keep the following points in mind? (1) For the most part I have chosen "weak" definitions, that is, those with the widest possible extension so long as they exclude what I do not mean; but therefore they give the least concrete information. (2) I am sensible that this way of defining is as annoying to some people as it is entertaining to others. But there is no doubt that from time to time it pays off in a surprising insight not easily attainable in any other way. (3) I have not tried to be logically systematic; the glossary is meant as an index to the text, not the text as an application of the theory of the glossary. My guess is that the theory here sketched could be developed from the undefined primitives "Combination," "Time," and a list of the "Material Parts" of the medium. But it will be noticed that I occasionally employ quite different basic ideas, "Attention," "Background," etc. I think that these approaches are compatible. References are to pages.]

ABSOLUTE, 174–75: Persisting uncombinable part. *See* Sublime.

ABSURD, 84: Combinable with anything. *See* Laughter.

ACTION (*Verb*): Sequence whereby the parts involved are different from then on.

ACTIVELY PARTICIPANT, 108–9: Involved in the plot but safe from reversal.

ACTUAL EXPERIENCE, 3, 4, 20: Attending to the presentation that meets the attention.

ADAPTATION, TRANSLATION, 225–66: Plot with an alteration of medium or manner.

ADMIRATION, 73: Achievement of an exploit. *See* Emotion.

ADVENTURE STORY, 129–30: Sophisticated isolation of sentiment in an action. *See* "Humorous."

AESTHETIC SURFACE, 4, 16: Reality restricted to actual experience of a medium. *See* Imitation.

AGENT: Character of an action.

ALLEGORY, 173, 218, 253: Sophisticated symbol of which a part is not in the aesthetic surface.

ANTAGONIST, 33–34, 150–51: The hidden protagonist as another actor on the scene. *See* Complex.

APPARENT PLOT, 33–35: The strand of the complex plot with unity of time and scene.

APPERCEPTION, MODE OF, 100, 162–63: Character of relating wholes and parts in actual experience.

ATONEMENT, 53: Giving-up of the retarding sin.

BAD WORK, 21, 245–46, 258: Failure of combination where the critic can see through to the nonpoetic causes. *See* Psychology.

BASE, 80, 92: Safely deflatable foreground of underlying drives.

BEGINNING, 13, 89, 151: System of nontemporal implications that is a source of probability.

BOOK-REVIEWING, 21–22: Looking for a structure in the unfamiliar, in the ongoing community of letters.

BUFFOON, 84: Deflatable without normal residue.

CATHARSIS, 42–43: Removal in the resolution of elements that cannot be redintegrated.

CHAPTER (*of a Novel*), 135–36: Removal of an alternative to fixation.

CHARACTER, 14, 114, 118, 128–29, 239, 252, 257: Part of the beginning that persists as a source of probability during the plot.

CLASSIC, 23–24, 123: Work whose parts are familiar but that is not read as a unique structure and so ceases to be the experience of a man. *See* History of Literature.

CLIMAX: Ending of feeling.

COMIC, 80–126: Deflatable accidental connection releasing underlying drives.

COMIC INTRIGUE, 82–87, 236–44: Expanding comic combination.

COMIC REVERSAL, 86: Sudden succession of one comic intrigue to another.

COMMITMENT, 129–30: Action succeeding a sentimental sequence.

COMMUNICATION, 12, 216: Identity of structure of aesthetic surface between artist and audience.

COMPASSION, 51: Effective denial of something that cannot be integrated. *See* Gratuitous Probability.

COMPLEX, 27, 54, 60, 65, 105–6, 147, 176–77, 206, 254: Combining an apparent and hidden plot of the same character.

COMPOUNDING, 28, 31–33, 38, 104, 128: Completed whole as a new beginning.

CONTEMPT, 92–93: Safety after the deflation.

CONVENTION, 91, 102, 122: Noncombinable limit of experience, or necessity-from-the-beginning.

CONVERSION, 55: Change of character from impasse to miracle.

CREDIBILITY, 9, 76: Continuing to present something that fills the attention. *See* Actual Experience.

CYCLICAL, 141–42: Part of the beginning as part of the ending. *See* Compounding.

DEFLATION, 86: Reduction of the comic intrigue to absolutely naught.

DESPAIR, 55, 148, 172: Completion of a serious impasse.

DEUS EX MACHINA, 55, 89: Agent of a miracle.

DIALECTIC, 200: Thought sequence of thoughts.

DICTION, 46, 48–49, 57, 77–78, 97–100, 114–16, 192–96, 226–27, 246: Implications of speech. *See* Medium.

DIRECT, 190–91: Combination without vehicles.

DISCOVERY, 35: Emergence of the hidden plot to the unity of time and scene. *See* Complex.

FRAILTY, 35–36, 135: Possibility of the emergence of the hidden plot. *See* Complex.

FRAMEWORK (*Story-Framework*), 124–25: A temporal vehicle to give occasions for nontemporal parts.

GENERIC CRITICISM. *See* Genre.

GENETIC ANALYSIS, 2, 6, 257–58: Explanation of a work by answering, "Where do the parts come from?"

GENRE, GENERIC CRITICISM, 18–20, 233: Structures of the aesthetic surface abstractly considered. Application to particulars of an organon of such structures.

GLORYING, 94, 108, 120: Change from a humor to a wit.

GOODNESS, 35–36, 60: Seriousness of the protagonist in the apparent plot.

GRATUITOUS PROBABILITY, 52, 54–55, 88: Uncombined power of probability in an impasse. *See* Poetic Justice.

HABIT (*Virtue*), 68, 70: Repeatable character.

HIDDEN PLOT, 33–35, 177: The strand of the complex plot that does not occupy the unity of time and scene but appears as a sporadic sequence of breaks in the apparent plot.

HIERARCHY OF PARTS, 122–23: Tendency to combine in wholes in an ordered series.

HINDRANCE (*Retardation*), 52–53, 161, 248–49: Principle that keeps agents from acting.

HISTORY, 59–60, 63, 70, 109: An action moved by characters and also by an historical theory-from-the-beginning.

HISTORY OF LITERATURE, 24–25: A sequence of genetic and final analyses, relating the parts to the social background, but regarding each work as a whole experience and therefore partly as an ending and a beginning.

HUMOR (*Comic Mask*), 83, 106–7, 115, 236: Character of comic expansion.

"Humorous" (*Sense of Pirandello*), 130: Sophisticated emphasis of retardation. *See* Adventure Story.

Image. *See* Metaphor.

Imitation, 6–9, 200: Anything repeated as an aesthetic surface. In formal analysis the structure of the imitation is not that of the model but of the aesthetic surface.

Impasse, 55, 58, 145: An action that cannot proceed though the probabilities have not been exhausted.

Implication, 15, 121: Tendency of parts to combine.

Important, 74: What must be attended to. (In the long run, importance is given by the Narrator.)

"In" the Play; Not "in" the Play, 95, 100: Relation of the aesthetic surface to the actual experience.

Inductive Formal Analysis, 22–25: Finding the structure in the actual experience.

Infatuation, 36–38, 53, 265: Continuance of complexity.

"Ingénu," 102: Sympathetic agent in a comedy.

Irony, 34, 49: Diction meaningful in both strands of a complex plot.

Isolated, 121–22: Combining to a point but no further. *See* Neutralize; Sophistication.

Joy, 55: Succession of action to necessary inaction.

Laughter, 80–81, 91–94: The "meaningless" interval in comic reversals or between deflation and normalcy; emergence of the underlying drives. *See* Absurd; Glorying; Malice.

License, 88: Continuance of comic probability.

Lyric, 177, 184–85, 234: Imitation of feeling.

Madness, 263: Character always in passion.

Magnitude, 18, 113, 172: Combination of many and widely contrasting parts.

MALICE, 80–81, 92: Deflation of a humor.

MANNER (*Narrative and Dramatic*), 76–77, 158–62, 185, 218–19, 235, 238–39: Relation of parts to the unity of time and scene.

MEDIUM, 235–36: The presentable material parts underlying all combinations (e.g., speech, scene, or designates of signs). *See* Texture.

MELODRAMA, 34–86: Accidental convergence of several serious plot strands.

METAPHOR, IMAGE, SYMBOL, 216–20, 248: Combining of parts as a part.

METER, 48, 98, 186–88, 231–32: Character by counting the medium.

MIDDLE, 14, 90, 152: Passage from the probable to the necessary.

MIRACLE, 53–55, 58, 175, 206, 254: Gratuitously probable action after an impasse.

MIXTURE, 81, 113–14, 163–64, 190: Combining different genres.

MODIFICATION, 186–90, 207–14: Alteration of the persisting.

MONTAGE, 238, 242–43: The unity of time as a part.

MOTION OF THOUGHT, 119–204, 250–51: Relation of thought to the unity of time.

MYSTERY, 254–57: Sublime symbol.

NARRATION (*of Reversal*), 40: Withdrawal of the plot from the unity of scene, saving the spectacle for the ending.

NARRATOR, 73–76, 117–19, 158–60, 223: Structure of the unity of time when parts of the plot are not in that unity. *See* Manner.

NATURALISM, 117: Sophisticated emphasis of environmental parts.

NATURALIZED, 196: The conventional made probable.

NECESSITY, 14, 85: Probability when there are no alternatives.

NEUTRALIZE, 16, 114, 121–22, 190: Keeping parts of the aesthetic surface from implying anything.

NORMAL, 45: Of the same genre but not involved in the character-change of the plot; serious but not tragic; lively but not comic; sympathetic but not sentimental; feelingful but not increasing; etc.

NOVEL, 69, 127–83: Imitation of sentiment.

OCCASION, 130–32: Vehicle for sentiment, comedy, etc.

PACE, 244–45: Relation of the unity of time to a norm.

PARODY, 117, 121, 235: Sophisticated emphasis of the comic in a mixture of the serious and comic.

PART, 15–16: Anything in the aesthetic surface that combines. *See* Neutralize.

PASSION, 39, 73, 131, 163, 198: Disintegration of character.

PATHETIC, 99: Seriousness blocked in combining.

PENALTY, 42–43: Contrary of the infatuation.

PHILOSOPHY, 43–45, 59, 94, 107, 110, 121, 152: Thought of the resolution.

PITY, 41, 60, 108: Succession of the hidden to the apparent plot. *See* Emotion.

PLAUSIBLE: A weak combination that is part of a strong combination.

PLOT, 16–17, 125, 183: Structure of parts continuous from the beginning to the ending.

POETIC JUSTICE: Tendency to wholeness of actual experience.

PORNOGRAPHY, 27: Underlying drives emerged and surviving the ending.

PRAYER, 52: Gratuitous probability in a steady will for the impossible.

PRIDE, 74: Performance of an exploit by a representative.

PROBABILITY, 14, 198: Falling into place of following elements in a temporal whole.

PROPER MAGNITUDE, 17, 90–91: Working out the given possibilities of combination.

PROSE, 114–16: Rhythm without meter.

PSYCHOLOGY, SOCIOLOGY, ETC., 135, 151, 173, 206, 250, 258: Combination (by critic) not in the aesthetic surface.

PUBLIC (*Representative Crowd*), 96: Normal limit (on the scene) to comic expansion or tragic action. *See* Convention.

RECKLESSNESS, 39, 131, 163: Disintegration of the serious protagonist as the strands of the complex plot converge.

RECREATION, 11: Absorption in safe actual experience. *See* Aesthetic Surface; Imitation.

RESOLUTION, 42–45, 265: Redintegration of elements in the ending.

RETARDATION, 127, 161: Continuance of the sentimental sequence.

REVERSAL, 35, 40, 147: Change in the protagonist at the destruction of the apparent plot and emergence of the hidden plot.

RHYTHM, 49, 171, 186–90, 207–14, 217, 247: Structuring by diction of the unity of time as a part.

SATIRE, 92–93, 119: Sophisticated contempt by isolation of the base.

SCENE-CHANGE, 160: Emergence of the Narrator by separating the unities of time and scene.

SENTIMENT, 60, 73, 102, 123–29: Randomness of a sentimental disposition. *See* Sentimental Sequence.

SENTIMENTAL COMEDY, 100–102: Mixture of sympathetic and comic strands.

SENTIMENTAL DISPOSITION, 127, 162, 166: Character with a hindrance.

SENTIMENTAL HERO, 133–35, 159: The sentimental disposition shared in by the Narrator.

SENTIMENTAL INTERESTS, 131, 133: Part of the sentimental disposition that leads to situations.

TEXTURE, 192–96: The medium as a part.

THEME, 157, 234, 236–37: Narrator's theory.

THEORY, 59–65, 113: Philosophy-from-the-beginning as a source of probability.

THOUGHT, 43–45, 156–57, 199–200: Combination of meanings. *See* Motion of Thought.

TOPICAL: Discussion of properties to get at the essence.

TRAGIC, 26–79, 174: Destruction of the serious.

TRANSLATION. *See* Adaptation.

TRIVIAL, 90, 190, 249: Withdrawal from actual experience.

UNDERLYING DRIVES, 81, 84, 93, 99: Background importance of the comic. *See* Laughter.

UNITY OF TIME AND SCENE, 97, 160–62, 222: Continuous time and place of the actual experience.

UNIVERSAL, 95, 111, 166–67: Character surviving the ending for a sequel or as a philosophy.

UNSYMPATHETIC, 95: Destructible without redintegration.

URBANE, 83: Agent of comic resolution, not involved in the intrigue.

VEHICLE, 189–90: A merely plausible part.

VERSE, 48, 98, 186–88: Rhythm with meter.

VERSE FORM, 196–99, 202–4, 230–31: Conventional framework of meter.

WHOLE (*Closure*): Exhaustive actuality of the combinable.

WINDFALL, 88: Removal of grounds of nondeflatable comic probability. *See* Ending.

WIT, 83, 106–7, 115: Agent that can survive deflation.

WONDER, 55: Succession of the miracle.

# Index of Works and Authors

PRINTED IN U·S·A·